econometric theory and applications

David A. Katz

University of Dayton

Prentice-Hall, Inc., Englewood Cliffs, New Jersey 07632

Library of Congress Cataloging in Publication Data

KATZ, DAVID A.
Econometric theory and applications.

Bibliography: p.
Includes index.
1. Econometrics. I. Title.
HB139.K37 330′.028 81-12051
ISBN 0-13-223313-4 AACR2

Editorial/production supervision and interior design by Steven Young
Cover design by Mario Piazza
Manufacturing buyer: Ed O'Dougherty

Printed in the United States of America
10 9 8 7 6 5 4 3 2 1

ISBN 0-13-223313-4

Prentice-Hall International, Inc., *London*
Prentice-Hall of Australia Pty. Limited, *Sydney*
Prentice-Hall of Canada, Ltd., *Toronto*
Prentice-Hall of India Private Limited, *New Delhi*
Prentice-Hall of Japan, Inc., *Tokyo*
Prentice-Hall of Southeast Asia Pte. Ltd., *Singapore*
Whitehall Books Limited, *Wellington, New Zealand*

contents

3

the two-variable regression model 50

4

the multiple regression model 105

5

forecasting 158

6

the importance of time and lags in a regression model 177

7

simultaneous equations models 194

8

introduction to simulation 223

appendix A introduction to the computer and to BASIC programming 242

appendix B statistical tables 266

selected bibliography 273

index 277

preface

Until recently, econometrics was mainly studied by advanced students at the graduate level. Consequently, most of the textbooks have been developed with these students in mind. The primary goal of *Econometric Theory and Applications* is to present an elementary, but comprehensive, treatment of econometrics for undergraduates and beginning graduate students. Some research in the area of economic education suggests that attempting to cover fundamental principles within an introductory course, as opposed to the whole body of knowledge, can significantly increase understanding and retention. Thus, the basic philosophy of the book is that beginning students gain more by understanding the most important concepts extremely well than by spreading themselves out among a much larger set of knowledge. Gaining this breadth of knowledge can be better left to later courses which might use some of the more advanced textbooks listed in the Bibliography.

A secondary goal is to provide—for those who so desire—the capability to use interactive computer programs in conjunction with assigned exercises. None of the existing econometrics textbooks provide this capability. Given the rapid growth of interactive computing, the programs in this book may prove increasingly valuable.

Several other features of this book distinguish it from most of the other econometrics textbooks, the foremost of which is the writing style, which attempts to present econometric theory and applications in a form that can be understood without resort to mathematical proofs or derivations. Gaining an intuitive understanding of important mathematical concepts is emphasized, although a few of the more important proofs and derivations are contained in optional sections.

Another unique feature of the book is the use of "computer demonstrations" to illustrate the probabilistic nature of the regression model and other theoretical and applied aspects of econometrics. Computers have powerful teaching abilities, which can be used to enhance the quality of instruction. A computer is, of course, no substitute for a skilled instructor, but rather a tool for assisting an instructor.

Chapter 8 is unique in that it covers simulation, especially computer simulation. Although simulation models can be extremely difficult to work with algebraically, their solutions can often be easily obtained by a computer. In fact, the reader may find that the interactive computer programs in Chapter 8 are surprisingly easy, given the difficulty of the simulation models discussed in the chapter. Even if the reader does not have access to interactive computer facilities, Chapter 8 provides a brief introduction to simulation for those interested. In any event Chapter 8 is optional.

This book may be used in either of two ways, or a combination of both. The first method is that used at most colleges and universities—the classroom discussion approach in which the student reads the textbook and works the exercises. This may involve the use of a computer package such as SPSS (Statistical Package for the Social Sciences) to solve a statistical or regression problem. However, such packages are often not available in an interactive mode, thereby making it difficult or impossible to obtain quick feedback. The second method is similar to the first except that several exercises are worked on an interactive computer terminal, a device resembling a typewriter and permitting immediate access to and feedback from a computer. Consequently the book contains two sets of exercises—one for the traditional and one for the interactive approach. The latter involves running (*not writing*) computer programs written in BASIC, a language available at almost all computer installations. Every attempt has been made to use a BASIC that will work on any machine, including minicomputers. The first section of Appendix A explains how to work the computer exercises. But regardless of which approach is chosen, it is hoped that the reader will share the author's enthusiasm for econometrics.

I would like to thank my editor, David Hildebrand, Professor Thomas D. Bible of Oregon State University, Professor Thomas F. Cargill of the University of Nevada, Professor Steven A. Y. Lin of Southern Illinois University, Professor M. Ray Perryman of Baylor University, and Professor David E. Spencer of Washington State University. All provided numerous and invaluable suggestions during the writing of this book.

David A. Katz

1

introduction to econometrics

a definition of econometrics

One of the foremost econometricians of our time, Gerhard Tintner, has defined *econometrics* as the "... application of mathematical statistics to economic data to lend empirical support to the models constructed by mathematical economics and to obtain numerical results."[1] The "numerical results" represent an attempt to "measure" the mathematical relationship between or among economic variables, and therefore this explains the literal meaning of econometrics, which is "economic measurement."

In a way, as suggested by Tintner's definition, an econometrician must be a jack-of-all-trades. He or she must have a knowledge not only of statistics but also of mathematical economics. In addition, an understanding of the techniques of data collection and computer processing and programming may be required for some econometric problems. For example, mathematical economists have formulated equations that mathematically represent economic theories, but then so have econometricians. Statisticians have developed ways to measure the relationship between two variables, but then so have econometricians. Computer scientists have written computer programs to solve an equation, but then so have econometricians. It is this eclecticism that in part makes econometrics such an exciting discipline to study.

[1]Gerhard Tintner, *Methodology of Mathematical Economics and Econometrics* (Chicago: University of Chicago Press, 1968), p. 74.

the employment of econometricians

Because of the wide application of econometrics to problems in business and government, econometricians are in great demand today. Econometricians are employed by all sizes of corporations and all levels of government. In addition, there are several private consulting firms that offer their econometric skills to both individuals and institutions. Economists employed at colleges and universities often receive research grants to study particular economic problems that involve econometric work. In fact, college and university professors often find it extremely difficult to publish research that does not have empirical support such as that which can be provided by econometric methods. "Econometrics or perish" is the slogan of many an aspiring economics professor.

However, the high salaries that econometricians are now earning do not necessarily mean that you should rush out and become an economist specializing in econometrics. As more than one econometrician has demonstrated, the market for such professional labor groups as economists moves in a "cobweb" cycle.[2] Thus, when salaries are high in a particular field, more students choose that field, thereby having a depressing influence on salaries when they graduate. But declining salaries reduce future supply and increase demand, thereby raising salaries; the cobweb cycle begins anew. Of course, factors other than market conditions significantly contribute to the success of an individual (for example, dedication and enthusiasm). Should the reader discover that he or she shares the author's enthusiasm for econometrics, it is hoped that the employment opportunities in econometrics will be seriously considered.

econometrics and the computer

Some econometricians are primarily involved in the development and refinement of econometric theory, while others focus on the empirical testing of economic theory. The latter requires the availability of data and a computer to analyze these data. It is not an overstatement to say that econometricians owe their existence to the invention of the computer. Should the computers decide to strike, econometricians would lose their jobs.

Consequently, it is important that you gain some understanding of the role of the computer in econometric work. To accomplish this goal, the textbook utilizes two educational tools. First, we make liberal use of "computer demonstrations" to provide an intuitive idea of the meaning of an important mathematical theory, explain a difficult problem, or present numerical results. *Computer demonstration* is defined as "the output of a computer program" and

[2]Charles E. Scott, "The Market for Ph.D. Economists: The Academic Sector," *American Economic Review*, 69 (May 1979), 137–47; and R. B. Freeman, "Supply and Salary Adjustments to the Changing Science Manpower Market: Physics, 1948–1973," *American Economic Review*, 65 (March 1975), 27–39.

is abbreviated by the word *demo*. Since your instructor may require you to use a computer package such as SPSS (Statistical Package for the Social Sciences) to work an econometric problem, some of the computer demonstrations will help to acquaint you with this form of computer output.

Second, the chapters contain "computer exercises," which are optional. The computer exercises involve running (not writing) computer programs written in BASIC (Beginners All-Purpose Symbolic Instructional Code), a language available at almost all computer installations. Although there are several forms of BASIC, the computer programs contained in the computer exercises are written in a simplified version of BASIC and therefore should run on most computers. These programs are also written to work on any size computer, including minicomputers. Normally, BASIC programs are run on an interactive computer terminal, a device resembling a typewriter and permitting immediate access to and feedback from a computer. Some of these terminals are equipped with a television screen (CRT) instead of or in addition to a paper printer. Many of the home computers being sold today use BASIC; the reader who owns one of these may be able to work the exercises on it. If you desire to work the computer exercises, you should read the first section of Appendix A, which explains how to run BASIC programs. Should you desire to modify or add programs not in the textbook, Appendix A also provides an introduction to BASIC programming. Careful study of this Appendix should enable you to write computer programs intermediate in difficulty. But without considerable practice, do not expect to become an expert.

An alternative to a computer is a calculator. Some calculators are even programmable, thereby having some of the capabilities of computers. For example, some have the ability to perform the calculations associated with a "two-variable regression model" automatically, a topic covered in Chapter 3. Interestingly, these calculators are relatively inexpensive because of major technological breakthroughs in this industry in recent years. In any event, the purchase of a calculator will undoubtedly be a valuable investment regardless of whether you choose to work the computer exercises.

the methodology of econometrics

specifying

The methodology of econometrics consists of specifying, estimating, and verifying an economic model. If a model is successfully verified, it may be used for purposes of projection or prediction. *Specification* of an econometric model involves expressing an economic theory in the form of a mathematical equation. Although nonlinear models are not ruled out, the econometrician usually specifies models that are "linear in their parameters."

As an example, suppose we read in the financial news: "Stock market prices have been rising because corporate profits have been rising." The writer of this newspaper article has a theory about what causes stock prices to change, namely, changes in corporate profits. This theory may be expressed in mathematical notation:

$$Y = \alpha + \beta X \qquad (1.1)^3$$

where Y = stock market prices
X = corporate profits
α, β = population parameters (Greek letters are used for population parameters)

The parameters α and β are constants that we wish to estimate. The first parameter, α, is the constant term, or the value of Y when $X = 0$. The second parameter, β, is the slope of the line, or the change in Y per one-unit change in X. This is illustrated in Figure 1.1 for a positive value of β. If β were negative, the line would be downsloping, as in Figure 1.2. Which figure agrees with the

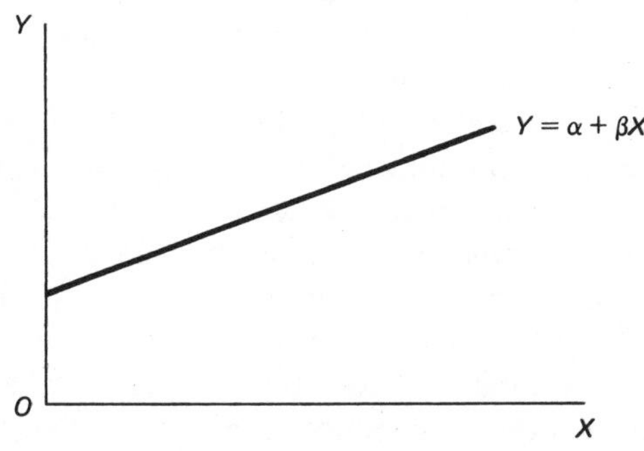

figure 1.1. $\beta > 0$

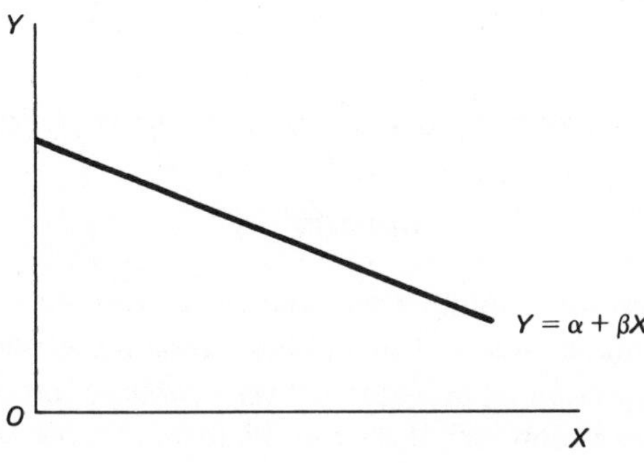

figure 1.2. $\beta < 0$

[3]An error term has been omitted from this equation for expositional reasons. This will be discussed in Chapter 3.

theory? Since the theory postulates a positive relationship between Y and X (increasing profits cause stock prices to increase, not decrease), Figure 1.1 is in conformance with the theory. Y is termed the *dependent variable* because we are assuming that stock market prices "depend" on corporate profits, not the other way around. X is the *independent variable*, or *explanatory variable*. Equation (1.1) is termed *linear* because the parameters are not raised to a power. For example, Equation (1.2) is nonlinear in the parameter β, but not α:

$$Y = \alpha + \beta^2 X \tag{1.2}$$

Because they are extremely difficult to estimate, we will not deal with equations of the form of (1.2) in this book. However, as will be discussed in a later chapter, an econometric model may be specified that is nonlinear in X, though its estimation may not be difficult. For example, Equation (1.3) is linear in its parameters, but nonlinear in X:

$$Y = \alpha + \beta X^2 \tag{1.3}$$

estimating

Estimation of the econometric model specified in Equation (1.1) involves an attempt to determine approximately the values of α and β, the "population parameters." In this case, the population consists of all corporate stocks. Usually, data are not readily available on an entire population, or if they are, high costs may preclude a computer analysis of the entire population. Consequently, we are usually content with "sampling" the population, that is, selecting at random certain members of the population.

The sample data may be "cross-section" or "time-series." For example, data on the current stock market price and profit of one hundred corporations are cross-section, since these data are only from one time period. Alternatively, we might have data on total profits of all corporations over a period of time (time-series) and on the overall level of stock market prices as measured by a stock-price index such as the Dow Jones Industrial Average or the Standard and Poor's Index.

Data collection is often the most difficult part of econometric work. Although governments and private organizations collect and disseminate a large volume of economic data, selecting exactly what you need and coding it for the computer can be a monumental and costly task. If the data are not available, knowledge of survey and sampling techniques will probably be required, not to mention the financial cost of collecting your own data. Econometric work is often criticized on the basis of the mathematical techniques' being superior to the data being analyzed. This criticism is undoubtedly valid in many cases.

Assuming that the data problem has been resolved, Equation (1.1) may now be estimated using *regression* analysis, a major econometric technique discussed later in this book. At the heart of regression analysis is the obtaining of regression coefficients, A and B, which estimate the population parameters α and β. The regression equation is of the following form:

$$Y = A + BX \qquad (1.4)^4$$

verifying

Verification of an econometric model involves determining the "statistical significance" of the regression equation or model. One obvious type of verification is to examine the sign (positive or negative) on B. Since our theory would predict a positive sign (stock prices increase when corporate profits increase), a negative B regression coefficient as an estimate of the population parameter β would lead us to seriously question the theory or the data used to estimate the model. Alternatively, an error in model specification might have occurred. For example, Equation (1.3) might be a more realistic depiction of the real world than Equation (1.1).

In addition to whether or not B is of the expected sign, we are interested in knowing whether B is significantly different from zero. If not, then there is no statistically significant relationship between the dependent and independent variables. This latter situation is portrayed in Figure 1.3. Another aspect of verifying a model is how well the model "fits" the data. One measure of this is the *coefficient of determination*, which is introduced in Chapter 3.

forecasting

If we find that there is a statistically significant relationship between Y and X, the model might serve for purposes of projection or prediction. Although the words *projection* and *prediction* are often used interchangeably, some econometricians distinguish between them. Projection may imply that the future course

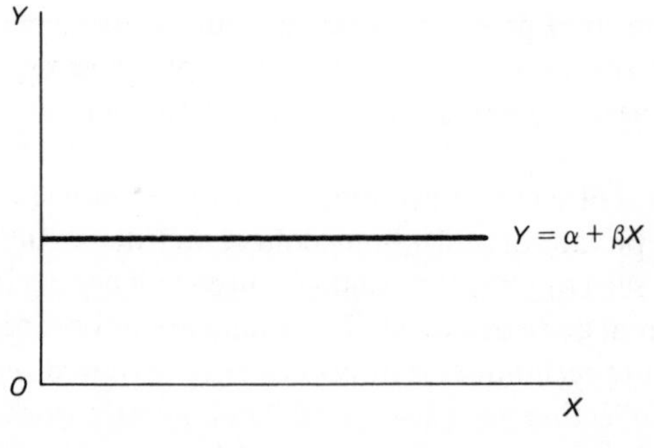

figure 1.3. $\beta = 0$

[4]A residual term has been omitted from this equation for expositional reasons. This will be discussed in Chapter 3.

of a variable is being forecast, while prediction may not involve consideration of the time dimension.

To demonstrate the distinction between projection and prediction, let us consider another example. Suppose a college wishes to predict the performance of its applicants and specifies a model of the form of Equation (1.1), where Y is college grade-point average and X is SAT (Scholastic Aptitude Test) score. The underlying theory of this model is that entering students with higher SAT scores will probably get higher grades in college than those with lower SAT scores. Since time is not considered, this is an example of prediction.

However, if we were to use our stock price–corporate profits model to forecast the future course of the stock market, this would be an example of projection because time (the future) is being considered. When time is being considered in a model, the t (or T) subscript is often used, as in Equation (1.5):

$$Y_t = A + BX_t \tag{1.5}$$

The subscript t refers to a particular time period. For example, we might be projecting prices for the year 1985 ($t = 1985$).

In this book, we classify projection and prediction under the general heading of "Forecasting." Preparing a forecast and determining its accuracy are important aspects of econometric work. The living of many econometricians depends on their ability to forecast the course of economic activity with some level of precision. Although there are many cynics who question whether the future can ever be forecast, the response of econometricians is that the benefits of imperfect projections far outweigh the costs, and that many buyers of their skills have benefited by being able to make more intelligent decisions. In a later chapter we will devote a considerable amount of time to discussing forecasting.

The above methodology, which is illustrated in Figure 1.4, might lead one to reject or revise an existing theory, or develop a new theory. However, when a theory is "rejected" by statistical evidence, it only indicates one particular sample, one particular methodology, and one particular instance for which the theory was in error. Theory should only be modified when it fails in repeated statistical tests using alternative samples and methodologies.

knowledge prerequisites

A major goal of this book is to introduce undergraduates or first-year graduate students to econometrics. To understand the mathematical models presented in this book, (1) at least one year of economic theory (macro-micro sequence) would seem to be required. Furthermore one course in elementary statistics is normally considered a prerequisite to the study of econometrics. Chapter 2 provides a brief review of some important statistical concepts and is optional for the reader who feels a review is unnecessary. The knowledgeable

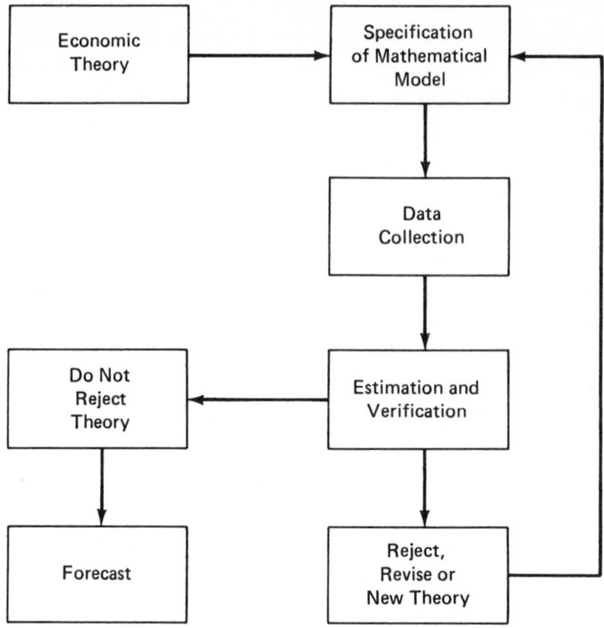

figure 1.4. Methodology of Econometrics

reader may be content with working the rather extensive set of exercises at the end of Chapter 2.

organization of the book

The organization of the book is straightforward. As mentioned above, Chapter 2 reviews the key statistical concepts that must be understood in order to follow the presentation of econometric theory in the remainder of the book. Chapter 3 develops the two-variable regression model, and Chapter 4 the multiple (more than two variables) regression model. Because matrix algebra is often used in advanced econometrics courses, Chapter 4 introduces the reader to the concept of a matrix and demonstrates how matrix algebra is used to perform the calculations in the three-variable case. Chapter 4 focuses on the problems associated with detecting and correcting for multicollinearity, autocorrelation, and heteroscedasticity. Chapter 5 shows how a regression model can be used for purposes of forecasting, and Chapter 6 discusses the importance of time and lags in a regression model.

Whereas the first six chapters analyze models containing a single equation, Chapter 7 is devoted to *multiequation,* or *simultaneous equations,* models. Because *simulation* has become an increasingly important aspect of econometric work, Chapter 8 introduces the reader to difference equations. A simulation model is a multiequation model that contains a set of difference equations. The emphasis in Chapter 8 is on obtaining a solution by computer (*computer simulation*) because the mathematical solution is often extremely difficult.

The chapters contain two sets of exercises. The first set contains exercises of a theoretical and applied nature. A calculator is required to work the applied exercises. The second set ("computer exercises") requires access to a computer terminal and interactive BASIC. The computer exercises are optional. To learn anything requires practice, and econometrics is no exception. It is hoped that the working of some or all of the exercises will provide the reader with sufficient practice.

summary

Econometrics is a discipline that combines knowledge from the fields of mathematical economics, statistics, survey research, and computer science. Thus, econometricians must have a broad background in order to practice their trade. Econometricians are employed in business, government, and academe. Consequently, the market for econometricians is not limited by a single market. Salaries are sufficiently high to attract people into the profession, although the cobweb nature of the market clouds the picture with regard to future employment opportunities.

Econometricians may work in either the theoretical or the applied area (or a combination of both). The theoretical area is concerned with the development and refinement of econometric theory, while the applied area deals with the empirical testing of economic theory. The methodology of the latter area consists of four steps: (1) specification, (2) estimation, (3) verification, and (4) forecasting. The purpose of this book is to introduce you to econometric theory and its applications.

exercises

1. What are the major sources of economic data in your library?

2. Develop an economic theory (involving only two variables) that you would like to test. Can you find any data that would allow you to test the theory?

3. A downward-sloping demand curve (Q increases as P decreases) represents a theory of demand. Specify the equation for a demand curve where Q is the dependent and P is the independent variable. Following the convention that the dependent variable is measured along the vertical axis and the independent variable along the horizontal axis, graph your equation. Do you find anything strange regarding how the axes are labeled?

4. If you estimated the equation specified in Exercise 3 and found that B was not significantly different from zero, would you reject or revise the theory of demand? Is the single equation specified in Exercise 3 sufficient to describe a market?

5. Keynes's consumption function may be specified by an equation of the form

$$Y = \alpha + \beta X$$

where Y is consumption and X is income. If this equation were estimated, what would you expect the value of B to be? What about the value of A?

6. Consider the following two sets of hypothetical data. Which is time-series and which is cross-section? How many observations are there in each data set?

data set a:

	Consumption for 1980	Income for 1980
Family #1	12,000	15,000
2	13,600	17,000
3	9,600	12,000
4	40,000	50,000
5	48,000	60,000
6	36,000	45,000
7	28,000	35,000
8	20,000	25,000
9	15,200	19,000

data set b:

	Consumption (billions)	Income (billions)
1970	1,350	1,500
1971	1,440	1,600
1972	1,485	1,650
1973	1,530	1,700
1974	1,620	1,800
1975	1,688	1,875
1976	1,710	1,900
1977	1,732	1,925
1978	1,728	1,920
1979	1,800	2,000

7. Graph the data in Data Set A (Y = consumption and X = income). What is the slope (B) of the line and the height (A) at which the line intersects the Y axis?

8. A production function is of the form

$$Y = \alpha X^{\beta}$$

Can you think of a way of making this into a linear equation of the form of Equation (1.1)? (*Hint:* Take the log of both sides.)

computer exercises

1. Read the first section of Appendix A.

2. Familiarize yourself with the computer environment at your school. Obtain a computer number and have someone show you how to log on and off a computer terminal.

3. The most simple type of computer program is one that can perform the calculations of an average calculator. Knowledge of the following symbols is needed to write such a program:

Arithmetic Operation	BASIC Symbol
Addition	+
Subtraction	−
Multiplication	*
Division	/
Exponentiation	**

The following BASIC program and run calculates: 5^2

```
10 PRINT 5**2
RUN
  25
```

The following program and run calculates: $10 \div 2$

```
10 PRINT 10/2
RUN
  5
```

Think up your own problem and run it on the computer. (*Note:* Some computers have a calculator mode that does not require defining a program name. Check with someone in your computer center to see if a calculator mode is available.)

2

a brief review of some important statistical concepts

Without an understanding of certain important statistical principles, it would be impossible to follow the presentation of econometric theory that begins in the next chapter. Since it is assumed that the reader has taken a statistics course, this chapter reviews some of the more important statistical concepts normally considered prerequisites to the study of econometrics. This chapter is of course no substitute for an introductory course in statistics, but rather it attempts to provide the reader with an opportunity to refresh his or her memory.

The key statistical concepts reviewed in this chapter are descriptive and inferential statistics, the meaning of a variable, frequency distribution, measures of location and dispersion, probability theory, sampling theory, and hypothesis testing and confidence intervals. There are many excellent books on statistics. A more extensive discussion of these concepts can be found in the selected statistical references listed in the Bibliography at the end of this book.

descriptive versus inferential statistics

Introductory statistics courses normally distinguish between *descriptive* and *inferential* (also termed *inductive*) statistics. Descriptive statistics are used to present and summarize data in an easily understandable form. This is usually the first step in data analysis. For example, every ten years the Census Bureau collects data on the population of the United States. This collection of data requires the employment of several thousand workers and is therefore very expensive. In fact, the major cost of many, if not most, economic studies is that of data collection. Once the data are collected, they are fed into a computer and stored on tape. Individuals working for the Census Bureau may then use this tape to construct tables, charts, and graphs that describe the data. For instance, a table of the population of all cities and towns is prepared and published by the Census Bureau for use by interested individuals and government officials. These published reports help determine the share of government funds that cities and towns receive from certain government grants and are therefore vitally important to almost everybody. The most important descriptive statistics discussed in this chapter are the arithmetic mean, median, mode, standard deviation, variance, kurtosis, skewness, range, minimum, maximum, and frequency distribution.

Researchers often go far beyond the description of data. *Statistical inference* can be defined as the use of sample data in order to form general conclusions regarding a population. For example, the Bureau of Labor Statistics (BLS) uses a random sample of over fifty thousand households to estimate the unemployment rate each month. The "true" unemployment rate could only be known by surveying the many millions of households in the country each month. Yet the BLS attempts to infer from this sample the true unemployment rate, which is termed the *population parameter*. The estimate of the population parameter is termed the *sample statistic*. Knowledge of the unemployment rate is crucial for the successful operation of the federal government's economic policies. Many millions of dollars are saved by relying on inferential statistics instead of attempting to survey the entire population.

An economist may have a particular hypothesis or question that he or she wishes to explore. The techniques of inferential statistics are often used to test a hypothesis. For example, it might be hypothesized that individuals with low incomes have relatively lower life expectancies than those with high incomes. Sample data could be collected, and the techniques of inferential statistics could be applied to this question. If the hypothesis is accepted, a "statistically significant difference" is said to exist between those with low incomes and those with high incomes. Econometricians are primarily involved with inferential statistics, although descriptive statistics allow them to gain a better understanding of the underlying data. Probability and sampling theory, and hypothesis testing and confidence intervals, are the important inferential statistical concepts reviewed in this chapter.

the meaning of a variable

Data represent numerical information that is defined in the form of a *variable*. A variable refers to any quantity that may take on more than one value. For example, population is a variable because it is not fixed or constant. The distinction between *descriptive* and *inferential* statistics is sometimes explained by noting that descriptive statistics measure the size of the variation in a particular variable, while inferential statistics attempt to explain the cause of the variation. Thus, the unemployment rate (a variable) may vary from a low of 2 percent to a high of 10 percent in the major metropolitan areas (descriptive). The cause of this variation might be explained by other economic variables, such as government spending (inferential). If everything were constant or certain, there would be no need for statisticians or econometricians.

The unemployment rate may take on any value from 0 percent to 100 percent. The latter are termed the *possible values* of the variable. However, some of the possible values may never be observed. During the Great Depression of the 1930s, unemployment reached a high of about 25 percent. Although we have never observed a value higher than 25 percent in this country, this does not mean that such a value is impossible.

A variable may be either *discrete* or *continuous.* A variable is discrete if its possible values have jumps or breaks, and continuous if there are no jumps or breaks. The distinction between discrete and continuous may in part depend on physical realities or units of measurement. For example, population is a discrete variable because it is measured in whole units or integers: 1, 2, 3, not 1.1, 1.2, 1.3. In contrast, unemployment is a continuous variable because it need not be measured in units that have breaks in them.

frequency distribution

Every set of data can be described in terms of how frequently certain values occur or in the form of a *frequency distribution.* In the discussion that follows, consider the hypothetical stock-price data in Table 2.1.

table 2.1. Selling Price of XYZ, Inc., Stock at the End of Each Month, Fiscal Year 1977–78

Month	Price
July	$27.25
August	28.50
September	30.00
October	29.25
November	30.50
December	28.00
January	28.50
February	29.50
March	30.25
April	29.75
May	30.25
June	28.75

A frequency distribution may be either *grouped* or *ungrouped.* If the number of values (or *observations*) is relatively small, an ungrouped frequency distribution, as presented in Table 2.2, may be more desirable.

table 2.2. Ungrouped Frequency Distribution

Price	Frequency
$27.25	1
28.00	1
28.50	2
28.75	1
29.25	1
29.50	1
29.75	1
30.00	1
30.25	2
30.50	1

For a large number of observations, an ungrouped frequency distribution would be impractical. For example, ten years of stock-price data would consist of 120 monthly observations. The stock-price data are grouped in Table 2.3. The class intervals are arbitrary.

table 2.3. Grouped Frequency Distribution

Stock Price ($)	Frequency
27.00–27.75	1
28.00–28.75	4
29.00–29.75	3
30.00–30.75	4

measures of location and dispersion

In addition to a frequency distribution, other statistics may be used to describe or summarize data. In this section we review some of the most important descriptive statistics and apply them to the stock-price data in Table 2.1.

The *arithmetic mean* or simply *mean* ($\bar{X}$) is defined as the average of all values. In mathematical notation:

$$\bar{X} = \frac{\sum_{I=1}^{N} X_I}{N} \tag{2.1}$$

where

$$\sum_{I=1}^{N} X_I$$

means $X_1 + X_2 + X_3 + \cdots + X_N$ (X_1 is the first stock price, 27.25; X_2 is 28.50; etc.), and N is the number of observations (12). Because they are implied, the subscripts are often omitted: $\bar{X} = \sum X/N$. The mean or average of the twelve monthly stock prices is 29.21.

The *median* is defined as the middle value and is found by ordering the stock prices from lowest to highest and selecting the value in the middle. The prices so ordered are 27.25, 28.00, 28.50, 28.50, 28.75, 29.25, 29.50, 29.75, 30.00, 30.25, 30.25, and 30.50. Since there are an even number of stock prices, the middle value is either the sixth or seventh value—29.25 or 29.50. In this case, the *median* is defined as the average of the two middle values, or 29,375. Obviously, there is no such problem in the case of an odd number of observations. The *mode* is defined as the value occurring most frequently; 28.50 and 30.25 each occur twice and no other value occurs more than twice. Therefore, a unique mode does not exist for the stock-price data.

The *standard deviation* (S) is a measure of the spread of the stock market prices and is defined by the formula

$$S = \sqrt{\frac{\sum_{I=1}^{N} (X_I - \bar{X})^2}{N - 1}} \tag{2.2}$$

where

$$\sum_{I=1}^{N} (X_I - \bar{X})^2$$

means $(X_1 - \bar{X})^2 + (X_2 - \bar{X})^2 + (X_3 - \bar{X})^2 + \cdots + (X_N - \bar{X})^2$. The *variance* is another measure of the spread of the data. Much statistical analysis beyond the descriptive level represents an attempt to explain variance, or why values deviate from their mean. For example, stock prices may vary because profits vary. The variance is equal to the square of the standard deviation:

$$\text{Variance} = S^2 \tag{2.3}$$

Demo 2.1 presents a computer printout of each $(X_I - \bar{X})$ and $(X_I - \bar{X})^2$, $\sum (X_I - \bar{X})^2$, and the values for the mean, standard deviation, and variance.

Note the use of the "E notation" in Demo 2.1. The fourth number in the second column, .173606E − 2, is equal to .00173606. Thus, the decimal point is moved two places to the left and two zeros are added. If this number had instead been .173606E2, then the decimal place would be moved two places to the right: 17.3606. Similarly, the eighth number in the second column, .850691E − 1, is equal to .0850691. Because the "E notation" is frequently used in research, especially for very small and very large numbers, the reader should become familiar with it.

$X_I - \bar{X}$	$(X_I - \bar{X})^2$
−1.95833	3.83507
−.708334	.501737
.791666	.626735
.041666	.173606E−2
1.29167	1.6684
−1.20833	1.46007
−.708334	.501737
.291666	.850691E−1
1.04167	1.08507
.541666	.293402
1.04167	1.08507
−.458334	.21007

$$\sum (X_I - \bar{X})^2 = 11.3542$$

MEAN = 29.2083

S = 1.01597

VARIANCE = 1.0322

demo 2.1. Calculations for Mean, Standard Deviation, and Variance

The descriptive statistics reviewed above are often discussed alongside the *normal distribution,* the most commonly used frequency distribution in statistics and econometrics. The properties of the normal distribution, or normal curve (Figure 2.1), are as follows:

1. It is bell-shaped and symmetrical.
2. The mean lies at the center.
3. The sum of the area under the curve equals one. (This principle is discussed below in the section on probability theory.)

The normal distribution is often used as a model of the frequency distribution of a population because it effectively represents the relative frequencies observed.

If data are normally distributed, then the standard deviation permits us to

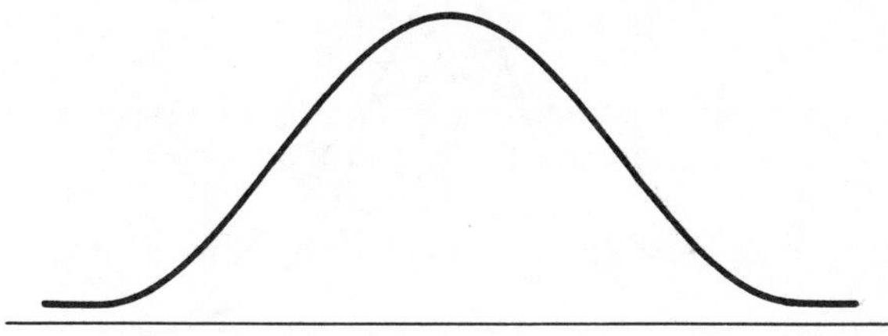

figure 2.1. Normal Curve

make conclusions regarding the frequency of particular observations. For example, a perfect normal distribution has 68.2 percent of the observations lying within one (plus or minus) standard deviation of the mean, 95.4 percent within two standard deviations, and 99.8 percent within three standard deviations (Figure 2.2). In the statistical tables at the end of this book is a table giving the areas under the normal curve. The use of this table is explained in a later section. Note that in Figure 2.2, Greek symbols are used to represent population parameters (μ and σ), while $\bar{X}$ and S are "estimators" of μ and σ, respectively. We will explain the properties of estimators in the next chapter.

Kurtosis (Figure 2.3) is a measure of the general peakedness of a distribution. A perfect normal distribution has a value of zero, while a distribution with a greater percentage of values clustered about the mean has positive kurtosis (*leptokurtic*); a distribution with a lower percentage of values clustered about the mean has negative kurtosis (*platykurtic*). Two distributions with the same variance can have markedly different values of kurtosis. For example, a leptokurtic (more peaked) distribution has longer tails than the platykurtic (flatter) distribution with the same variance. Kurtosis is defined by the formula

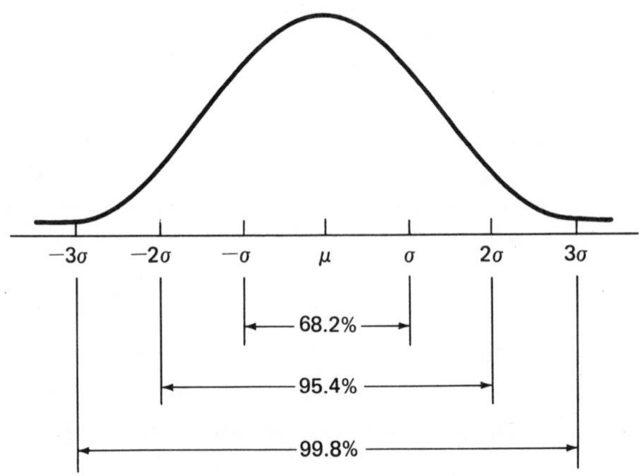

figure 2.2. Perfect Normal Distribution

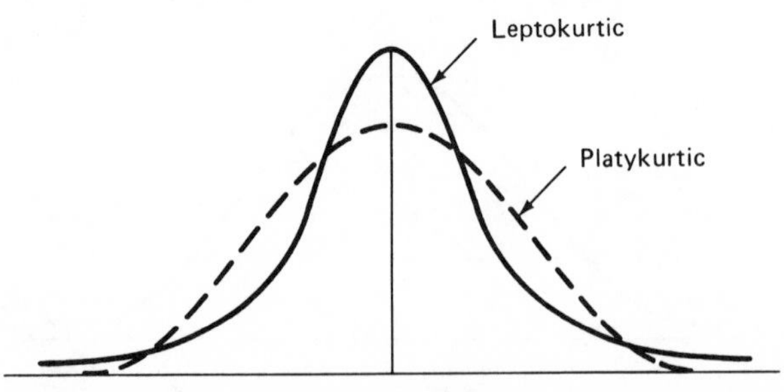

figure 2.3. Kurtosis

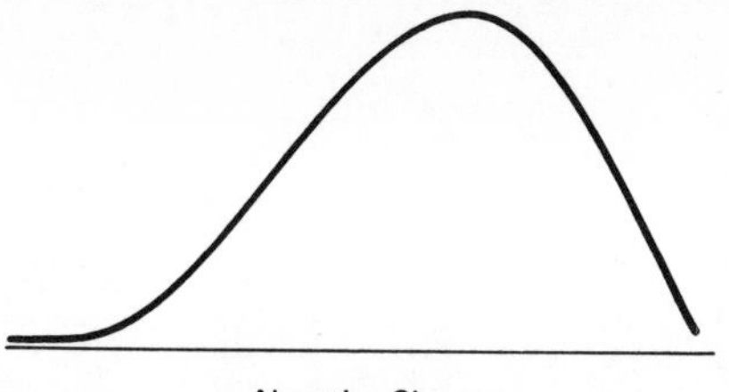

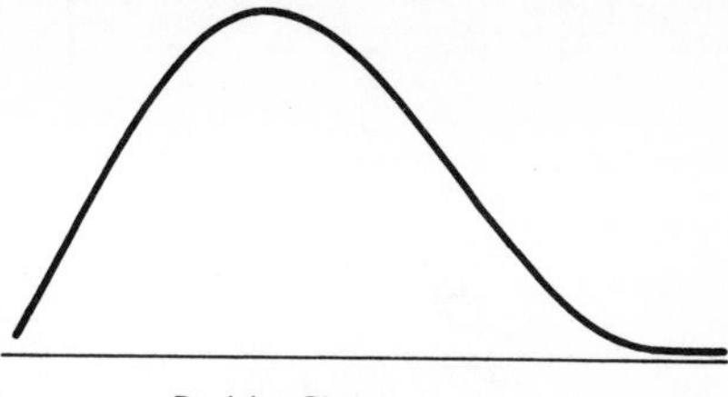

figure 2.4. Skewness

$$K = \frac{\sum_{I=1}^{N} \left(\frac{X_I - \bar{X}}{S} \right)^4}{N} - 3 \tag{2.4}$$

Skewness (Figure 2.4) measures the extent to which one tail of a distribution exceeds the other—i.e., whether or not the curve is symmetrical. It is positive if high values are farther away from the mean than low values, is negative if low values are farther away, and has a value of zero for the perfectly symmetrical distribution. The formula defining skewness (SK) is

$$SK = \frac{\sum_{I=1}^{N} \left(\frac{X_I - \bar{X}}{S} \right)^3}{N} \tag{2.5}$$

The *minimum* is defined as the lowest value of the variable, and the *maximum* as the highest value. The *range* is simply the difference between the maximum and the minimum and is another measure of the spread or variability of the data. The financial section of a newspaper regularly reports the minimum and maximum values for stocks listed on the New York Stock Exchange. In the present example the minimum is 27.25, the maximum is 30.50, and the range is 3.25.

probability theory

Consider an experiment that involves the tossing of a coin hundreds or even thousands of times. This experiment would ordinarily be rather difficult to perform because of the large amount of time and effort required. However, you can easily perform this experiment by using the *random-variable function* on a computer, which generates random numbers in the range of zero to one (or any specified range). Demo 2.2 presents the output from a computer "run" that generated ten "random" numbers. *Random variable* may be defined as a variable whose value is determined by chance. The reason we make use of the random-variable function is that it allows us to discuss probability theory without resort to advanced mathematics.

Since there is, theoretically, an equal probability of obtaining a number

.204935
.229581
.533074
.132211
.995602
.783813
.741854
.397713
.709588
.67811

demo 2.2. Random Numbers Generated in Sample Run

between 0 and .5, and between .5 and 1, any time the computer generates a number less than .5, we assign a head to that event, and a tail for numbers greater than .5. What if the computer came up with a number precisely equal to .5? Although this possibility is remote, this would represent the event of the coin standing on edge. In Demo 2.3 the computer program that simulates this experiment is run for 25, 50, 100, 200, 300, 400, 500, 600, 700, 800, 900, 1,000, 2,000, 3,000, 4,000, and 5,000 coin tosses. Duplicating this experiment with an actual coin would obviously be a formidable task, but it is accomplished in a few seconds on a computer.

What happens to the percentage of heads as the number (N) of coin tosses increases? If would appear from Figure 2.5 that, as N increases, the relative fre-

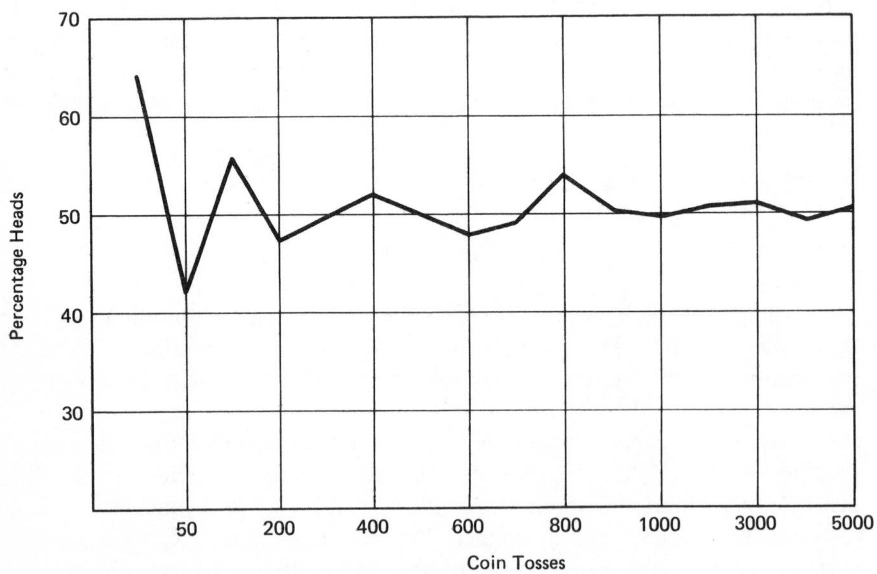

figure 2.5. Graph of Coin-Tossing Experiment

```
RUN
NUMBER OF COIN TOSSES
? 25
NUMBER OF HEADS= 16
NUMBER OF TAILS= 9
PERCENTAGE HEADS= 64

RUN
NUMBER OF COIN TOSSES
? 50
NUMBER OF HEADS= 21
NUMBER OF TAILS= 29
PERCENTAGE HEADS= 42

RUN
NUMBER OF COIN TOSSES
? 100
NUMBER OF HEADS= 56
NUMBER OF TAILS= 44
PERCENTAGE HEADS= 56

RUN
NUMBER OF COIN TOSSES
? 200
NUMBER OF HEADS= 95
NUMBER OF TAILS= 105
PERCENTAGE HEADS= 47.5

RUN
NUMBER OF COIN TOSSES
? 300
NUMBER OF HEADS= 149
NUMBER OF TAILS= 151
PERCENTAGE HEADS= 49.6667

RUN
NUMBER OF COIN TOSSES
? 400
NUMBER OF HEADS= 208
NUMBER OF TAILS= 192
PERCENTAGE HEADS= 52

RUN
NUMBER OF COIN TOSSES
? 500
NUMBER OF HEADS= 250
NUMBER OF TAILS= 250
PERCENTAGE HEADS= 50

RUN
NUMBER OF COIN TOSSES
? 600
NUMBER OF HEADS= 286
NUMBER OF TAILS= 314
PERCENTAGE HEADS= 47.6667

RUN
NUMBER OF COIN TOSSES
? 700
NUMBER OF HEADS= 345
NUMBER OF TAILS= 355
PERCENTAGE HEADS= 49.2857

RUN
NUMBER OF COIN TOSSES
? 800
NUMBER OF HEADS= 431
NUMBER OF TAILS= 369
PERCENTAGE HEADS= 53.875

RUN
NUMBER OF COIN TOSSES
? 900
NUMBER OF HEADS= 458
NUMBER OF TAILS= 442
PERCENTAGE HEADS= 50.8889

RUN
NUMBER OF COIN TOSSES
? 1000
NUMBER OF HEADS= 499
NUMBER OF TAILS= 501
PERCENTAGE HEADS= 49.9

RUN
NUMBER OF COIN TOSSES
? 2000
NUMBER OF HEADS= 1012
NUMBER OF TAILS= 988
PERCENTAGE HEADS= 50.6

RUN
NUMBER OF COIN TOSSES
? 3000
NUMBER OF HEADS= 1527
NUMBER OF TAILS= 1473
PERCENTAGE HEADS= 50.9

RUN
NUMBER OF COIN TOSSES
? 4000
NUMBER OF HEADS= 1956
NUMBER OF TAILS= 2044
PERCENTAGE HEADS= 48.9

RUN
NUMBER OF COIN TOSSES
? 5000
NUMBER OF HEADS= 2519
NUMBER OF TAILS= 2481
PERCENTAGE HEADS= 50.38
```

demo 2.3. Computer Simulation of Coin-Tossing Experiment

quency of heads becomes more stable. In other words, its amplitude declines. The *probability* of an *event* (a head) can be defined as that value of relative frequency obtained as N approaches infinity. Is the random-number function "unbiased?" Another way of asking this question is, on the average, do we get .5 when a random number is generated? Or, do we "expect" to get .5 on the average?

The "expected" result (E) of an experiment is simply the mean of its frequency (also termed *probability*) distribution, or .5 in the case of the computer-simulated coin-tossing experiment. E is actually a weighted average of all possible outcomes of an experiment. If we let $X_1 = 1$ for heads and $X_2 = 0$ for tails, then $E(X) = .5(1) + .5(0) = .5$. More generally, the expected value or mean of a random variable is

$$E(X) = \mu = P_1X_1 + P_2X_2 + \cdots + P_NX_N = \sum_{I=1}^{N} P_IX_I \tag{2.6}$$

where P_I = probability that X_I occurs
μ = population mean

Population is defined as all possible outcomes of an experiment. In research we seldom know the true population mean (μ) or the true population standard deviation (σ). Consequently, we use the sample mean ($\bar{X}$) and the sample standard deviation (S) to "estimate" the true population parameters. Much statistical analysis involves attempting to measure how close the sample statistics estimate the population parameters.

In the discrete case (X takes on a finite number of values), as in the coin-tossing experiment, the population consists of heads or tails. However, the random-number function itself generates numbers from an infinite population consisting of all numbers between zero and one. The equation for this frequency distribution is

$$\begin{aligned} F(X) &= 1 \qquad 0 < X < 1 \\ &= 0 \qquad \text{elsewhere} \end{aligned} \tag{2.7}$$

The graph of this equation is shown in Figure 2.6. $F(X)$ is continuous in the range of zero to one. The fact that the graph of $F(X)$ is horizontal means that there is the same probability of selecting a number in all intervals of a given width that lie between zero and one. The probability of selecting any particular number is zero.

A geometrical interpretation of probability can be gained by noting that the area under the curve is equal to one (a square of dimension one by one). Thus, the total probability of selecting a random number between zero and one is equal to one. If this square is sliced into ten equal rectangles, as in Figure 2.7, the area of each represents the probability of selecting a number between 0 and .1, .1 and .2, and so forth. This probability is obviously .1(.1 × 1). Given that the area underneath a graph of any frequency distribution (not just the random-

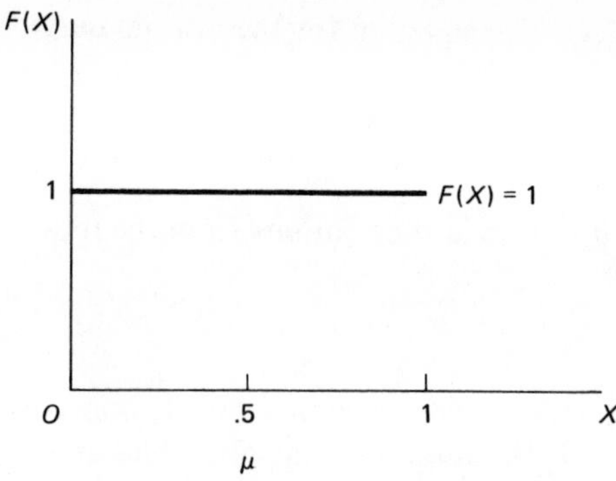

figure 2.6. Graph of Random-Number Distribution

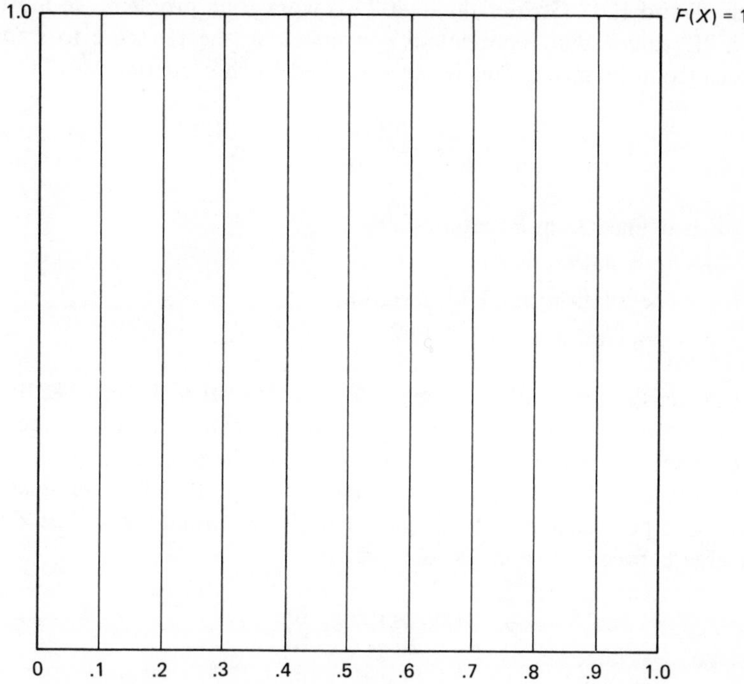

figure 2.7. Geometrical Interpretation of Probability Using Random-Number Function

number function) equals one by definition, the following equation holds:

$$\sum_{I=1}^{N} P_I = 1 \tag{2.8}$$

The most important distribution in statistics and econometrics is the normal distribution (Figure 2.1). The equation for the normal curve is

$$F(Z) = \frac{e^{-Z^2/2}}{\sqrt{2\pi}} \tag{2.9}$$

where Z is measured in standard deviations from the mean
$e = 2.71828$
$\pi = 3.14159$

The evaluation of the area under this curve is much more complicated than that of the random-number distribution. Fortunately, tables and computer programs are available to do the work for us. As an example, suppose that IQ is normally distributed with a mean of 100 and a standard deviation of 20. What is the probability that a person selected at random has an IQ between 100 and 120? Between 85 and 120? Greater than 140? To work each problem, we must calculate a "Z value" that represents a conversion of the IQ score to standard deviations from the mean. This is accomplished by the equation

$$Z = \frac{X - \mu}{\sigma} \tag{2.10}$$

where Z is defined as in Equation (2.9)
μ = population mean
σ = population standard deviation
X = population value (IQ score)

In the discussion that follows, the reader should refer to Figure 2.8. Because the normal curve is symmetrical, the area to the right of the mean equals .5, and the area to the left of the mean also equals .5. The table of areas under the normal curve gives the areas for the right half only, and therefore we must work out the above problems in terms of each half of the normal curve. The Z value for the area between 100 and 120 is

$$Z = \frac{120 - 100}{20} = \frac{20}{20} = 1$$

According to Statistical Table 1, the area is .3413, or the probability is .3413 of selecting a person at random with an IQ between 100 and 120. The Z value for the area between 85 and 100 (we must consider each half of the curve separately) is

$$Z = \frac{100 - 85}{20} = \frac{15}{20} = .75$$

The area associated with a Z value of .75 is .2734; the probability is .2734 of

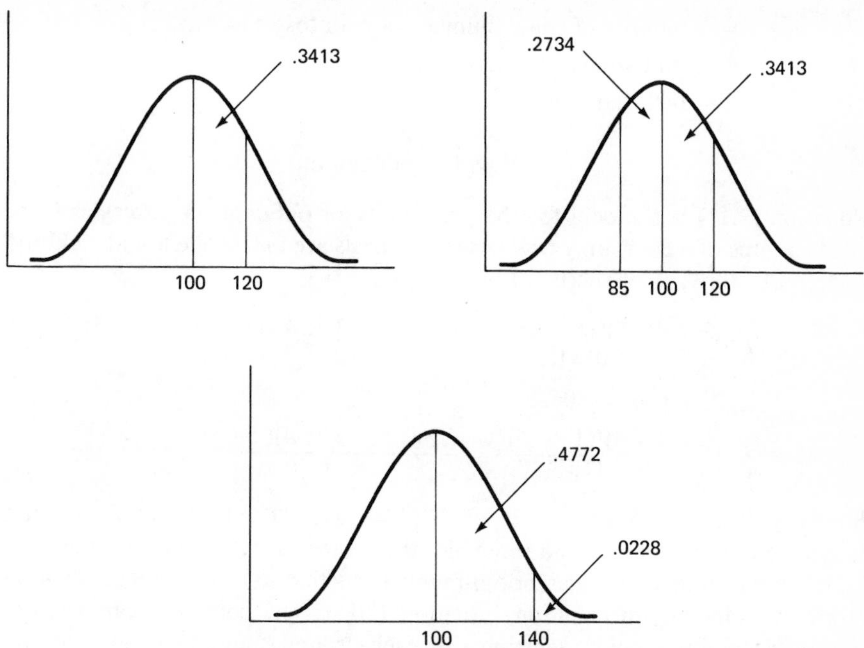

figure 2.8. Illustration of Normal-Curve Problems

selecting a person with an IQ between 85 and 100. Therefore, the probability is .6147 (.3413 + .2734) of selecting a person with an IQ between 85 and 120. The Z value for the area between 100 and 140 is

$$Z = \frac{140 - 100}{20} = \frac{40}{20} = 2$$

The associated area is .4772, or the probability is .4772 of selecting a person with an IQ between 100 and 140. But what about a person with an IQ greater than 140? Since the total area to the right of the mean is .5, the answer must be .0228 (.5 − .4772).

Another commonly used probability distribution is the binomial distribution. It applies in the discrete case in which there are only two possible values, such as in the coin-tossing problem. Suppose we wish to know the probability of obtaining 0, 1, 2, 3, or 4 heads in four flips of a coin. The equation for calculating these probabilities is

$$P(X) = \frac{N!P^X(1-P)^{N-X}}{X!(N-X)!} \qquad (2.11)$$

where X = number of heads (0, 1, 2, 3, 4)

$P(X)$ = probability of X successes (a head)

N = number of trials (number of coin tosses = 4)
P = probability of a success (.5)
$!$ = factorial; e.g., $3! = 1 \times 2 \times 3$
$4! = 1 \times 2 \times 3 \times 4$
$0! = 1$ (by definition)

Equation (2.11) is a model for the probability of obtaining X successes (e.g., heads in flips of a coin) in N trials when the trials are independent and yield the same probability, P, of success. For example:

$$P(0) = \frac{4!(.5)^0(1-.5)^4}{0!4!} = \frac{(1 \times 2 \times 3 \times 4)(1)(.5)^4}{(1)(1 \times 2 \times 3 \times 4)}$$

$$= (.5)^4 = .0625$$

$$P(1) = \frac{4!(.5)^1(1-.5)^3}{1!3!} = \frac{(1 \times 2 \times 3 \times 4)(.5)(.5)^3}{6} = .25$$

Similarly, $P(2) = .375$, $P(3) = .25$, and $P(4) = .0625$. The binomial distribution is symmetrical for $P = .5$ and resembles the normal distribution for large N.

It is interesting to use the random-number function to experimentally demonstrate the binomial-distribution Equation (2.11). The computer can be programmed to flip a coin four times in each "round," and there can be any number of rounds, as in Demo 2.4.

```
NUMBER OF HEADS=1 ON ROUND 1
NUMBER OF HEADS=2 ON ROUND 2
NUMBER OF HEADS=2 ON ROUND 3
NUMBER OF HEADS=2 ON ROUND 4
NUMBER OF HEADS=3 ON ROUND 5
NUMBER OF HEADS=4 ON ROUND 6
NUMBER OF HEADS=2 ON ROUND 7
NUMBER OF HEADS=2 ON ROUND 8
NUMBER OF HEADS=0 ON ROUND 9
NUMBER OF HEADS=3 ON ROUND 10
NUMBER OF HEADS=3 ON ROUND 11
NUMBER OF HEADS=1 ON ROUND 12
NUMBER OF HEADS=1 ON ROUND 13
NUMBER OF HEADS=3 ON ROUND 14
NUMBER OF HEADS=3 ON ROUND 15
NUMBER OF HEADS=0 ON ROUND 16
NUMBER OF HEADS=2 ON ROUND 17
NUMBER OF HEADS=2 ON ROUND 18
NUMBER OF HEADS=1 ON ROUND 19
NUMBER OF HEADS=2 ON ROUND 20
NUMBER OF HEADS=0 ON ROUND 21
NUMBER OF HEADS=1 ON ROUND 22
NUMBER OF HEADS=2 ON ROUND 23
NUMBER OF HEADS=1 ON ROUND 24
NUMBER OF HEADS=4 ON ROUND 25
```

demo 2.4.

How close is our experiment to the theoretically expected results of .0625, .25, .375, .25, and .0625? If we count the number of rounds that zero heads, one head, two heads, three heads, and four heads occurred, the respective results are 3, 6, 9, 5, and 2, which translate into probabilities (dividing by 25) of .12, .24, .36, .20, and .08. These experimental results are actually surprisingly close considering that there are only twenty-five rounds. If there had been a hundred or a thousand rounds, our experimental results would probably have been much closer to the theoretically expected results. However, this experiment clearly demonstrates that the probability of an event's occurring is defined in the abstract (as N approaches infinity); the reality need not and probably will not conform to the precise theoretical expectation.

sampling theory

An interesting question is whether or not the "coin" we were tossing in the preceding section is unbiased. Since our coin was the random-number generator on a computer, this question is equivalent to asking whether or not the mean of the population of random numbers is equal to .5. In this section and the next we develop the theory necessary to answer this question. At the heart of this theory is the science of sampling. Either because of physical impossibility (the number of random numbers is infinite) or because of the lack of time and money, the researcher rarely attempts to study the entire population. Instead he or she must be content with "sampling" the population. We then hope to estimate the population mean (μ) using the sample mean ($\bar{X}$).

Suppose we draw a sample of ten random numbers. Demo 2.5 shows one run of a computer program that generates ten random numbers and calculates their mean and standard deviation. Given that the mean of these numbers is .540 (rounded), not .5, should we conclude that the random-number function is biased? Or is it possible that these numbers could have been drawn from a

```
        .30052
        .803081
        .113802
        .455083
        .706284
        .141954
        .495166
        .693415
        .703993
        .983225
MEAN=   .539652
SD=     .288751
```

demo 2.5. Sample of Ten Random Numbers Along with Their Mean and Standard Deviation

population with a mean of .5? Understanding what is meant by the "sampling distribution of means" is the key to answering this question.

Instead of generating just one sample mean (.540), as in Demo 2.5, we could use the same program to generate a large number of sample means. The result would be a sampling distribution of means. In Demo 2.6 we have generated twenty-six sample means. Each number (e.g., .367 is the first sample mean) represents the mean of ten random numbers. Thus, twenty-six sets of ten random numbers (total of 260) are generated, but only the mean of each set is printed. Then the grand mean (the mean of the twenty-six sample means) and the standard deviation of the twenty-six sample means are printed: .466462 and .07876, respectively. The "standard deviation of a sampling distribution" is termed the *standard error*.

Now consider the graph of the frequency distribution of the random-number function (Figure 2.6). As this distribution is a horizontal line rather than bell shaped, the population of random numbers is obviously not normally distributed. Although we will save a demonstration of this concept for one of the exercises, the sampling distribution of means in Demo 2.6 is normally distributed

```
     .367
     .464
     .344
     .491
     .506
     .470
     .517
     .547
     .437
     .375
     .612
     .495
     .542
     .356
     .487
     .458
     .609
     .567
     .476
     .491
     .453
     .391
     .521
     .322
     .455
     .375
MEAN= .466462
SD= .07876
```

demo 2.6. Sampling Distribution of Means Along with Grand Mean and Standard Error

(Figure 2.9). What we have discovered is one of the most important theorems in statistics—the central limit theorem—which states that the means of repeated samples (the sampling distribution of means) tend toward normality even if these samples are not drawn from a normally distributed population. This theorem allows us to make conclusions about the probability of drawing sample means within a certain distance from the assumed population mean (.5 in this case). From a knowledge of the normal distribution, we can state the following conclusion: 68.2 percent of the sample means lie within one (plus or minus) standard error of the true population mean, 95.4 percent lie within two standard errors, and 99.8 percent lie within three standard errors. Of course, these percentages are approximations for any real-world experiment.

Intuitively, it may seem logical to the reader that error would vary directly with the standard deviation (a measure of variability) and inversely with the sample size. This is actually the case, as the equation for the standard error is

$$SE = \frac{\sigma}{\sqrt{N}} \tag{2.12}$$

where σ is the standard deviation of the population and N is the sample size. If we make the simplifying assumption that σ is equal to .289 (from Demo 2.5), then the standard error is equal to

$$\frac{.289}{\sqrt{10}} = \frac{.289}{3.162} = .091$$

If the true mean of the population of random numbers is .5 and the actual standard deviation of all random numbers is .289, then 68.2 percent of the samples of $N = 10$ will have means in the range of plus or minus .091 of .5: .409 to .591; 95.4 percent of the sample means will lie within the range of .318 to .682; and 99.8 percent in the range of .227 to .773.

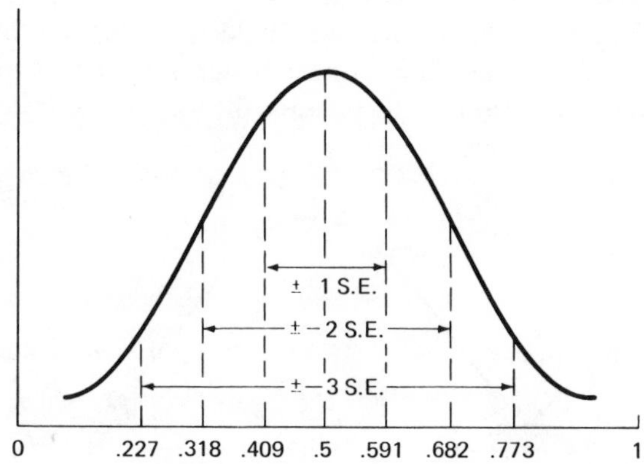

figure 2.9. Sampling Distribution of Means

The basic problem in sampling is that a sample that is not representative of the entire population might accidentally be selected, thereby causing us to make the wrong conclusion with respect to the value of the population mean. For example, there is a 4.6-percent chance (100 — 95.4) of selecting a sample mean below .318 or above .682. In the next section we will discuss how to deal with this problem.

hypothesis testing and confidence intervals

The hypothesis we wish to test is whether or not the mean of the random-number function is equal to .5. This hypothesis actually consists of two hypotheses. The first is known as the "null" hypothesis—$H_0: \mu = .5$. If we do not reject H_0, then it is assumed that any difference between the sample mean and the assumed population mean occurred because of random-sampling error. The second hypothesis is known as the "alternate" and is abbreviated $H_1: \mu \neq .5$. If we reject H_0, H_1 is automatically accepted; it is highly unlikely that the difference between the sample mean and the assumed population mean occurred because of chance random-sampling error.

A *critical region* must be chosen that measures the *level of risk* we are willing to take with respect to rejecting the null hypothesis. This critical region is illustrated in Figure 2.10 for a "two-tailed" test. Thus, if our sample mean lies "too far" away from the assumed population mean, it lies in the critical region. The notion of "too far" is measured by the number of standard errors the sample mean lies from the assumed population mean.

For example, suppose that the size of each tail of the critical region is 0.1 percent; for both tails this is a total of 0.2 percent. Since 99.8 percent of the sampling distribution of means (Figure 2.9) fall within plus or minus three standard errors of the mean, if we selected a sample of ten random numbers with a mean of less than .227, the sample mean would lie in the left tail of the critical region. Similarly, a mean greater than .773 would lie in the right-hand tail. At the 0.2-percent level of risk, we would reject the null hypothesis if the sample mean were less than .227 or greater than .773. The level of risk is also termed the *level of significance*. If, instead, the size of the critical region were

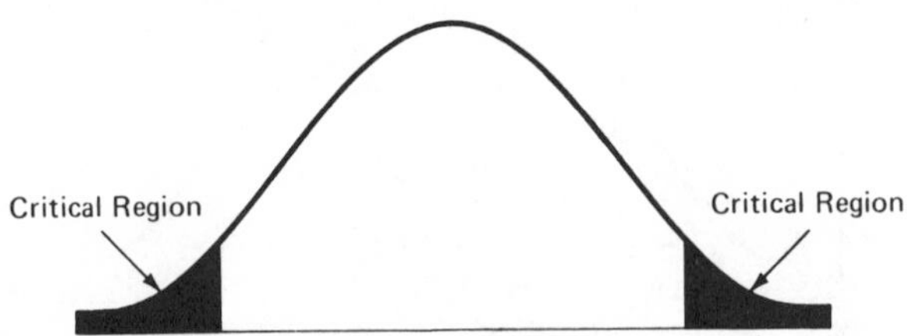

figure 2.10. Illustration of Critical Region for Two-Tailed Test

4.6 percent (plus or minus two standard errors), a sample mean less than .318 or greater than .682 would lie in the critical region. What about a 68.2-percent critical region? This is equivalent to plus or minus one standard error, and therefore a sample mean less than .409 or greater than .591 would lie in the critical region.

A major problem in hypothesis testing is the choice of the size of the critical region. For example, a .05 critical region (.025 for each tail) means that there is a .05 (5-percent) probability of rejecting the null hypothesis when it is actually true. That is, 5 percent of the time we will draw a sample mean that lies in the critical region, thereby causing us to reject the null hypothesis even though it is true. If this should occur, we have committed a "Type I" error. The smaller the critical region or the level of risk, the less likely is the sample mean to lie in the critical region, and the smaller the probability of rejecting the null hypothesis and committing a Type I error.

However, suppose that the null hypothesis is false and therefore the alternate hypothesis is true. If we reduce the probability of rejecting the null hypothesis by setting an extremely low level of risk for committing a Type I error, we increase the probability of rejecting the alternate hypothesis even though it is true. Rejecting the alternate hypothesis when it is true is known as a "Type II" error. Thus, the smaller the risk of a Type I error, the greater is the risk of committing a Type II error.

Because the probability of making a Type II error is somewhat difficult to calculate and because few computer programs are available that calculate probabilities of Type II errors, econometricians are generally content with arbitrarily setting the probability of committing a Type I error and hoping for the best. Although this procedure may not be completely satisfactory, most published economic research considers only the probability of a Type I error.

Since the choice of the appropriate level of significance (risk of Type I error) involves a trade-off, the economist might make the choice depending on the relative cost of committing either error. Suppose the null and alternate hypotheses are:

H_0: It will not rain today.
H_1: It will rain today.

Since our clothes may be ruined and our health affected if it does rain and we do not take an umbrella, whereas there is little cost in bringing the umbrella with us if it does not rain, we would be inclined in this example to set an extremely high probability of committing a Type I error. The high probability attached to a Type I error means that we are more likely to reject the null hypothesis and less likely to make a Type II error. Although the choice of the appropriate level of significance is arbitrary, normally the choice is made at either the 1-, 5-, or 10-percent levels of risk.

To observe the process of hypothesis testing, consider the sample of ten random numbers in Demo 2.5 with a mean of .54 and a sample standard deviation of .289. The hypotheses are

$$H_0: \mu = .5$$
$$H_1: \mu \neq .5$$

It must be pointed out that since σ is not usually known in econometric work, the Z distribution cannot be used. An alternative is the T (or student's t) distribution, which approximates Z for large N ($N > 30$). In fact, the numerical difference between T and Z is trivial for most econometric problems. However, for a small sample of ten random numbers, the difference between T and Z is not trivial. T is defined as

$$T = \frac{|\bar{X} - \mu|}{SE} \tag{2.13}$$

where $SE = S/\sqrt{N}$. The T test has $(N - 1)$ "degrees of freedom," which refer to the number of "unconstrained observations" from the sample.

Equation (2.13) means that we should take the absolute value of the difference between the sample mean and the assumed population mean and divide by the standard error. T measures the number of standard errors that the sample mean lies from the population mean. If T is greater than a certain critical value, the null hypothesis is rejected; if T is less than this critical value, the null hypothesis is accepted. The critical values can be obtained from a T table (see Statistical Table 2). For a sample size of ten ("degrees of freedom" $= N - 1 = 9$), the critical values with the significance levels in parentheses are 3.250 (.01), 2.262 (.05), and 1.833 (.1). Note that the critical values fall as the level of significance increases. For a sample of ten random numbers with a mean of .54 and a standard deviation of .289, T is equal to

$$\frac{|.54 - .5|}{.289/\sqrt{10}} = \frac{.04}{.091} = .440$$

Since .440 is less than any of the above critical values, it really does not matter which level of significance is chosen. The null hypothesis is not rejected; the mean of the population of random numbers is equal to .5.

Another method of testing the null hypothesis is to construct what is termed a *confidence interval.* A confidence interval contains the area outside the critical region (the middle area in Figure 2.10). Thus, a .95 (95-percent) confidence interval is equivalent to a .05 level of significance. The interpretation of this confidence interval is that we are 95-percent certain (.95 "level of confidence") that the true mean of the population lies within this interval. A confidence interval is calculated by first multiplying the appropriate critical T value by the standard error. Then this result is added to the sample mean to give the upper bound of the interval. The lower bound of the interval is obtained by subtracting the same result from the sample mean. The 90-, 95-, and 99-percent confidence intervals are calculated as follows:

90% Confidence Interval:
$1.833 \times (.091) = .167$
Upper Bound $= .54 + .167 = .707$
Lower Bound $= .54 - .167 = .373$
Therefore: $.373 < \mu < .707$

95% Confidence Interval:
$2.262 \times (.091) = .206$
Upper Bound $= .54 + .206 = .746$
Lower Bound $= .54 - .206 = .334$
Therefore: $.334 < \mu < .746$

99% Confidence Interval:
$3.250 \times (.091) = .296$
Upper Bound $= .54 + .296 = .836$
Lower Bound $= .54 - .296 = .244$
Therefore: $.244 < \mu < .836$

The null hypothesis is tested by seeing if the confidence interval contains the assumed mean of the population (.5). If so, then the null hypothesis is accepted; if not, it is rejected. Since all of the above confidence intervals contain .5, we can accept the null hypothesis at the .1, .05, and .01 levels of significance. The confidence-interval test should always arrive at the same conclusion as the T test (Equation (2.13)).

summary

Statistics is a prerequisite of the study of econometrics. The reader should have a good comprehension of the concepts presented in this chapter before proceeding with the remainder of the book. The exercises are designed to freshen the memory and provide needed practice. Statistics and econometrics are not easy disciplines to study, and therefore the reader should not be surprised to discover that considerable practice is needed in order to understand the concepts discussed in this book.

The science of statistics may be separated into two branches—*descriptive* and *inferential.* The descriptive branch consists of summarizing and presenting data in a form that can be easily comprehended. Tables, figures, and graphs are important descriptive tools. For example, a table may be in the form of a frequency distribution that presents the mean, standard deviation, and other measures of location and dispersion. Although the use of descriptive statistics is often the first step in data analysis, econometricians are primarily interested in using data to test theories or hypotheses. It is this latter area that in part constitutes the second branch of statistics—inferential.

Hypothesis testing requires a knowledge of probability and sampling theory. As the coin-tossing experiment demonstrated, the *probability* of an event is defined in terms of the relative frequency obtained as N (the number of trials or observations) approaches infinity. Therefore, we should not be surprised if our experimental or empirical results do not exactly coincide with those predicted by probability theory. However, we can expect the amount of error (the amplitude in Figure 2.5) to be reduced as N increases.

The most important probability distribution in econometrics is the normal curve, or normal distribution. A "Z value" associated with the normal curve measures the number of standard deviations a particular value of a normally distributed population lies from the mean. For example, 68.2 percent of the values lie within plus or minus one standard deviation of the mean, 95.4 percent within two standard deviations, and 99.8 percent within three standard deviations. Probabilities associated with other Z values can be calculated by using the Z statistical table at the end of the book. If a variable takes on only two values, then the binomial distribution is applicable. The binomial distribution resembles the normal curve for large N.

Data must be available in order to test a hypothesis. The cost of data collection can be greatly reduced by relying on sampling, instead of attempting to survey an entire population. An important aspect of sampling theory is the "sampling distribution of means," which consists of all possible samples of a particular size. For example, Figure 2.9 shows a graph of all possible sample means that may be drawn from a population of random numbers; the sample size is equal to ten for the infinite number of possible samples (the population of random numbers is infinite).

Because the sampling distribution of means is normally distributed (central limit theorem), it is possible to test hypotheses regarding the population parameters (μ and σ) by using the sample statistics ($\bar{X}$ and S). The equations presented for $\bar{X}$ and S—Equations (2.1) and (2.2)—are used to estimate the usually unknown population parameters (μ and σ) from sample data. Thus, $\bar{X}$ and S are "estimators" of the population parameters. Some of the properties of estimators are considered in the next chapter.

One set of hypotheses that may be tested consists of a "null" and an "alternate" hypothesis. If the null hypothesis is not rejected, then we conclude that the population parameter is equal to an assumed value. Acceptance of the alternate instead of the null hypothesis means that our sample estimate is "too far" away from the assumed value of the population parameter and thus very unlikely for the difference to be due to chance random-sampling error; consequently, the null hypothesis is rejected. The notion of "too far" is measured by T, which is equal to the number of standard errors from the assumed value and is defined by a *critical region*. Although the appropriate critical region is arbitrary, normally a 1-, 5-, or 10-percent critical region is established for purposes of decision making.

The null and alternate hypotheses may also be tested by constructing a *confidence interval*. The population parameter is contained within the interval with a particular probability defined by the level of confidence chosen (usually 90, 95, or 99 percent).

Hypothesis tests and confidence intervals are affected by the sample size. This is because the standard error falls as the sample size increases (see Equation (2.12)). The decline in standard error associated with increased sample size is analogous to the declining amplitude illustrated in Figure 2.5 for the coin-tossing experiment. Thus, we can have greater confidence in our decisions as the sample size increases.

We now present several examples that should help the reader to better understand the material presented in this chapter. Throughout the textbook, the reader is encouraged to study the examples carefully before proceeding with the exercises.

examples

example 1

a. Calculate $\sum (X_i - \bar{X})$ where X takes on the values 1, 3, 5, and 7. That is, $X_1 = 1$; $X_2 = 3$; $X_3 = 5$; and $X_4 = 7$.

$$\bar{X} = \sum X_i/N = (1 + 3 + 5 + 7)/4 = 4$$

$$\begin{aligned} X_1 - 4 &= 1 - 4 = -3 \\ X_2 - 4 &= 3 - 4 = -1 \\ X_3 - 4 &= 5 - 4 = 1 \\ X_4 - 4 &= 7 - 4 = 3 \\ & \qquad\qquad\; 0 = \text{Answer} \end{aligned}$$

b. Calculate $\sum_{i=1}^{5} i^2$

$$1^2 + 2^2 + 3^2 + 4^2 + 5^2 = 1 + 4 + 9 + 16 + 25 = 55$$

c. Calculate $\sum X_i^2$ where X takes on the values 1, 2, 3, 4, and 5.

$1^2 + 2^2 + 3^2 + 4^2 + 5^2 = 55$, or same answer as in Part b of this example.

example 2

You have the following family-income data:

$25,000
18,000
20,000
22,000
100,000

Calculate the mean and median. Which is the preferred measure of family income?

$$\begin{aligned}\bar{X} &= \sum X_i/N \\ &= (25{,}000 + 18{,}000 + 20{,}000 + 22{,}000 + 100{,}000)/5 \\ &= 37{,}000\end{aligned}$$

To calculate the median, the data must be ordered:

18,000 20,000 22,000 25,000 100,000

The median is the middle value (\$22,000). The median is often used instead of the mean to summarize income data because it is not affected by extreme values such as the \$100,000 figure.

example 3

Calculate the standard deviation of the income data in Example 2. Is income normally distributed?

To calculate the standard deviation:

The income data can be expressed in thousands to make the calculations easier: 25, 18, 20, 22, 100.

$$S = \sqrt{\frac{\sum (X_I - \bar{X})^2}{N - 1}}$$

$$\begin{aligned}(25 - 37)^2 &= 144 \\ (18 - 37)^2 &= 361 \\ (20 - 37)^2 &= 289 \\ (22 - 37)^2 &= 225 \\ (100 - 37)^2 &= \underline{3{,}969} \\ & 4{,}988\end{aligned}$$

$$S = \sqrt{\frac{4{,}988}{4}} = \sqrt{1{,}247} = 35.32$$

$= \$35{,}320$ (multiplying by 1,000, since original data were in thousands)

The data are skewed positively and are therefore not normally distributed:

$$SK = \frac{\sum \left(\frac{X_I - \bar{X}}{S}\right)^3}{N}$$

$$\begin{aligned}\left(\frac{25 - 37}{35.32}\right)^3 &= -.04 \\ \left(\frac{18 - 37}{35.32}\right)^3 &= -.16 \\ \left(\frac{20 - 37}{35.32}\right)^3 &= -.11 \\ \left(\frac{22 - 37}{35.32}\right)^3 &= -.07\end{aligned}$$

$$\left(\frac{100 - 37}{35.32}\right)^3 = \begin{array}{r} 5.64 \\ \hline 5.26 \end{array}$$

$$SK = \frac{5.26}{5} = 1.05$$

Note: The answer is not multiplied by 1,000 because, for example:

$$\left(\frac{25{,}000 - 37{,}000}{35{,}320}\right) = \left(\frac{25 - 37}{35.32}\right)$$

example 4

Suppose a lottery consists of 100 tickets and you buy one of them. Each ticket costs $1 and the prize is $25. What is the mathematical expectation?

To calculate the mathematical expectation:

The probability of winning is .01 (1/100), and the probability of losing is .99 (99/100):

$$P_1 = .01$$
$$P_2 = .99$$

If you win, the net payoff is $24 (25 − 1). If you lose, the loss is the price of the ticket, or $1:

$$X_1 = \$24$$
$$X_2 = -\$1$$

Therefore:

$$E(X) = .01(\$24) + .99(-\$1)$$
$$= .24 - .99 = -\$.75$$

Thus, the lottery management can expect to earn $.75 on every ticket sold, or a total of $75.

example 5

Assume that family income is normally distributed with a mean of $20,000 and a standard deviation of $4,000. What is the probability that a family selected at random will have an income between $20,000 and $22,000?

$$\mu = \$20{,}000$$
$$\sigma = 4{,}000$$
$$Z = (X - \mu)/\sigma$$
$$= \frac{22{,}000 - 20{,}000}{4{,}000} = .5$$

The area of the normal curve associated with a Z value of .5 is .1915. Thus, about 19 percent of the families have incomes between $20,000 and $22,000.

What about between \$19,000 and \$20,000?

$$Z = \frac{19{,}000 - 20{,}000}{4{,}000} = -.25$$

$$= .25 \text{ (minus signs are meaningless, since area under normal curve is positive)}$$

The area associated with a Z value of .25 is .0987, or about 10 percent of the families have incomes between \$19,000 and \$20,000.

example 6

A random sample of 144 families in a major city finds that the mean family income is \$17,500 and the sample standard deviation is \$3,600. Test the null and alternate hypotheses:

$$\mu = \$20{,}000$$

$$\mu \neq \$20{,}000$$

First, the level of significance must be chosen (this is arbitrary). For example, the critical values at the .01, .05, and .1 levels are 2.576, 1.96, and 1.645, respectively. These are for degrees of freedom equal to infinity (∞). The degrees of freedom for the T test are defined as one less than the sample size ($N - 1$). However, the critical values do not decline beyond a sample size of 121. Thus, the row marked "infinity" can be used for a sample size of 144.

The standard error is equal to

$$SE = \frac{3{,}600}{\sqrt{144}} = \frac{3{,}600}{12} = 300$$

Therefore:

$$T = \frac{|17{,}500 - 20{,}000|}{300} = \frac{2{,}500}{300} = 8.33$$

Since 8.33 is greater than the above critical values, the null hypothesis is rejected regardless of what level of risk is chosen. The alternate hypothesis is accepted:

$$\mu \neq \$20{,}000$$

example 7

Use the data in the preceding example to construct 90-, 95-, and 99-percent confidence intervals.

First, multiply the standard error by the appropriate critical value:

$$90\%: \quad 300 \times 1.645 = 493.5$$

$$95\%: \quad 300 \times 1.96 = 588$$

$$99\%: \quad 300 \times 2.576 = 772.8$$

The resulting values can then be used to construct the relevant ranges:

$$90\%: \quad 17{,}500 \pm 493.5$$
$$95\%: \quad 17{,}500 \pm 588$$
$$99\%: \quad 17{,}500 \pm 772.8$$

Thus:

$$90\%: \quad 17{,}006.5 < \mu < 17{,}993.5$$
$$95\%: \quad 16{,}912 < \mu < 18{,}088$$
$$99\%: \quad 16{,}727.2 < \mu < 18{,}272.8$$

exercises

1. Calculate the mean, standard deviation, kurtosis, and skewness of the following set of data.

Selling Price of *XYZ*, Inc.,
Stock at the End of Each Month,
Fiscal Year 1978–79

Month	Price
July	$30.50
August	31.25
September	30.00
October	29.25
November	29.75
December	28.50
January	27.25
February	26.75
March	27.00
April	27.50
May	28.00
June	28.25

2. Work out a frequency distribution for the combined data for 1977–78 and 1978–79 (see Table 2.1). Calculate the median, mode, maximum, minimum, and range.

3. In a throw of a fair die, there are six possible outcomes. What is the expected value of this experiment? What is its mean?

4. What would be the equation of the random-number function if it generated numbers between zero and two with an equal probability? Graph the function. (*Hint:* The area under the curve must equal one.)

5. Construct a frequency distribution for a throw of two dice.

6. If income is normally distributed with a mean of \$15,000 and a standard deviation of \$3,000, what is the probability that a person will have an income between \$16,000 and \$18,000? Greater than \$25,000? Given your answer to the last question, do you think that income is normally distributed?

7. If the mean lifetime of a battery is 1,050 hours with a standard deviation of 225 hours, what is the probability that a battery will last no longer than 800 hours? Between 900 and 1,200 hours? Longer than 1,200 hours?

8. A form of Russian roulette consists of putting one bullet in a six-shooter and spinning the chamber before each person pulls the trigger on himself. If a person is killed, another bullet is put in the gun and the revolver continues going around the table until everyone there has pulled the trigger once. If there are six people at the table, what is the probability that zero, one, two, three, four, five, or six people will be killed if the revolver goes around the table once?

9. Suppose that a population consists of the four numbers 1, 3, 8, and 12. Are these numbers normally distributed? List all the possible samples of $N = 2$ that could be selected from these four numbers and calculate the mean of each sample. Is the sampling distribution symmetrical? What is the mean of the sampling distribution? What is the mean of the population?

10. The standard error of the twenty-six sample means (see Demo 2.6) is .079. What percentage of the sample means lie within one, two, and three standard errors of the grand mean (.466)? Would it appear that the sampling distribution is normally distributed? What is the relationship between the standard deviation (.289) in Demo 2.5 and the standard error?

11. What is the effect of sample size on the standard error?

12. What is the effect of sample size on the T test and confidence interval?

13. Can you explain why the critical values (T test) fall as the level of significance increases?

14. Why does the size of the confidence interval increase as the level of confidence increases?

15. A random sample of one hundred families finds their average income to be \$14,000 with a standard deviation of \$1,500. Test the null hypothesis $\mu =$ \$14,300 at the .01, .05, and .1 levels of significance. Construct confidence intervals at the .90, .95, and .99 levels. Given that income is not normally distributed, is your work meaningful?

16. The following random numbers were generated by a computer: .205, .230, .533, .132, .996, .784, .742, .398, .710, and .678. Test the null hypothesis $\mu = .5$ at the .01, .05, and .1 levels of significance. Construct confidence intervals at the .90, .95, and .99 levels.

computer exercises

1. Use the following program to calculate the mean, standard deviation, kurtosis, and skewness for the combined stock-price data for 1977–78 and 1978–79 (see Table 2.1 and Exercise 1). Statement 105 should read:

```
105 DATA 24
```

and a DATA statement must be added at 108 to contain the 1978–79 data:

```
108 DATA 30.5,31.25,30,29.25,29.75,28.5,27.25,26.75,27,27.5,28,28.25
```

This program is dimensioned to run on up to one hundred observations. Statement 5 must be changed should you desire to increase the number of observations.

```
5DIM X(100)
15READ N
20FOR I=1 TO N
30READ X(I)
40LET S1=S1+X(I)
50NEXT I
60LET S1=S1/N
70FOR I=1 TO N
80LET S2=S2+(X(I)-S1)**2
90NEXT I
95PRINT "MEAN=";S1
97LET S2=SQR(S2/(N-1))
100PRINT "S=";S2
105DATA 12
107DATA 27.25,28.5,30,29.25,30.5,28,28.5,29.5,30.25,29.75,30.25,28.75
110LET S=0
115LET S5=0
120FOR I=1 TO N
130LET S=S+((X(I)-S1)/S2)**4
135LET S5=S5+((X(I)-S1)/S2)**3
140NEXT I
150LET S3=S/N-3
160PRINT "K=";S3
210LET S4=S5/N
220PRINT "SK=";S4
230END
RUN
MEAN=      29.2083
S=          1.01597
K=         -1.20013
SK=        -.396222
```

demo 2.7. Basic Program and Run for 1977–78 Data. Mean, Standard Deviation, Kurtosis, and Skewness Are Calculated.

2. Use the following program to work Exercise 2 above. Statement 755 should be revised to contain the number of observations:

```
755DATA 24
```

and Statement 765 should be added:

```
765DATA 30.5,31.25,30,29.25,29.75,28.5,27.25,26.75,27,27.5,28,28.25
```

This program is dimensioned to run on up to one hundred observations. (Statement 100 must be changed should you desire to increase the number of observations.)

```
100DIM D(100),S(100),C(100)
110READ N
120FOR I=1 TO N
130READ D(I)
140NEXT I
150FOR I=1 TO N
160LET C(I)=1
170NEXT I
180LET S(1)=D(1)
190LET L=1
200FOR I=2 TO N
210FOR J=1 TO L
220IF D(I)=S(J) THEN 270
230NEXT J
240LET L=L+1
250LET S(L)=D(I)
260GOTO 280
270LET C(J)=C(J)+1
280NEXT I
290LET P=L-1
300FOR K=1 TO P
310LET E=1
320LET O=L-K+1
330FOR I=2 TO O
340IF S(I)>S(E) THEN 360
350GOTO 370
360LET E=I
370NEXT I
380LET T=S(E)
390LET S(E)=S(O)
400LET S(O)=T
410LET T=C(E)
420LET C(E)=C(O)
430LET C(O)=T
```

demo 2.8. Basic Program and Run for 1977–78 Data. Number of Unique Points, Frequency Distribution, Mode, and Median Are Calculated.

```
440NEXT K
450PRINT "UNIQUE POINTS=";L
460PRINT "FREQUENCY DISTRIBUTION"
470FOR I=1 TO L
480PRINT S(I),C(I)
490NEXT I
500LET M=N/2
510LET A=0
520FOR I=Q TO L
530LET A=A+C(I)
540IF A=M THEN 570
550IF A>M THEN 590
560NEXT I
570LET Y=(S(I+1)+S(I))/2
580GOTO 600
590LET Y=S(I)
600LET J=1
610FOR I=2 TO L
620IF C(I)>C(J) THEN 640
630GOTO 650
640LET J=I
650NEXT I
660LET Z=S(J)
670LET F=J+1
680IF F>L THEN 720
690FOR I=F TO L
700IF C(J)=C(I) THEN 740
710NEXT I
720PRINT "MODE=";Z
730GOTO 750
740PRINT "MODE IS UNDEFINED"
750PRINT "MEDIAN=";Y
755DATA 12
760DATA 27.25,28.5,30,29.25,30.5,28,28.5,29.5,30.25,29.75,30.25,28.75
770END

RUN
UNIQUE POINTS= 10
FREQUENCY DISTRIBUTION
 27.25                 1
 28                    1
 28.5                  2
 28.75                 1
 29.25                 1
 29.5                  1
 29.75                 1
 30                    1
 30.25                 2
 30.5                  1
MODE IS UNDEFINED
MEDIAN= 29.375
```

demo 2.8. Continued

3. Duplicate Demo 2.3 by running the following program. Are your results the same?

```
5PRINT "NUMBER OF COIN TOSSES"
10INPUT N
20RANDOM
30LET H=0
40FOR I=1 TO N
50LET X=RND
60IF X>.5 THEN 80
70LET H=H+1
80NEXT I
90PRINT "NUMBER OF HEADS=";H
100PRINT "NUMBER OF TAILS=";N-H
110PRINT "PERCENTAGE HEADS=";H/N*100
120PRINT
130END
```

demo 2.9. Listing of Coin-Tossing Program

Change Statement 60 to read: 60IF X > .9 THEN 80. Run this program again a few times. Can you explain your results?

4. Work Exercises 6 and 7 above with the following program in which you input the mean, the standard deviation, and the left-most and right-most values. For example, in Exercise 6, the left-most value is 16000 and the right-most value is 18000 (numbers typed into the computer should never have a comma in them). This program actually calculates the integral of Equation (2.9) to an accuracy of about two decimals.

```
10PRINT "MEAN"
20INPUT M
30PRINT "STANDARD DEVIATION"
40INPUT S
50PRINT "LEFT-MOST VALUE OF RANGE"
60INPUT A
70PRINT "RIGHT-MOST VALUE OF RANGE"
80INPUT B
90LET C=(A-M)/S
100LET D=(B-M)/S
110FOR X=C TO D STEP .001
120LET S1=S1+((1/SQR(2*PI))*EXP(-X**2/2))*.001
130NEXT X
140PRINT "PROBABILITY=";S1;"IN RANGE OF";A;"TO";B
150END

RUN
MEAN
? 100
```

demo 2.10. Program and Run for Normal-Curve Probability Problems

```
STANDARD DEVIATION
? 20
LEFT-MOST VALUE OF RANGE
? 100
RIGHT-MOST VALUE OF RANGE
? 120
PROBABILITY= .341666 IN RANGE OF 100 TO 120

RUN
MEAN
? 100
STANDARD DEVIATION
? 20
LEFT-MOST VALUE OF RANGE
? 85
RIGHT-MOST VALUE OF RANGE
? 120
PROBABILITY= .61499 IN RANGE OF 85 to 120

RUN
MEAN
? 100
STANDARD DEVIATION
? 20
LEFT-MOST VALUE OF RANGE
? 100
RIGHT-MOST VALUE OF RANGE
? 140
PROBABILITY= .477422 IN RANGE OF 100 to 140
```

demo 2.10. Continued

5. Work Exercise 8 above using the following program in which you input *P* and *N*.

```
10PRINT "THE PROBABILITY OF A SUCCESS"
20INPUT P
30LET Q=1-P
40PRINT "NUMBER OF TRIALS"
50INPUT N
60LET F1=1
70FOR I=1 TO N
80LET F1=F1*I
90NEXT I
100LET O=Q**N
110PRINT "THE PROBABILITY OF 0 SUCCESSES IS";O
120FOR I=1 TO N
130LET R=N-I
140LET F2=1
150LET F3=1
160FOR J=1 TO R
```

demo 2.11. Program and Run for Binomial-Distribution Problem

```
170 LET F2=F2*J
180NEXT J
190FOR B=1 TO I
200LET F3=F3*B
210NEXT B
220LET T=(F1*(P**I)*(Q**N(N-I)))/(F2*F3)
230PRINT "THE PROBABILITY OF";I;"SUCCESSES IS";T
240LET M=M+T
250NEXT I
260LET M=M+O
270PRINT "TOTAL PROBABILITY IS";M
280END

RUN
THE PROBABILITY OF A SUCCESS
? .5
NUMBER OF TRIALS
? 4
THE PROBABILITY OF 0 SUCCESSES IS .0625
THE PROBABILITY OF 1 SUCCESSES IS .25
THE PROBABILITY OF 2 SUCCESSES IS .375
THE PROBABILITY OF 3 SUCCESSES IS .25
THE PROBABILITY OF 4 SUCCESSES IS .0625
TOTAL PROBABILITY IS 1
```

demo 2.11. Continued

6. In selecting a random sample, we must often generate random numbers that are integers and lie within a specified range. For example, the random selection of twenty-five students out of a total of one thousand would require whole numbers generated in the range of one to one thousand. The following program generates any number of random numbers in any specified range. The program is run for the above problem (thirty numbers are generated to account for the possibility of duplication). Run this program for any desired range and for any size *N*.

```
10PRINT "NUMBER OF RANDOM NUMBERS"
20INPUT N
30PRINT "LEFT-MOST VALUE OF RANGE"
40INPUT A
50PRINT "RIGHT-MOST VALUE OF RANGE"
60INPUT B
70RANDOM
80FOR I=1 TO N
90PRINT INT((B-A)*RND+A)
100NEXT I
110END
```

demo 2.12. Program and Run for Generating Random Numbers in Any Specified Range

```
RUN
NUMBER OF RANDOM NUMBERS
? 30
LEFT-MOST VALUE OF RANGE
? 1
RIGHT-MOST VALUE OF RANGE
? 1000
 574
 442
 488
 953
 326
 372
 299
 444
 976
 864
 399
 608
 65
 910
 884
 110
 700
 219
 8
 79
 407
 728
 714
 729
 944
 102
 111
 752
 512
 307
```

demo 2.12. Continued

7. The following program generates one hundred sample means of one hundred random numbers (ten thousand total) and calculates the percentage of the sample means that lie within one and two standard deviations of the mean (grand mean) of the one hundred sample means. Run this program a few times. Can you explain your results?

```
5RANDOM
10DIM T(100)
20DIM P(100)
```

demo 2.13. Listing of Program That Demonstrates Central Limit Theorem

```
30LET S1=0
40LET S2=0
50DIM X(100)
60FOR J=1 TO 100
70LET A=0
80FOR I=1 TO 100
90LET X(I)=RND
100LET A=A+X(I)
110NEXT I
120LET A=A/100
130LET P(J)=A
140LET S1=S1+P(J)
150NEXT J
160LET S1=S1/100
170PRINT "MEAN OF 100 SAMPLE MEANS=";S1
180FOR J=1 TO 100
190LET S2=S2+(P(J)-S1)**2
200NEXT J
210LET S2=SQR(S2/100)
220PRINT "STANDARD DEVIATION OF SAMPLING DISTRIBUTION=";S2
230LET C1=0
240LET C2=0
250FOR J=1 TO 100
260IF S1+S2<P(J) THEN 300
270IF S1-S2>P(J) THEN 300
280LET C1=C1+1
290 GO TO 320
300IF S1+2*S2<P(J) THEN 330
310IF S1-2*S2>P(J) THEN 330
320LET C2=C2+1
330NEXT J
340PRINT C1/100*100;"% WITHIN ONE STD.DEV."
350PRINT C2/100*100;"% WITHIN TWO STD.DEV."
360END
```

demo 2.13. Continued

8. The following program generates any desired number of random numbers and calculates their mean, standard deviation, standard error, and *T* value. Run this program twenty-five times for any fixed *N*. What percentage of the time does a Type I error occur? (Choose any level of significance.)

```
10RANDOM
20PRINT "NUMBER OF RANDOM NUMBERS"
30INPUT N
40LET S=0
50DIM X(100)
60FOR I=1 TO N
```

demo 2.14. Listing of *T*-Test Program for Random-Number Function

```
70LET X(I)=RND
80LET S=S+X(I)
90NEXT I
100LET S1=S/N
110PRINT "MEAN OF";N;"RANDOM NUMBERS=";S1
120LET S2=0
130FOR I=1 TO N
140LET S2=S2+(X(I)-S1)**2
150NEXT I
160LET S3=SQR(S2/(N-1))
170PRINT "S=";S3
180LET S4=S3/SQR(N-1)
190PRINT "SE=";S4
200PRINT "T=";ABS((S1-.5)/S4)
210END
```

demo 2.14. Continued

3

the two-variable regression model

In this chapter we discuss the role of *regression* analysis in econometric work. As mentioned in Chapter 1, a single-equation regression model consists of one dependent variable, and one or more independent variables. We begin with the two-variable case (*simple regression*) and then extend the analysis to more than two variables (*multiple regression*) in the next chapter.

First we examine some of the theoretical properties of estimators. Then we explain three purely mathematical techniques used in regression analysis (covariation and correlation analysis, ordinary least squares, and the coefficient of determination). In the remainder of the chapter we discuss the major assumptions of the regression model and the consequences of their violation, hypothesis tests and confidence intervals, and mathematical forms of regression models.

theoretical properties of estimators

A two-variable regression model is of the form

$$Y = \alpha + \beta X \tag{3.1}$$

where Y is the dependent variable, X is the independent variable, and α and β are the unknown population parameters that we desire to estimate.[1] If the

[1]There is an error term missing from Equation (3.1); this will be discussed later.

population parameters were known with certainty, there would be no need to apply the estimation techniques covered in this chapter. In fact, there would be no need for econometric theory. Unfortunately (fortunately for econometricians), the values for the population parameters are rarely known, and therefore they must be estimated from sample data. Consequently, it is necessary to know something about the properties of estimators of population parameters. Three general theoretical properties are defined and explained in this section:

1. Bias
2. Efficiency
3. Consistency

bias

If B is an estimator of β, *bias* may be defined as

$$\text{Bias} = E(B) - \beta \tag{3.2}$$

where $E(B)$ is the "expected" value of B.[2] $E(B)$ is the mean of the sampling distribution of B. In other words, if we were to take repeated samples of the population, each sample would be associated with a particular estimate of β, B. The mean or average of the B's generated by all the samples is equal to $E(B)$.

For example, suppose that the population consists of all the odd numbers between zero and ten: 1, 3, 5, 7, and 9. Furthermore, we wish to estimate the population parameter, μ, by selecting a random sample of 2. The value of this parameter is equal to 5:

$$\mu = (1 + 3 + 5 + 7 + 9)/5 = 5$$

Of course, as already stated, we normally do not know the value of the population parameter and therefore estimate it by selecting a random sample. If the sample selected is the 7 and 9, we can estimate μ by calculating $\bar{X}$:

$$\bar{X} = (7 + 9)/2 = 8$$

Obviously, 8 is not very close to the true parameter value, 5. Is $\bar{X}$ a biased estimate of the population parameter? While you might be inclined to answer yes, remember that bias is defined by Equation (3.2) in terms of the sampling distribution of $\bar{X}$:

$$\text{Bias} = E(\bar{X}) - \mu$$

Let us list all the possible samples of $N = 2$ and calculate $E(\bar{X})$, the mean of the sampling distribution of $\bar{X}$. The bias can then be calculated. All the possible

[2]See Chapter 2 for a review of E and sampling distributions.

samples of $N = 2$ are listed in Table 3.1, along with their means. The mean of all the sample means ("grand mean") is equal to 5; consequently, $E(\bar{X}) = 5$ and $\bar{X}$ is an unbiased estimate of μ:

$$\text{Bias} = 5 - 5 = 0$$

table 3.1. Demonstration of Unbiased Estimator

	X	$\bar{X}$
Sample # 1	1,3	2
# 2	1,5	3
# 3	1,7	4
# 4	1,9	5
# 5	3,5	4
# 6	3,7	5
# 7	3,9	6
# 8	5,7	6
# 9	5,9	7
#10	7,9	8
		50

Grand mean $= E(\bar{X}) = 50/10 = 5$

Bias is illustrated in Figure 3.1. Note that the center of the sampling distribution for the unbiased estimator is at β, while the center of the distribution for the biased estimator lies to the right of β.

To demonstrate how an estimator may be biased, consider the equation for the population standard deviation, σ:

$$\sigma = \sqrt{\frac{\sum (X - \mu)^2}{N}} \tag{3.3}$$

Equation (2.2) was given in Chapter 2 to estimate σ:

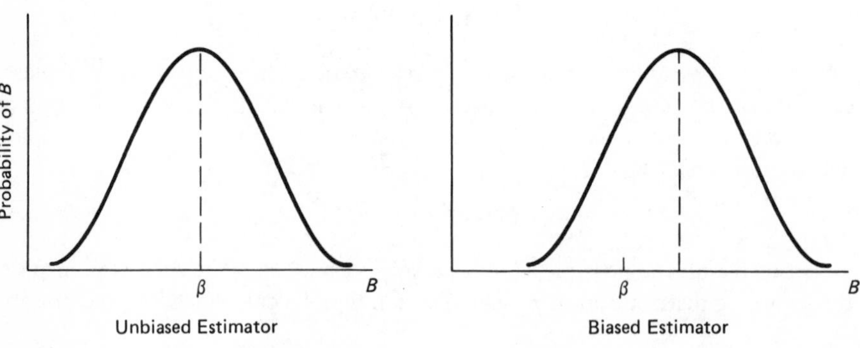

figure 3.1. Illustration of Bias

$$S = \sqrt{\frac{\sum (X - \bar{X})^2}{N - 1}} \tag{2.2}$$

Suppose that we divided by N instead of $N - 1$:

$$S_1 = \sqrt{\frac{\sum (X - \bar{X})^2}{N}} \tag{3.4}$$

S_1 is a biased estimator of σ.

To show this, let us calculate S and S_1 for all the samples presented in Table 3.1. The true standard deviation, σ, is equal to 2.8. However, as can be seen in Table 3.2a, $E(S_1) = 2$ and $E(S) = 2.8$. Thus, S is an unbiased estimator of σ, while S_1 is a biased estimator:

$$\text{Bias} = E(S_1) - \sigma = 2 - 2.8 = -.8$$

table 3.2a. Demonstration of Biased Estimator

	$\sum (X - \bar{X})^2$	S_1	S
Sample # 1	2	1	1.4
# 2	8	2	2.8
# 3	18	3	4.2
# 4	32	4	5.6
# 5	2	1	1.4
# 6	8	2	2.8
# 7	18	3	4.2
# 8	2	1	1.4
# 9	8	2	2.8
#10	2	1	1.4
		20	28.0

$$E(S_1) = 20/10 = 2$$
$$E(S) = 28/10 = 2.8$$

table 3.2b. Calculation of σ for 1, 3, 5, 7, 9

$X - \mu$	$(X - \mu)^2$
−4	16
−2	4
0	0
2	4
4	16
	40

$$\sigma = \sqrt{\frac{40}{5}} = \sqrt{8} = 2.8$$

For this reason, we should divide by $N - 1$, not N, in calculating the sample standard deviation.

efficiency

An estimator may be unbiased, but not as "efficient" as another estimator. Efficiency is defined by the variance (Var) of the sampling distribution of the estimator:

$$\text{Var}(\bar{X}) = \sigma_{\bar{X}}^2 \tag{3.5}$$

For the estimator $\bar{X}$, Equation (3.5) is equivalent to (see Equation (3.3)):

$$\sigma_{\bar{X}}^2 = \frac{\sum (\bar{X} - \mu)^2}{N} \tag{3.6}$$

where $\bar{X}$ is the mean of each sample and N is the number of samples in the sampling distribution. Equation (3.6) is calculated for the ten samples of Table 3.1 and presented in Table 3.3. Since the variance is equal to 3, $\bar{X}$ is said to be more efficient than another estimator only if the latter's variance is greater than 3. Thus, efficiency is a relative term.

table 3.3. Calculation of Variance of Estimator $\bar{X}$

	$\bar{X}$	$\bar{X} - \mu$	$(\bar{X} - \mu)^2$
Sample # 1	2	−3	9
# 2	3	−2	4
# 3	4	−1	1
# 4	5	0	0
# 5	4	−1	1
# 6	5	0	0
# 7	6	1	1
# 8	6	1	1
# 9	7	2	4
#10	8	3	9
			30

$$\text{Var}(\bar{X}) = \frac{30}{10} = 3$$

Efficiency is illustrated in Figure 3.2. The estimator with the smaller variance is B_1. Because we can have greater confidence in an estimator with a smaller

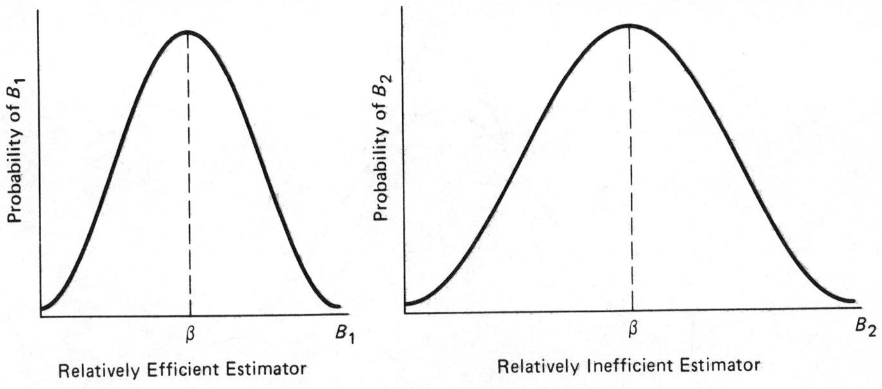

figure 3.2. Illustration of Efficiency

variance, B_1 is to be preferred over B_2 even though both are unbiased estimators (note that the center of both distributions coincides with β).

consistency

It is interesting to note that the variance of the original population, σ^2, is greater than the variance of the estimator, $\sigma_{\bar{X}}^2$:

$$\sigma^2 = (2.8)^2 = 7.8$$

$$\sigma_{\bar{X}}^2 = 3$$

Thus, the distribution of a sampling distribution is less spread out than the original population. This is illustrated in Figure 3.3. Furthermore, as the sample size becomes larger, the variance of the sampling distribution becomes smaller and smaller. This latter property is known as "consistency" and is illustrated in

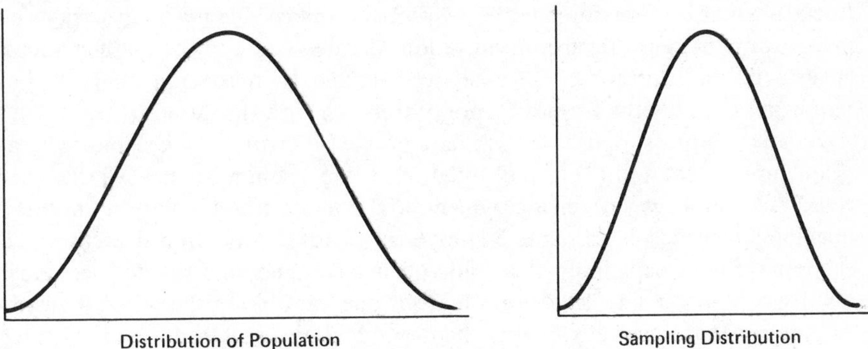

figure 3.3. Distribution of Population versus Sampling Distribution

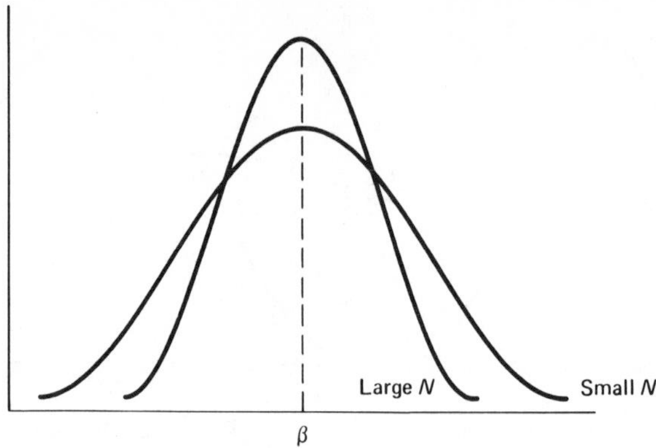

figure 3.4. Illustration of Consistency

Figure 3.4. An estimator that becomes a single point (equal to the population parameter) as the sample size approaches infinity is termed *consistent*.

In a later section the major assumptions of the regression model are developed. The technique used to estimate the regression coefficients is *ordinary least squares*. If the assumptions of the regression model hold, then the least squares estimators are "best linear unbiased estimators" (BLUE) of the population parameters. They are "best" in the sense that no other linear unbiased estimators are more efficient. The theoretical basis for proving that the least squares estimators are BLUE is provided by the Gauss-Markov theorem. The Gauss-Markov theorem is proven in Appendix 3.1.

covariance and correlation analysis

A regression model specifies a line of causation from the independent variable (X) to the dependent variable (Y). This line of causation is based upon an economic theory; in the absence of theory, it is impossible to infer causation. In contrast with regression analysis, *covariance* and *correlation* analysis does not involve any inference regarding causation. Because some of the mathematics of covariance and correlation analysis are applied to regression analysis, it is important to study the former before proceeding with the latter.

As an example, suppose we have data on the following two variables: (1) rate of unemployment and (2) rate of inflation. Many economists believe that there is a trade-off between unemployment and inflation. As inflation increases, unemployment decreases; as unemployment increases, inflation decreases. The economic forces explaining this trade-off are complex and do not necessarily involve any direct line of causation from one variable to the other. Thus, we cannot say that unemployment is the dependent and inflation the independent variable, or vice versa.

However, we can measure the *linear association* between the rates of inflation and unemployment by way of covariance and correlation analysis. The estimating equation for covariance is

$$\text{Cov}(X, Y) = \frac{\sum (X - \bar{X})(Y - \bar{Y})}{N - 1} \tag{3.7}$$

where X and Y are arbitrarily assigned to each variable, since one is not assumed dependent on the other. For example, X can equal the unemployment rate and Y the inflation rate. The numerator in Equation (3.7) will be positive if $(X - \bar{X})$ tends to have the same sign as $(Y - \bar{Y})$, and negative if the two terms tend to have the opposite sign. Thus, the covariance will be positive if the two variables tend to move in the same direction, and negative if they move in the opposite direction. In the case where the two variables show no discernible pattern of movement with each other, the covariance will be close to zero.

Consider the hypothetical data in Table 3.4 and the graph of these data in Figure 3.5. Quite clearly, the linear relationship is negative and suggests a

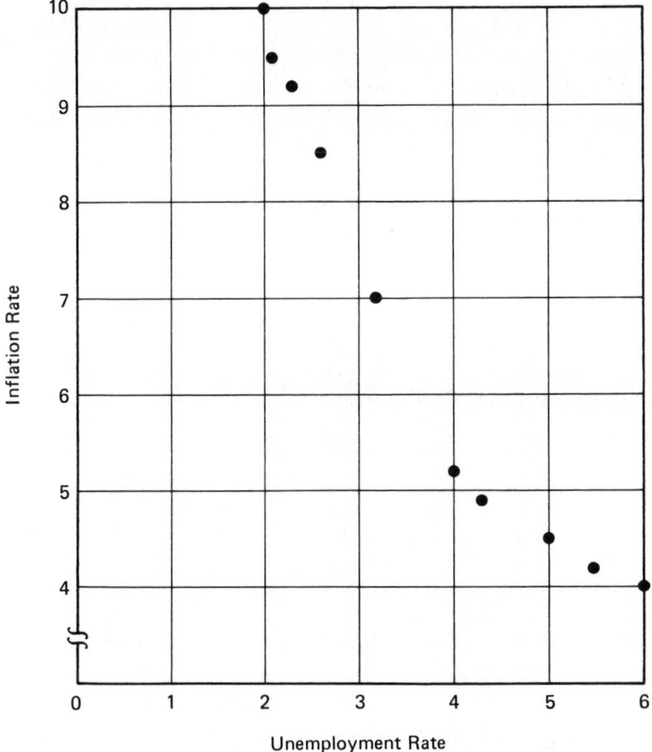

figure 3.5. Graph of Unemployment and Inflation Rates

table 3.4. Unemployment and Inflation Rates

Unemployment Rate (X)	Inflation Rate (Y)
2.0	10.0
2.1	9.5
2.3	9.2
2.6	8.5
3.2	7.0
4.0	5.2
4.3	4.9
5.0	4.5
5.5	4.2
6.0	4.0
$\bar{X} = 3.7$	$\bar{Y} = 6.7$

covariance less than zero. The calculations for the covariance are presented in Table 3.5. As expected, the covariance is negative (−3.42).

Because it depends on the units of measurement, the value for the covariance is difficult to interpret. Does −3.42 represent a weak or a strong negative relationship between the rates of unemployment and inflation? This question can be answered by the process of *normalization*, which is accomplished by dividing the covariance by the product of both standard deviations. The result is the *correlation coefficient*:

$$R = \frac{\text{Cov}\,(X, Y)}{S_X S_Y} \tag{3.8}$$

table 3.5. Covariance Calculations

$X - \bar{X}$	$Y - \bar{Y}$	$(X - \bar{X})(Y - \bar{Y})$
−1.7	3.3	−5.61
−1.6	2.8	−4.48
−1.4	2.5	−3.50
−1.1	1.8	−1.98
−0.5	0.3	−0.15
0.3	−1.5	−0.45
0.6	−1.8	−1.08
1.3	−2.2	−2.86
1.8	−2.5	−4.50
2.3	−2.7	−6.21
		−30.82

$\text{Cov}\,(X, Y) = -30.82/9 = -3.42$

where S_X and S_Y are the respective standard deviations of X and Y. R has a range of -1 to $+1$; a value of -1 indicates a perfect negative relationship, $+1$ indicates a perfect positive relationship, and zero implies no linear association. R is calculated in Table 3.6 and is equal to $-.97$, which suggests a strong negative relationship between the rate of inflation and the rate of unemployment.

table 3.6. Correlation Calculations

$(X - \bar{X})^2$	$(Y - \bar{Y})^2$
2.89	10.89
2.56	7.84
1.96	6.25
1.21	3.24
0.25	0.09
0.09	2.25
0.36	3.24
1.69	4.84
3.24	6.25
5.29	7.29
19.54	52.18

$$S_X = \sqrt{\frac{19.54}{9}} = \sqrt{2.17} = 1.47$$

$$S_Y = \sqrt{\frac{52.18}{9}} = \sqrt{5.80} = 2.41$$

$$R = \frac{-3.42}{(1.47)(2.41)} = \frac{-3.42}{3.54} = -.97$$

The finding of a linear relationship between the rate of inflation and the rate of unemployment may help to provide support for an economic theory, but it is not based upon a regression model in which one variable is dependent and the other independent. After explaining the method of ordinary least squares and the coefficient of determination, we will discuss the theory and application of regression models in econometric work.

the method of ordinary least squares (OLS)

Suppose we have collected data on the income and IQ of ten individuals. Table 3.7 presents these data.

table 3.7. Income-IQ Data

Income	IQ
$ 5,000	80
6,000	95
7,000	100
8,000	101
9,000	103
10,000	115
11,000	105
12,000	116
13,000	120
14,000	110
Mean = $9,500	Mean = 104.5

Presuming there is a linear relationship between income and IQ, where income is the dependent variable and IQ the independent variable, can a line be fitted to these data? One method is to simply graph the points and draw a line through the center of these points, as in Figure 3.6. The major problem with this method is obvious. The position of the line depends on the individual perceptions of the person drawing it. Thus, we need a more scientific procedure for drawing this line. The method of ordinary least squares (OLS) is one way of solving this

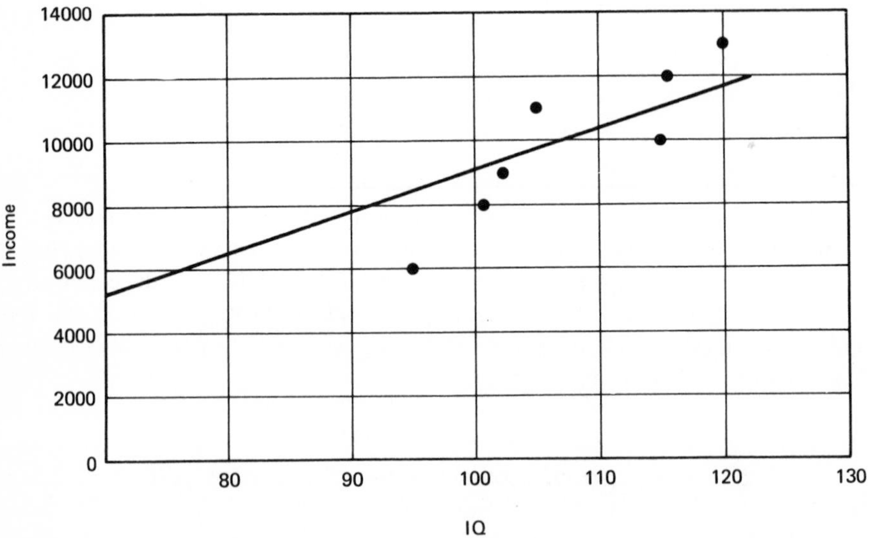

figure 3.6. Graph of Income-IQ Relationship Line Drawn with Naked Eye

problem. As will be discussed later in the chapter, the major reason that OLS is used is that it has certain desirable statistical properties.

The method of OLS consists of passing a straight line through the points such that the sum of the squared vertical deviations from this line is minimized:

$$\text{Minimize} \sum_{I=1}^{N} (Y_I - Yc_I)^2 \tag{3.9}$$

where Y_I is each value of Y (income): 5,000, 6,000, etc.; and Yc_I (Y calculated) is each calculated Y value derived from the equation

$$Yc_I = A + BX_I \tag{3.10}$$

where X_I is each value of X (IQ): 80, 95, etc. These concepts are illustrated in Figure 3.7. Yc is the desired OLS line.

Thus, we must find an A and a B such that Equation (3.9) is satisfied. The following equations were derived with the aid of differential calculus. The derivations are given in Appendix 3.1. By substituting into these equations, the values of A and B that minimize Equation (3.9) can be obtained.

$$B = \frac{\sum (X - \bar{X})(Y - \bar{Y})}{\sum (X - \bar{X})^2} \tag{3.11}$$

$$A = \bar{Y} - B\bar{X} \tag{3.12}$$

These calculations are presented in Table 3.8.

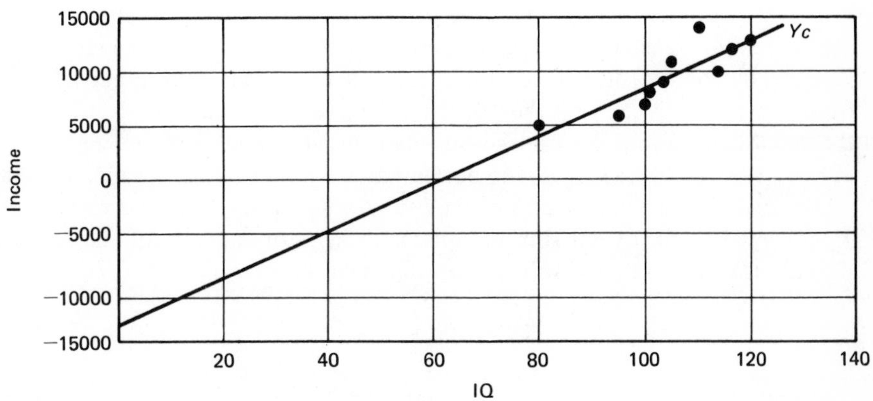

figure 3.7. Graph of OLS Line

table 3.8. Calculations of A and B for Income-IQ Data

$X_I - \bar{X}$	$Y_I - \bar{Y}$	$(X_I - \bar{X})(Y_I - \bar{Y})$	$(X_I - \bar{X})^2$
−24.5	−4,500	110,250	600.25
− 9.5	−3,500	33,250	90.25
− 4.5	−2,500	11,250	20.25
− 3.5	−1,500	5,250	12.25
− 1.5	− 500	750	2.25
10.5	500	5,250	110.25
0.5	1,500	750	0.25
11.5	2,500	28,750	132.25
15.5	3,500	54,250	240.25
5.5	4,500	24,750	30.25
		274,500	1,238.50

$$B = \frac{274{,}500}{1{,}238.50} = 221.639$$

$$A = 9{,}500 - 221.639(104.5) = -13{,}661.284$$

Therefore:

$$Yc_I = -13{,}661.284 + 221.639X_I \tag{3.13}$$

the coefficient of determination (R^2)

Since B is positive in Equation (3.13), the relationship between income and IQ is direct; that is, increases in IQ tend to be associated with increases in income. If B had been negative, this would have indicated an inverse relationship—increases in IQ would have been associated with decreases in income. However, this tells us nothing about how close the line fits the data. The latter can be measured by the *coefficient of determination*, R^2, which is the square of the correlation coefficient. The R^2 measures the *variation* in the dependent variable that is "explained" by the independent variable. The range of R^2 is from zero to one. The closer the calculated Yc line fits the data points, the higher the R^2. For example, Yc for the first data point is equal to $-13{,}661.284 + 221.639(80) = 4{,}069.85$. This is to be compared with an actual Y value of 5,000.

Variation is defined in terms of the "sum of squares." The *total variation* in Y is defined as the "total sum of squares (TSS)," or the sum of the squared deviations of the actual Y values from the mean of Y:

$$\text{TSS} = \sum_{I=1}^{N} (Y_I - \bar{Y})^2 \tag{3.14}$$

The error (e) or "residual sum of squares (RSS)" is equal to the sum of the squared deviations of Yc from the actual Y values:

$$\text{RSS} = \sum_{I=1}^{N} (Y_I - Yc_I)^2 = \sum e^2 \tag{3.15}$$

The "explained sum of squares (ESS)" is equal to the sum of the squared deviations of the calculated Y values from the mean of Y:

$$\text{ESS} = \sum_{I=1}^{N} (Yc_I - \bar{Y})^2 \tag{3.16}$$

The total sum of squares is equal to the explained sum of squares plus the residual sum of squares:

$$\text{TSS} = \text{ESS} + \text{RSS} \tag{3.17}$$

These concepts are illustrated in Figure 3.8. The R^2 is the explained variation, or the ratio of the explained sum of squares to the total sum of squares:

$$R^2 = \frac{\text{ESS}}{\text{TSS}} \tag{3.18}$$

Dividing Equation (3.17) by TSS, the following relationship can be derived:

$$1 = \frac{\text{ESS}}{\text{TSS}} + \frac{\text{RSS}}{\text{TSS}} \tag{3.19}$$

Thus, the sum of the explained variation and the unexplained variation is equal to one. Under what conditions will the R^2 equal one? Obviously the unexplained variation (RSS/TSS) must equal zero, and this can only occur if the ordinary least squares line perfectly fits the data points.

The calculations are presented in Table 3.9. The R^2 is equal to .737. This means that 73.7 percent of the total variation in income is "explained" by IQ. As mentioned above, the square root of R^2 is defined as the "coefficient of

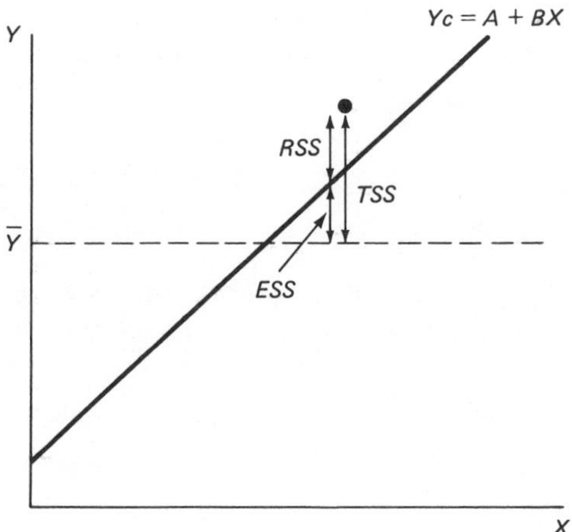

figure 3.8. Total, Explained, and Residual Variation of Y

table 3.9. Calculations of Unexplained and Explained Variation (R^2)

Yc_I	$Y_I - Yc_I$	$(Y_I - Yc_I)^2$	$(Y_I - \bar{Y})^2$
4,069.85	930.15	865,179.03	20,250,000
7,394.44	−1,394.44	1,944,462.92	12,250,000
8,502.63	−1,502.63	2,257,896.92	6,250,000
8,724.27	− 724.27	524,567.04	2,250,000
9,167.55	− 167.55	28,073.01	250,000
11,827.22	−1,827.22	3,338,732.93	250,000
9,610.83	1,389.17	1,929,793.29	2,250,000
12,048.86	− 48.86	2,387.30	6,250,000
12,935.41	64.59	4,171.87	12,250,000
10,719.02	3,280.98	10,764,808.36	20,250,000
		21,660,072.67	82,500,000

$$\text{Unexplained variation} = \frac{21{,}660{,}072.67}{82{,}500{,}000.00} = .263$$

$$\text{Explained variation} = R^2 = 1 - .263 = .737$$

correlation (R)." It should be noted that if our model were turned around so that IQ were the dependent variable and income the independent variable, the R^2 and R values would still be the same. Thus, R^2 and R are measures of linear association only and do not imply causation.

An alternative calculating formula for R is

$$R = \frac{\sum xy}{\sqrt{\sum x^2 \sum y^2}} \tag{3.20}$$

where

$$\sum xy = \sum_{I=1}^{N} (X_I - \bar{X})(Y_I - \bar{Y}) = 274{,}500$$

$$\sum x^2 = \sum_{I=1}^{N} (X_I - \bar{X})^2 = 1{,}238.50$$

$$\sum y^2 = \sum_{I=1}^{N} (Y_I - \bar{Y})^2 = 82{,}500{,}00$$

Substituting into Equation (3.20), R is equal to .86. As a convention, x and y will always represent the deviations of X and Y about their means:

$$x = (X_I - \bar{X}) \tag{3.21}$$

$$y = (Y_I - \bar{Y}) \tag{3.22}$$

and we will drop the $I = 1$, N on the summation sign:

$$\sum = \sum_{I=1}^{N} \tag{3.23}$$

assumptions of the regression model

One of the most important mathematical relationships in macroeconomics is the Keynesian consumption function:

$$C = \alpha + \beta D \tag{3.24}$$

where C is consumption and D is disposable income. Equation (3.24) implies that there is an exact relationship between C and D. For example, if $\alpha = 2{,}000$, $\beta = .75$, and $D = \$20{,}000$, C is equal to \$17,000:

$$C = 2{,}000 + .75(\$20{,}000) = \$17{,}000$$

However, for reasons to be discussed below, economic relationships are rarely exact. Keynes's consumption theory is meant to apply on the "average." If there are one million families each with an income of \$20,000, the "average" consumption may be \$17,000, but the consumption of each of the one million families will not be exactly \$17,000.[3]

Consequently, the regression model is "probabilistic" in the sense that for any given observed value of X (the independent variable), there are many possible observations on Y (the dependent variable). The probabilistic nature of the regression model can be represented by an *error* or *disturbance* term:

$$Y_I = \alpha + \beta X_I + \epsilon_I \tag{3.25}$$

where ϵ = error. The error term is symbolized by a Greek letter because ϵ is the "true" regression error that is unknown but will be estimated.

The hypothetical data in Table 3.10 help to illustrate that a regression model represents an average or mean relationship, not an exact relationship. The entire

table 3.10. Family Consumption at Various Income Levels

	Income Level				
	\$10,000	*\$15,000*	*\$20,000*	*\$25,000*	*\$30,000*
	\$ 9,000	\$12,000	\$19,000	\$22,500	\$28,000
	10,000	9,000	8,000	21,000	24,000
	8,000	11,000	20,000	19,000	15,000
	5,000	13,000	17,500	20,500	24,000
	4,000	9,750	9,000	9,250	20,000
Mean consumption	\$7,200	\$10,950	\$14,700	\$18,450	\$22,200

[3]Another way of stating this proposition is that you can drown in a lake with an average depth of two feet.

population consists of twenty-five families divided evenly among five income categories: \$10,000, \$15,000, \$20,000, \$25,000, and \$30,000. For example, the consumption of the first family in the \$20,000 income category is \$19,000. The mean consumption for each income category is reported in the last row of the table. The true regression line passes through these means, as illustrated in Figure 3.9.[4]

There are several reasons why economic relationships are inexact. First, economics is a social science that studies the behavior of people. People do not always behave predictably, although on "average" we expect them to spend more as their incomes rise. Thus, while the mean consumption rises for each income group in Table 3.10, there is considerable overlap among income groups. For example, the lowest consumer expenditure in the \$30,000 income group is \$15,000; three families in the \$20,000 income group exceed this expenditure: \$19,000, \$20,000, and \$17,500. Furthermore, it would be absurd to expect a family to consume the same proportion of its income year after year.

Second, no model can include every variable that might explain the dependent

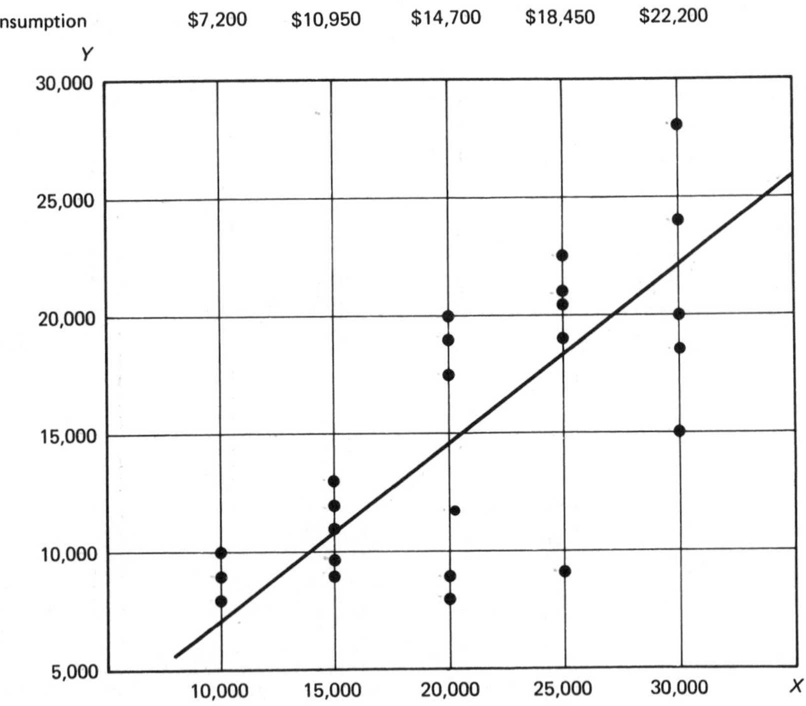

figure 3.9. Regression Model as a Mean Relationship

[4]In some advanced textbooks, each point on the regression line is symbolized by $E(Y \backslash X_I)$, which is the expected or mean value of Y given a particular X. Thus, a regression line may be defined as the straight line that passes through all of the "conditional" means of Y: $E(Y \backslash X)$.

variable. Such variables as wealth, education, family background, and sex—to mention only a few—may be determinants of consumption. Often because of a shortage of observations (small N) or lack of data, variables must be excluded from a model. But if it is assumed that the impact of omitted variables tends to cancel certain variables or is slight, then this source of error may not be serious. Of course, as discussed in the next chapter, a multiple-regression model may be specified, although this would not necessarily alleviate the problem.

Finally, errors result from measurement and data-collection problems. The use of a survey questionnaire often leads to measurement error because people are inclined to forget exactly what their consumption expenditure was, for example. Or a variable may be ambiguously or poorly defined, thereby causing measurement error. This problem may not be serious if there is an equal probability of positive and negative errors occurring.

However, errors may not cancel each other. If the alumni office of a college collects data by way of a survey on the income of graduates for the purpose of raising funds, people might underreport their income. They might overreport if the placement office was trying to determine the prosperity of its graduates. It is hoped that surveys can be designed to ensure that such errors in measurement and collection are random, instead of being biased in one direction. Given the foregoing reasons, the regression model must include an error component.

We now list the assumptions of the regression model:

1. The linear equation (3.25) describes the relationship between Y and X.
2. The X's are nonrandom (nonstochastic) and fixed.
3. The error term has zero expected value: $E(\epsilon) = 0$. That is, the mean of the disturbance associated with each level of X is zero.
4. The error term has constant variance for all observations: $E(\epsilon^2) = \sigma^2$. That is, the error term is "homoscedastic" as opposed to "heteroscedastic."
5. The error term of any one observation is uncorrelated with any other observation: $E(\epsilon_i \epsilon_j) = 0$ for $i \neq j$. That is, there is no "serial or autocorrelation."
6. The error term is uncorrelated with X: $E(X_i \epsilon_i) = 0$. This assumption is actually a corollary to Assumptions 2 and 3. A demonstration of this assumption will be saved for one of the exercises.
7. The error term is normally distributed. This assumption allows us to test hypotheses and construct confidence intervals.

We will now expand upon each of these assumptions.

The linearity assumption is made with respect to the parameters (α and β), not the variables (Y and X). For example, the equation $Y = \alpha + \beta X^2 + \epsilon$ is nonlinear in the variable X. Even so, the regression model still applies. However, the equation $Y = \alpha + \beta^2 X + \epsilon$ is nonlinear in the parameter β, and therefore this model cannot be estimated within the context of the classical regression model presented in this book. In a later section dealing with the mathematical forms of a regression model, we will further discuss the problem of linearity.

The regression model specifies that the Y's (and therefore the error term) are random, or *stochastic,* but that the X's are fixed, or *nonstochastic.* What this means is that in repeated samples on the same observations (for example, the fifty families in Table 3.10), Y will vary in a random manner for each fixed X. To illustrate the probabilistic nature of the regression model, suppose that Equation (3.26) describes a perfect relationship between Y and X, where Y and X take on the values in Table 3.11:

$$Y = -.045 + .1X \tag{3.26}$$

table 3.11. X and Y Values for Equation (3.26)

X	Y
1	.055
2	.155
3	.255
4	.355
5	.455
6	.555
7	.655
8	.755
9	.855
10	.955

Although the X values are fixed, the Y values are measured with error, as in Equation (3.25). Therefore, in repeated samples we can never expect to get exactly the true Y values in Table 3.11. Suppose we generate values for Y with a constant variance (within the same length of range) for each value of X. The Y range used for each fixed value of X is reported in Table 3.12.

Demo 3.1 presents the output of a computer program that generates random values for Y within the specified range in Table 3.12. The first column printed is the fixed X values, the second column is the random Y values, and the third column is the random error term. For example, for $X = 1$, $Y = .035$ and the error is $-.02$ $(.035 - .055)$; for $X = 10$, $Y = .956$ and the error is .001 $(.956 - .955)$. Also printed out is the sum of the errors for that one sample. It should be pointed out that Assumption 3 of the regression model implies that both the sum of errors for any one sample (in this sample the sum is .036) and the sum of errors for repeated samples of Y for any particular X tend toward zero. Of

table 3.12. Range of Y Values for Each Value of X

X	Range of Y	Midpoint of Range
1	.01 to .10	.055
2	.11 to .20	.155
3	.21 to .30	.255
4	.31 to .40	.355
5	.41 to .50	.455
6	.51 to .60	.555
7	.61 to .70	.655
8	.71 to .80	.755
9	.81 to .90	.855
10	.91 to 1.0	.955

course, we cannot expect to get exactly zero in an experiment such as this one. Because there is an equal probability of generating any number within the specified range for each X, Assumption 4 is equivalent to saying that the ranges of Y for each X are equal.

X	Y	Error
1	.035	−.020
2	.169	.014
3	.251	−.004
4	.382	.027
5	.479	.024
6	.543	−.012
7	.636	−.019
8	.747	−.008
9	.888	.033
10	.956	.001

SUM OF ERRORS = .036

demo 3.1. Illustration of Probabilistic Nature of Regression Model

Now suppose we generate twenty-five samples of $N = 10$ (as in Demo 3.1) and fit an OLS line to each of these samples. For each sample (K) we obtain values A and B, which are estimates of the true regression parameters, −.045 and .1 (α and β). We have done this in Demo 3.2, where K is the number of each sample. For each sample, B, A, $\sum xy$, $\sum x^2$, $\sum y^2$, R^2, and $\sum e^2$ (from Equation (3.15)) are printed in that order, Also, the standard deviation and mean of the twenty-five B's and the standard deviation and mean of the twenty-five A's are printed. Since this is a sampling distribution, the standard deviations are really

```
B= .104045 K= 1
A=-.658411E-1
SUMXY= 8.5837
SUMX2= 82.5
SUMY2= .897559
R2= .995019
SUME2= .447035E-2

B= .981727E-1 K= 2
A=-.447823E-1
SUMXY= 8.09925
SUMX2= 82.5
SUMY2= .803499
R2= .989578
SUME2= .837374E-2

B= .102815 K=3
A=-.601246E-1
SUMXY= 8.48223
SUMX2= 82.5
SUMY2= .878947
R2= .992211
SUME2= .684631E-2

B= .989717E-1 K= 4
A=-.477056E-1
SUMXY= 8.16517
SUMX2= 82.5
SUMY2= .813836
R2= .992978
SUME2= .571495E-2

B= .957686E-1 K= 5
A=-.311244E-2
SUMXY= 7.90091
SUMX2= 82.5
SUMY2= .761636
R2= .993465
SUME2= .497746E-2

B= .975022E-1 K= 6
A=-.333239E-1
SUMXY= 8.04393
SUMX2= 82.5
SUMY2= .791288
R2= .991171
SUME2= .698662E-2

B= .985508E-1 K= 7
A=-.459316E-1
SUMXY= 8.13044
SUMX2= 82.5
SUMY2= .809256
R2= .990121
SUME2= .799465E-2

B= .974213E-1 K= 8
A=-.296746E-1
SUMXY= 8.03726
SUMX2= 82.5
SUMY2= .786828
R2= .995136
SUME2= .382715E-2

B= .099207 K= 9
A=-.346629E-1
SUMXY= 8.18458
SUMX2= 82.5
SUMY2= .816889
R2= .993975
SUME2= .492144E-2

B= .096632 K= 10
A=-.369061E-1
SUMXY= 7.97214
SUMX2= 82.5
SUMY2= .775203
R2= .993758
SUME2= .004839

B= .989291E-1 K= 11
A=-.474704E-1
SUMXY= 8.16165
SUMX2= 82.5
SUMY2= .815839
R2= .989686
SUME2= .841492E-2

B= .960679E-1 K= 12
A=-.246666E-1
SUMXY= 7.9256
SUMX2= 82.5
SUMY2= .768284
R2= .991034
SUME2= .688827E-2

B= .980461E-1 K= 13
A=-.387668E-1
SUMXY= 8.0888
SUMX2= 82.5
SUMY2= .799487
R2= .99198
SUME2= .641173E-2

B= .096938 K= 14
A=-.166016E-1
SUMXY= 7.99739
SUMX2= 82.5
SUMY2= .781071
R2= .992549
SUME2= .581986E-2
```

demo 3.2. Sampling Distribution of *A* and *B*

```
B= .104123 K= 15
A=-.747082E-1
SUMXY= 8.59013
SUMX2= 82.5
SUMY2= .898654
R2= .995297
SUME2= .422633E-2

B= .993854E-1 K= 16
A=-.708343E-1
SUMXY= 8.1993
SUMX2= 82.5
SUMY2= .816189
R2= .998409
SUME2= .129831E-2

B= .102844 K= 17
A=-.646322E-1
SUMXY= 8.48462
SUMX2= 82.5
SUMY2= .881543
R2= .989846
SUME2= .895083E-2

B= .996858E-1 K= 18
A=-.382847E-1
SUMXY= 8.22408
SUMX2= 82.5
SUMY2= .824624
R2= .994179
SUME2= .480032E-2

B= .100883 K= 19
A=-.560179E-1
SUMXY= 8.32288
SUMX2= 82.5
SUMY2= .846123
R2= .992337
SUME2= .648361E-2

B= .944915E-1 K= 20
A=-.155456E-1
SUMXY= 7.79555
SUMX2= 82.5
SUMY2= .74151
R2= .993396
SUME2= .489712E-2

B= .100454 K= 21
A=-.331129E-1
SUMXY= 8.28742
SUMX2= 82.5
SUMY2= .836506
R2= .995211
SUME2= .400615E-2

B= .105389 K= 22
A=-.707667E-1
SUMXY= 8.69458
SUMX2= 82.5
SUMY2= .917535
R2= .998666
SUME2= .122428E-2

B= .938874E-1 K= 23
A=-.185844E-1
SUMXY= 7.74571
SUMX2= 82.5
SUMY2= .731291
R2= .994439
SUME2= .406665E-2

B= .999162E-1 K= 24
A=-.326056E-1
SUMXY= 8.24308
SUMX2= 82.5
SUMY2= .827738
R2= .995623
SUME2= .362098E-2

B= .983286E-1 K= 25
A=-.343738E-1
SUMXY= 8.11211
SUMX2= 82.5
SUMY2= .804125
R2= .99195
SUME2= .647336E-2

STD. DEV OF B'S= .29043E-2
STD. DEV OF A'S= .203504E-1
MEAN OF B'S= .991382E-1
MEAN OF A'S=-.415615E-1
```

demo 3.2. Continued

standard errors. The standard error of B is .0029 and for A, .02. The mean of the sampling distribution of B is .099 and for A, —.042.

At the beginning of the chapter it was stated that if the assumptions of the regression model hold, then the parameter estimates derived from ordinary least squares are best (most efficient) linear unbiased estimators of the population parameters (BLUE). They are best or most efficient in the sense that no other linear estimators have smaller standard errors. For example, if we chose the technique of minimizing the absolute deviations instead of the squared deviations, the standard errors of A and B would be greater. The least squares estimators are unbiased in the sense that the means of the sampling distributions of A and B equal their respective population parameters. Of course, in an experimental situation such as that in Demo 3.2, we cannot expect to get exactly the population parameters.

Assumption 7 is a direct consequence of the central limit theorem (see Chapter 2). Thus, the error term is normally distributed in Demo 3.2, even though the population of random numbers is not normally distributed. This permits us to test hypotheses and construct confidence intervals. As an example, suppose the null hypotheses are

$$\alpha = 0$$

$$\beta = 0$$

If β is not significantly different from zero, then it can be concluded that the slope of the regression line is equal to zero:

$$\frac{\Delta Y}{\Delta X} = 0$$

What this means is that changes in Y are not associated with changes in X. Thus, the independent variable does not "explain" the dependent variable. If α is not significantly different from zero, then the regression line passes through the origin (0, 0).

Following the methods developed in the preceding chapter, there are two ways to test the null hypotheses. First a T test can be constructed. If T exceeds a certain critical value, the null hypothesis is rejected and the alternate hypothesis accepted ($\alpha \neq 0$ or $\beta \neq 0$). Alternatively, a confidence interval can be calculated. If zero lies within this interval, the null hypothesis is accepted; if not, the alternate hypothesis is accepted.

To perform these hypotheses tests we must know the standard deviations of the sampling distributions (the standard errors). For example, in Demo 3.2 these are calculated for the twenty-five samples:

$$SE(B) = .0029$$

$$SE(A) = .02$$

Because it is impractical or impossible in most research problems to obtain estimates for the standard errors by repeated sampling, statisticians have developed equations to estimate them for any one sample:

$$SE(B) = s/\sqrt{\sum x^2} \tag{3.27}$$

$$SE(A) = s(\sqrt{\sum X^2/N \sum x^2}) \tag{3.28}$$

where $s = \sqrt{\sum e^2/(N-2)} = \sqrt{(\sum y^2 - B^2 \sum x^2)/(N-2)}$, and $\sum X^2 = 1^2 + 2^2 + \cdots + 10^2 = 385$ in Demo 3.2; $\sum x^2 = \sum (X - \bar{X})^2$ and $\sum y^2 = \sum (Y - \bar{Y})^2$. Note that s is termed the *standard error of estimate* and is a direct function of the error or residual sum of squares (RSS) defined earlier, and an inverse function of the sample size. Thus, the standard errors of A and B decrease as the RSS decreases and/or the sample size increases.

Let us calculate the standard errors for the first sample ($K = 1$) in Demo 3.2:

$$s = \sqrt{.004/8} = \sqrt{.0005} = .0224$$

$$SE(B) = .0224/\sqrt{82.5} = .0224/9.08 = .0025$$

$$SE(A) = .0224(\sqrt{385/(10 \times 82.5)}) = .0224\sqrt{.467} = .0153$$

It would appear that the sample estimates obtained from Equations (3.27) and (3.28) are very close to the standard deviations of the A's and B's of the sampling distribution.

We are now prepared to test the null hypotheses. First a T test can be constructed:

$$T(A) = \frac{|A - \alpha|}{SE(A)} = \frac{|A - 0|}{SE(A)} = \frac{|A|}{SE(A)} \tag{3.29}$$

$$T(B) = \frac{|B - \beta|}{SE(B)} = \frac{|B - 0|}{SE(B)} = \frac{|B|}{SE(B)} \tag{3.30}$$

Substituting into Equations (3.29) and (3.30), we test the null hypotheses for the first sample ($K = 1$):

$$T(A) = \frac{|-.0658|}{.0153} = 4.3$$

$$T(B) = \frac{.104}{.0025} = 41.6$$

The degrees of freedom for the two-variable regression model are $N - 2 = 8$. The critical values (see Statistical Table 2) for T are 1.86 (.1 level of significance), 2.306 (.05 level), and 3.355 (.01 level). Regardless of which level of significance is chosen, the null hypotheses are rejected; α and β are significantly different from zero.

Confidence intervals can also be calculated. We do so for β and leave those for α to one of the exercises:

90% Confidence Interval:
1.86(.0025) = .0046
Upper Bound = .104 + .0046 = .1086
Lower Bound = .104 − .0046 = .0994
Therefore: $.0994 < \beta < .1086$

95% Confidence Interval:
$2.306(.0025) = .0058$
Upper Bound $= .104 + .0058 = .1098$
Lower Bound $= .104 - .0058 = .0982$
Therefore: $.0982 < \beta < .1098$

99% Confidence Interval:
$3.355(.0025) = .0084$
Upper Bound $= .104 + .0084 = .1124$
Lower Bound $= .104 - .0084 = .0956$
Therefore: $.0956 < \beta < .1124$

Thus, we are 90-, 95-, and 99-percent certain that the true population parameter β lies in the respective ranges calculated above. On the basis of the confidence-interval test, the null hypotheses are again rejected.

If Assumptions 4 and/or 5 are violated, then it becomes more difficult to test the null hypotheses. First we demonstrate the consequences of heteroscedasticity and then those of autocorrelation. Suppose we generate values for Y as in Demo 3.1 except that the error variance increases as X increases. Consequently, the error term does not have constant variance for all observations, and therefore heteroscedasticity is present. The range of Y values for each fixed value of X is presented in Table 3.13. The reader will note that the error variance for

table 3.13. Range of Y for Heteroscedasticity Demonstration

X	Range of Y	Midpoint of Range
1	.055 to .055	.055
2	.150 to .160	.155
3	.245 to .265	.255
4	.340 to .370	.355
5	.435 to .475	.455
6	.530 to .580	.555
7	.625 to .685	.655
8	.720 to .790	.755
9	.815 to .895	.855
10	.910 to 1.000	.955

$X = 1$ is zero and steadily increases because the range of Y increases. The midpoint of each range is the same as in Table 3.12.

In Demo 3.3 we have again generated twenty-five random samples, but this time within the ranges specified in Table 3.12. B, A, R^2, $\sum e^2$, and the sample standard errors of B and A from Equations (3.27) and (3.28) are printed. For example, for the first sample ($K = 1$), $B = .100$, $A = -.047$, $R^2 = .998$, $\sum e^2 = .0017$, $SE(B) = .0016$, and $SE(A) = .0099$.

What is interesting about this experiment is the fact that the standard deviations of the twenty-five A's and twenty-five B's in Demo 3.3 are considerably

```
B= .100007 K= 1
A=-.467774E-1
R2= .997983
SUME2= .16678E-2
SAMPLE SE OF B= .158964E-2
SAMPLE SE OF A= .986348E-2

B= .987185E-1 K= 2
A=-.373487E-1
R2= .998117
SUME2= .151694E-2
SAMPLE SE OF B= .151604E-2
SAMPLE SE OF A= .940681E-2

B= .102187 K= 3
A=-.497632E-1
R2= .99884
SUME2= .100064E-2
SAMPLE SE OF B= .123131E-2
SAMPLE SE OF A= .764008E-2

B= .100355 K= 4
A=-.457737E-1
R2= .996202
SUME2= .316763E-2
SAMPLE SE OF B= .219076E-2
SAMPLE SE OF A= .135933E-1

B= .098142 K= 5
A=-.381062E-1
R2= .998021
SUME2= .157601E-2
SAMPLE SE OF B= .154528E-2
SAMPLE SE OF A= .958821E-2

B= .975327E-1 K= 6
A=-.038008
R2= .996712
SUME2= .258893E-2
SAMPLE SE OF B= .198056E-2
SAMPLE SE OF A= .122891E-1

B= .975973E-1 K= 8
A=-.338181E-1
R2= .996581
SUME2= .269634E-2
SAMPLE SE OF B= .202123E-2
SAMPLE SE OF A= .125414E-1

B= .09886 K= 9
A=-.370734E-1
R2= .995522
SUME2= .362688E-2
SAMPLE SE OF B= .23443E-2
SAMPLE SE OF A= .145454E-1

B= .100542 K= 10
A=-.467438E-1
R2= .99847
SUME2= .127774E-2
SAMPLE SE OF B= .139139E-2
SAMPLE SE OF A= .863337E-2

B= .998738E-1 K= 11
A=-.408031E-1
R2= .99931
SUME2= .56833E-3
SAMPLE SE OF B= .927958E-3
SAMPLE SE OF A= .575783E-2

B= .101702 K= 12
A=-.474575E-1
R2= .997355
SUME2= .226325E-2
SAMPLE SE OF B= .18518E-2
SAMPLE SE OF A= .114901E-1

B= .103711 K= 13
A=-.615179E-1
R2= .997847
SUME2= .191492E-2
SAMPLE SE OF B= .170335E-2
SAMPLE SE OF A= .010569
```

demo 3.3. Sampling Distribution in Presence of Heteroscedasticity

```
B= .100707 K= 7
A=-.424261E-1
R2= .997659
SUME2= .196314E-2
SAMPLE SE OF B= .172466E-2
SAMPLE SE OF A= .107012E-1

B= .101805 K= 15
A=-.496128E-1
R2= .998264
SUME2= .14869E-2
SAMPLE SE OF B= .150096E-2
SAMPLE SE OF A= .93132E-2

B= .972065E-1 K= 16
A=-.377655E-1
R2= .995565
SUME2= .347239E-2
SAMPLE SE OF B= .229373E-2
SAMPLE SE OF A= .142322E-1

B= .100208 K= 17
A=-.427422E-1
R2= .997192
SUME2= .233269E-2
SAMPLE SE OF B= .187999E-2
SAMPLE SE OF A= .116651E-1

B= .101541 K= 18
A=-.499095E-1
R2= .998213
SUME2= .15229E-2
SAMPLE SE OF B= .151902E-2
SAMPLE SE OF A= .942527E-2

B= .101436 K= 19
A=-.480927E-1
R2= .997773
SUME2= .189459E-2
SAMPLE SE OF B= .169428E-2
SAMPLE SE OF A= .105128E-1

B= .101898 K= 20
A=-.447035E-1
R2= .999446
SUME2= .47487E-3
SAMPLE SE OF B= .848234E-3
SAMPLE SE OF A= .526315E-2

B= .100827 K= 14
A=-.533235E-1
R2= .998954
SUME2= .878573E-3
SAMPLE SE OF B= .115376E-2
SAMPLE SE OF A= .715892E-2

B= .978577E-1 K= 21
A=-.340535E-1
R2= .994784
SUME2= .414276E-2
SAMPLE SE OF B= .250538E-2
SAMPLE SE OF A= .155455E-1

B= .989092E-1 K= 22
A=-.048656
R2= .999605
SUME2= .319362E-3
SAMPLE SE OF B= .695616E-3
SAMPLE SE OF A= .431618E-2

B= .100856 K= 23
A=-.481215E-1
R2= .99689
SUME2= .261784E-2
SAMPLE SE OF B= .199159E-2
SAMPLE SE OF A= .123575E-1

B= .102113 K= 24
A=-.521581E-1
R2= .997715
SUME2= .197059E-2
SAMPLE SE OF B= .172793E-2
SAMPLE SE OF A= .107215E-1

B= .101507 K= 25
A=-.498546E-1
R2= .996853
SUME2= .268388E-2
SAMPLE SE OF B= .201655E-2
SAMPLE SE OF A= .125124E-1

STD.DEV OF B'S= .169979E-2
STD.DEV OF A'S= .110902E-1
MEAN OF B'S= .100244
MEAN OF A'S=-.449845E-1
```

demo 3.3. Continued

smaller than those in Demo 3.2. Since the standard errors[5] are smaller, the confidence intervals are narrower and there is a greater probability of rejecting the null hypotheses. Thus, our estimates of the population parameters are more precise in the presence of heteroscedasticity. Unfortunately, our greater confidence is illusory because the existence of heteroscedasticity biases our estimates for the standard errors downward. This can easily be seen in Table 3.14, which presents the ratios of the standard errors in the presence and absence of heteroscedasticity.

table 3.14. Standard Deviations of *A*'s and *B*'s with and without Heteroscedasticity

	No Heteroscedasticity	Heteroscedasticity	Ratio
Standard deviation of *A*'s	.02	.01	.50
Standard deviation of *B*'s	.0029	.0017	.59

However, the means of the *A*'s and *B*'s in Demos 3.3 and 3.2 do not appear to differ significantly. We can therefore state the following conclusion and leave the formal proof to more-advanced books: Given the presence of heteroscedasticity, estimates of the standard errors of the regression parameters are biased downward, but the regression coefficients themselves are unbiased.

Heteroscedasticity is often a problem in cross-section studies in which data are collected from units that vary in size. For example, in a study of firm behavior, errors associated with larger firms may be greater than those in smaller firms, thus causing heteroscedasticity. Or in a study of family budgets, consumption and income may vary less for poorer families. Two cases of heteroscedasticity are illustrated in Figure 3.10. In Chapter 4 we discuss how to detect and correct for heteroscedasticity.

While heteroscedasticity more often occurs in cross-section analyses, autocorrelation more frequently occurs in time-series studies in which data are collected on variables over a period of time. Autocorrelation is almost always positive in such studies, and therefore we will primarily concern ourselves with this type of autocorrelation. With positive autocorrelation, observations in consecutive periods tend to lie above or below the estimated regression line. Positive and negative autocorrelation are illustrated in Figure 3.11.

The most common cause of autocorrelation in time-series analysis is the phenomenon of the business cycle. As is well known, time series such as employment, income, consumption, and stock prices are cyclical, ad infinitum. For example, when stock prices start to move up, the positive movement in this

[5]Remember that this is a sampling distribution. Therefore, the standard deviations of the twenty-five *A*'s and twenty-five *B*'s are also standard errors.

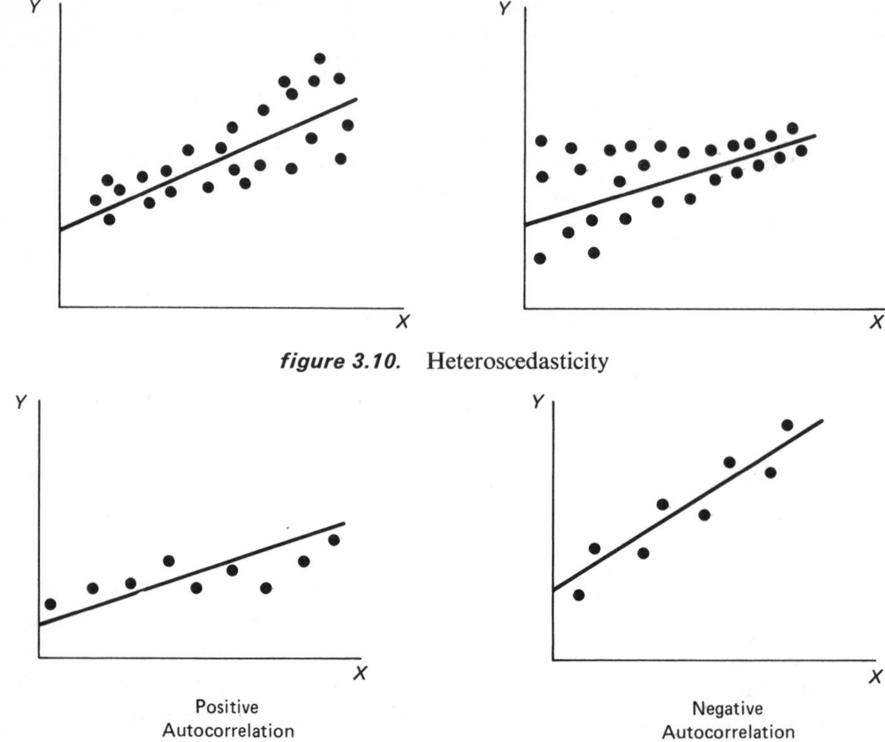

figure 3.10. Heteroscedasticity

figure 3.11. Positive and Negative Autocorrelation

period tends to be associated with a positive movement in the next period. Wesley Clair Mitchell, a noted authority on business cycles, has described this process: "The salient feature of the whole development is that each successive effect reacts to strengthen the causes that produced it, so that the movement toward prosperity gathers momentum as it proceeds."[6] As Mitchell indicates, one time series may also interact with another, a situation that Gerhard Tintner has termed "serial correlation."[7] Thus, autocorrelation is correlation of successive members of one series, and serial correlation is correlation between the lagged values of two different series. In this book we will use the terms *autocorrelation* and *serial correlation* interchangeably.

As an example, consider the regression line in Figure 3.12. The dependent variable is stock prices (Standard and Poor's), and the independent variable is time (the fourth quarter of 1968 to the first quarter of 1976). Positive autocorrelation is clearly present, as positive residuals tend to be followed by positive ones and negative residuals by negative ones. In addition to the business-cycle

[6]Mitchell, *Business Cycles and Their Causes* (Berkeley and Los Angeles: University of California Press, 1963), p. 25.

[7]Tintner, *Econometrics* (New York: John Wiley, 1965), p. 187.

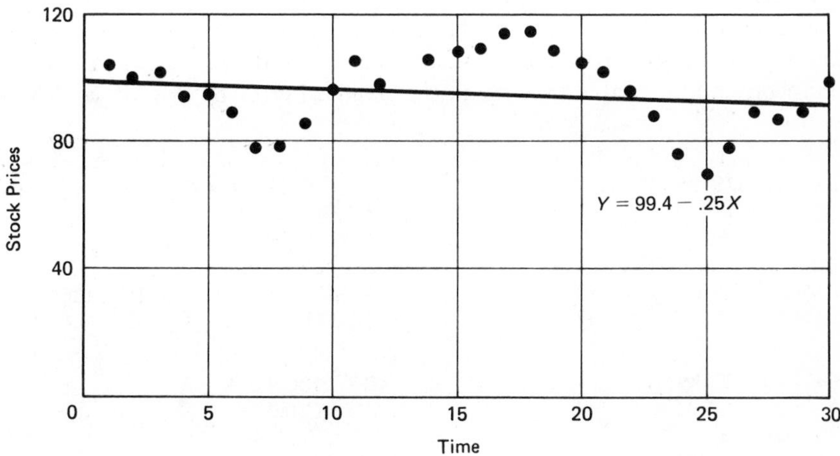

figure 3.12. Regression of Stock Prices on Time

phenomenon, another major cause of autocorrelation is an error in model specification. For example, the relationship between stock prices and time might be $Y = \alpha + \beta X^2 + \epsilon$. (The problem of the mathematical form of a regression model is treated in the next section.) Or an important variable such as the change in the money supply might be excluded from the model. (The next chapter extends the regression model to more than one independent variable.)

To demonstrate the consequences of autocorrelation, suppose we use the same stochastic model as in Demo 3.1, but this time for the first five values of X, the random numbers generated for Y lie below the true regression line; for the last five values of X, the generated Y values lie above the line. Table 3.15 presents the range and midpoint of Y values for each fixed value of X.

table 3.15. Range of Y for Autocorrelation Demonstration

X	Range of Y	Midpoint of Range
1	.01 to .055	.0325
2	.11 to .155	.1325
3	.21 to .255	.2325
4	.31 to .355	.3325
5	.41 to .455	.4325
6	.555 to .6	.5775
7	.655 to .7	.6775
8	.755 to .8	.7775
9	.855 to .9	.8775
10	.955 to 1.0	.9775

In Demo 3.4 we have generated twenty-five random samples of Y within the ranges specified in Table 3.15 and fitted a least squares line to each sample. Table 3.16 presents the ratios of the standard errors in the presence and absence of autocorrelation. In this experiment the standard error of B is biased down-

```
B= .106378 K= 1
A=-.749549E-1
R2= .997886
SUME2= .197768E-2
SAMPLE SE OF B= .173104E-2
SAMPLE SE OF A= .107408E-1

B= .105075 K= 2
A=-.698379E-1
R2= .995938
SUME2= .371486E-2
SAMPLE SE OF B= .237246E-2
SAMPLE SE OF A= .147207E-1

B= .105948 K= 3
A=-.732935E-1
R2= .995726
SUME2= .397474E-2
SAMPLE SE OF B= .245404E-2
SAMPLE SE OF A= .152269E-1

B= .106262 K= 4
A=-.799269E-1
R2= .994852
SUME2= .482047E-2
SAMPLE SE OF B= .270254E-2
SAMPLE SE OF A= .167688E-1

B= .109016 K= 5
A=-.916215E-1
R2= .998872
SUME2= .110686E-2
SAMPLE SE OF B= .129501E-2
SAMPLE SE OF A= .803534E-2

B= .109607 K= 6
A=-.10199
R2= .99831
SUME2= .167787E-2
SAMPLE SE OF B= .159444E-2
SAMPLE SE OF A= .989322E-2

B= .108059 K= 8
A=-.091218
R2= .998442
SUME2= .150353E-2
SAMPLE SE OF B= .150933E-2
SAMPLE SE OF A= .936514E-2

B= .108055 K= 9
A=-.870618E-1
R2= .996496
SUME2= .338697E-2
SAMPLE SE OF B= .226534E-2
SAMPLE SE OF A= .140561E-1

B= .107809 K= 10
A=-.836382E-1
R2= .995959
SUME2= .389028E-2
SAMPLE SE OF B= .242783E-2
SAMPLE SE OF A= .150643E-1

B= .108811 K= 11
A=-.914045E-1
R2= .995172
SUME2= .473905E-2
SAMPLE SE OF B= .267962E-2
SAMPLE SE OF A= .166266E-1

B= .105587 K= 12
A=-.788335E-1
R2= .997295
SUME2= .249493E-2
SAMPLE SE OF B= .194427E-2
SAMPLE SE OF A= .120639E-1

B= .105285 K= 13
A=-.742877E-1
R2= .996736
SUME2= .299466E-2
SAMPLE SE OF B= .213011E-2
SAMPLE SE OF A= .013217
```

demo 3.4. Sampling Distribution in Presence of Autocorrelation

```
B= .105279 K= 7
A=-.799554E-1
R2= .997518
SUME2= .227565E-2
SAMPLE SE OF B= .185687E-2
SAMPLE SE OF A= .115215E-1

B= .108895 K= 15
A=-.920661E-1
R2= .995841
SUME2= .408614E-2
SAMPLE SE OF B= .24882E-2
SAMPLE SE OF A= .154388E-1

B= .105076 K= 16
A=-.748203E-1
R2= .998144
SUME2= .169408E-2
SAMPLE SE OF B= .160408E-2
SAMPLE SE OF A= .99409E-2

B= .105258 K= 17
A=-.829926E-1
R2= .99712
SUME2= .264001E-2
SAMPLE SE OF B= .002
SAMPLE SE OF A= .124097E-1

B= .106904 K= 18
A=-.832454E-1
R2= .997624
SUME2= .224578E-2
SAMPLE SE OF B= .184464E-2
SAMPLE SE OF A= .114457E-1

B= .108564 K= 19
A=-.919963E-1
R2= .997483
SUME2= .245345E-2
SAMPLE SE OF B= .192804E-2
SAMPLE SE OF A= .119632E-1

B= .108586 K= 20
A=-.967838E-1
R2= .996121
SUME2= .378799E-2
SAMPLE SE OF B= .23957E-2
SAMPLE SE OF A= .148649E-1

B= .106856 K= 14
A=-.821492E-1
R2= .995107
SUME2= .463158E-2
SAMPLE SE OF B= .264907E-2
SAMPLE SE OF A= .016437

B= .107361 K= 21
A=-.852549E-1
R2= .996898
SUME2= .29586E-2
SAMPLE SE OF B= .211724E-2
SAMPLE SE OF A= .131372E-1

B= .104399 K= 22
A=-.654131E-1
R2= .998005
SUME2= .179768E-2
SAMPLE SE OF B= .165038E-2
SAMPLE SE OF A= .102403E-1

B= .106325 K= 23
A=-.795555E-1
R2= .997552
SUME2= .228918E-2
SAMPLE SE OF B= .186238E-2
SAMPLE SE OF A= .115557E-1

B= .105205 K= 24
A=-.813524E-1
R2= .997258
SUME2= .251049E-2
SAMPLE SE OF B= .195033E-2
SAMPLE SE OF A= .121015E-1

B= .106853 K= 25
A=-.945823E-1
R2= .998905
SUME2= .103265E-2
SAMPLE SE OF B= .125085E-2
SAMPLE SE OF A= .776131E-2

STD.DEV OF B'S= .149786E-2
STD.DEV OF A'S= .187255E-1
MEAN OF B'S= .106858
MEAN OF A'S=-.835294E-1
```

demo 3.4. Continued

ward, but that for A does not appear to be biased. However, the sample standard errors of A for many of the samples are biased downward. None is higher than .02, the standard error of A in the absence of autocorrelation.

table 3.16. Standard Deviations of A's and B's with and without Autocorrelation

	No Autocorrelation	Autocorrelation	Ratio
Standard deviation of A's	.02	.02	1.00
Standard deviation of B's	.0029	.0015	.52

Thus, Equations (3.27) and (3.28) lead to biased estimates of the standard errors when autocorrelation exists. Actually, the consequences of autocorrelation are the same as those of heteroscedasticity: Given the presence of autocorrelation, estimates of the standard errors of the regression parameters are biased downward, but the regression coefficients themselves are unbiased. This will lead to our having greater confidence in our regression estimators (coefficients) than warranted. Although it would appear that the regression parameters themselves are biased in Demo 3.4, this results solely because the generated Y values lie below the regression line for $X = 1$ to 5, and above the line for $X = 6$ to 10. If, instead, Y values had been generated above the regression line for $X = 1$ to 5 and below the line for $X = 6$ to 10, the parameters would have been biased in the opposite direction. Since both situations are likely to occur in time-series analysis (see Figure 3.12), on average the regression parameters are unbiased in the presence of autocorrelation.

The reader should refer to one of the more-advanced books in the Bibliography for a proof of the above. Techniques of detecting and correcting for autocorrelation are discussed in Chapter 4.

mathematical forms of regression models

Economic phenomena are not always so agreeable as to allow a straight line to be fitted to the X and Y data. Often a relationship is clearly nonlinear, yet there appears to be a certain predictable motion in the movement of X and Y. Consider the hypothetical data in Table 3.17, which are graphed in Figure 3.13. In each time period, GNP increases at the rate of 65 percent. Is there a way of expressing the relationship between GNP (Y) and time (X)?

The equation relating GNP to time is

$$Y = \rho e^{\beta X} \tag{3.31}$$

where ρ = constant; e = 2.71828, the "natural exponential." Clearly, Equation (3.31) is nonlinear in the parameter β, and therefore it cannot be estimated

table 3.17. Hypothetical GNP Data

Time	GNP ($billions)
1	12.18
2	20.09
3	33.12
4	54.60
5	90.02
6	148.41
7	244.69
8	403.43
9	665.14
10	1,096.63
11	1,808.04
12	2,980.96
13	4,914.77
14	8,103.08
15	13,359.70
16	22,026.50
17	36,315.50
18	59,874.10
19	98,715.80
20	162,755.00

within the context of the classical regression model presented in this chapter. However, Equation (3.31) can be converted to the following linear equation:

$$ln\, Y = \alpha + \beta X \tag{3.32}$$

where $\alpha = ln\, \rho$, a constant
ln = "natural logarithm"

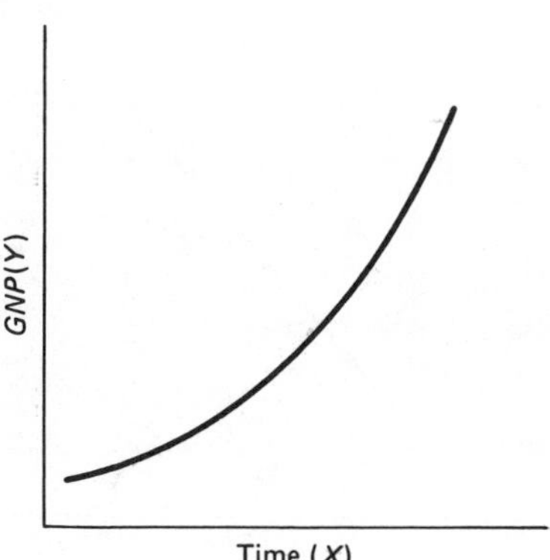

figure 3.13. Constant Percentage Growth Model

This function is graphed in Figure 3.14 and the transformed data are presented in Table 3.18. Equation (3.32) is a "semilog" model because only one of the variables is expressed in log form. The value for α is 2.0 and for β, .5. Note that $ln\ Y$ increases .5 for each X. The percentage increase in income (g) in each time period is given by the equation

$$g = (e^{\beta} - 1) \times 100 \tag{3.33}$$

table 3.18. *Ln Y* for Each *X*

Time	*Ln Y* (GNP)
1	2.5
2	3.0
3	3.5
4	4.0
5	4.5
6	5.0
7	5.5
8	6.0
9	6.5
10	7.0
11	7.5
12	8.0
13	8.5
14	9.0
15	9.5
16	10.0
17	10.5
18	11.0
19	11.5
20	12.0

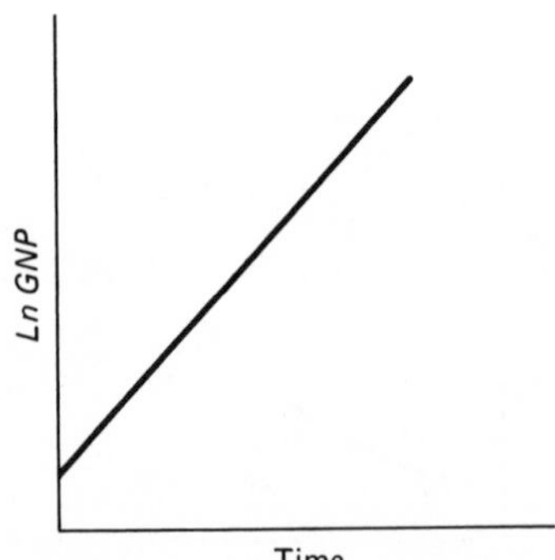

figure 3.14. Constant Percentage Growth Model in Semilog Form

Substituting into Equation (3.33) in this example:

$$g = (2.71828^{.5} - 1) \times 100 = (\sqrt{2.71828} - 1) \times 100$$
$$= (1.65 - 1) \times 100 = 65 \text{ percent}$$

Often in economic theory, a nonlinear demand curve is postulated as in Figure 3.15.[8] The data used to construct this curve are in Table 3.19. Note that the elasticity of demand (percentage change in quantity demanded divided by the percentage change in price) is constant and equal to −2.

The equation relating quantity (Y) to price (X) is

$$Y = \rho X^{\beta} \tag{3.34}$$

This can be converted to a "double-log" or "log-linear" form to permit estimation of the parameters by ordinary least squares:

$$\ln Y = \alpha + \beta \ln X \tag{3.35}$$

where $\alpha = \ln \rho$, a constant.

table 3.19. Hypothetical Demand Data

Quantity (Y)	Price (X)
1	$7.39
2	5.22
3	4.27
4	3.69
5	3.30
6	3.02
7	2.79
8	2.61
9	2.46
10	2.34
11	2.23
12	2.13
13	2.05
14	1.97
15	1.91
16	1.85
17	1.79
18	1.74
19	1.70
20	1.65

[8]It is common practice in econometric work to switch the traditional axes so that quantity is on the Y axis instead of the X axis. This makes sense, since quantity is in theory the dependent variable.

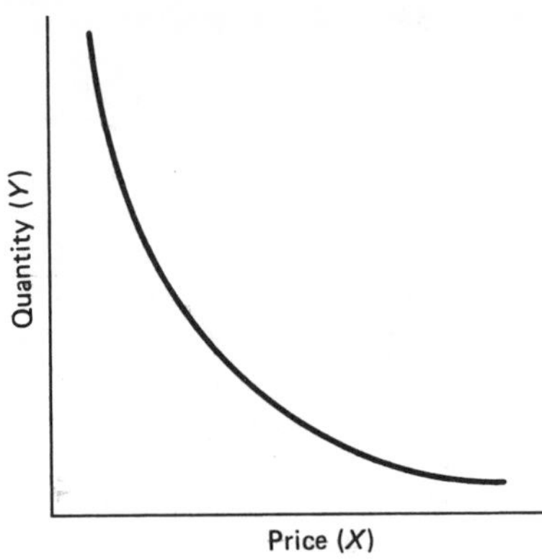

figure 3.15. Constant Elasticity of Demand Model

Equation (3.35) is graphed in Figure 3.16 and the transformed data are presented in Table 3.20. The value for α is 4 and for β, -2; thus, β measures the price elasticity of demand, one of the most important concepts in economic theory.

table 3.20. *Ln Y* and *Ln X*

***Ln Y* (Quantity)**	***Ln X* (Price)**
0.00	2.00
0.69	1.65
1.10	1.45
1.39	1.31
1.61	1.20
1.79	1.10
1.95	1.03
2.08	0.96
2.20	0.90
2.30	0.85
2.40	0.80
2.48	0.76
2.56	0.72
2.64	0.68
2.71	0.65
2.77	0.61
2.83	0.58
2.89	0.55
2.94	0.53
3.00	0.50

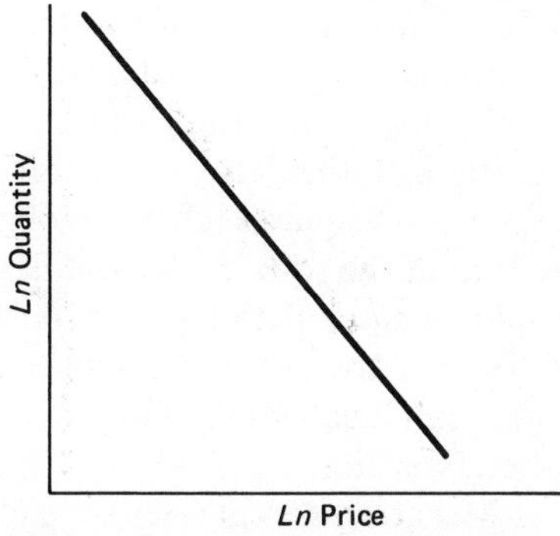

figure 3.16. Constant Elasticity of Demand Model in Double-Log Form

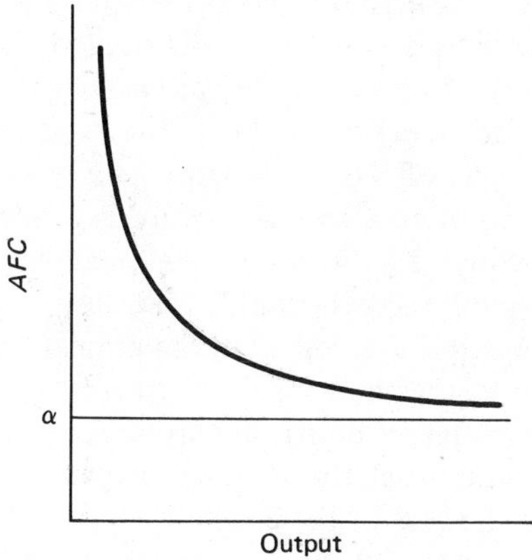

figure 3.17. Reciprocal Transformation Model

Another common mathematical form is the "reciprocal transformation" graphed in Figure 3.17, the equation of which is

$$Y = \alpha + \beta(1/X) \tag{3.36}$$

An example of Equation (3.36) in economic theory is the average fixed cost of production (AFC), which approaches a limit or asymptotic value measured by α. ($1/X$ goes to zero as X approaches infinity.)

summary

A two-variable regression model consists of one dependent and one independent variable. The dependence of one variable on another is based upon an underlying economic theory, not on the statistical measurement of the relationship between two variables. Thus, the statistical techniques developed in this chapter to measure the strength of the relationship between two variables (covariation and correlation analysis and the coefficient of determination) cannot be used to prove causation. Rather, they are merely suggestive.

The technique of ordinary least squares (OLS) involves fitting a line to the Y and X data such that the sum of the squared vertical deviations from the line is minimized. The usually unknown population parameters, α and β, are estimated by OLS. The estimators A and B are best linear unbiased estimators (BLUE) of the population parameters. The Gauss-Markov theorem provides the theoretical basis for proving this latter assertion.

The proof of the Gauss-Markov theorem (see Appendix 3.1) is based on certain assumptions: (1) the relationship between Y and X is linear; (2) the X's are nonstochastic and fixed; (3) the error term has zero expected value; (4) the error term is homoscedastic; (5) autocorrelation does not exist; and (6) the error term is uncorrelated with X. Furthermore, hypothesis tests are based on a seventh assumption: (7) the error term is normally distributed. The above assumptions constitute what is termed the *classical normal linear regression model.*

Two methods exist for testing the null hypotheses: $\alpha = 0$; $\beta = 0$. In the first method, the absolute value of the regression coefficient (A or B) derived from OLS is divided by its standard error. The result is termed T and is compared with the critical values in a T table with $N - 2$ degrees of freedom. For any given level of risk or significance, the null hypothesis is rejected if T exceeds the critical value, and accepted if T is less than the critical value. The logic behind this method is that T measures how far the regression coefficient (the estimator of the population parameter, α or β), lies from zero. Thus, a "low" T value would lead us to conclude that the population parameter is not statistically different from zero. In the case of the constant term α, this means that the line passes through the origin (0, 0). If the slope parameter β is not significantly different from zero, then X is not an important determinant of Y. The hypothesis test with respect to β is the more important unless the economic theory underlying the regression model would lead us to expect a positive or negative constant term. For example, because people tend to consume (out of savings) when their incomes are zero, we expect the constant term to be positive in a model in which consumption is the dependent and income the independent variable.

The second method is equivalent to the first and involves calculating a range that contains the true population parameter with a chosen level of confidence. The resulting range is termed a *confidence interval.* A confidence interval is constructed by multiplying the appropriate critical T value by the standard error, and then adding and subtracting this result from the regression coefficient. If the confidence interval contains zero, then the null hypothesis is accepted. Regardless of which method is chosen, the conclusion is the same.

Violation of two of the assumptions of the regression model—homoscedasticity and no autocorrelation—can have serious consequences for the testing of the null hypotheses. In either case, the standard errors of the regression coefficients are biased downward, although the regression coefficients themselves are unbiased. Consequently, if heteroscedasticity or autocorrelation exists, this increases the probability of rejecting the null hypotheses even though they might be true (Type I error). For example, a smaller standard error means a smaller confidence interval and therefore a lower probability that zero is contained within it. We will deal with the problems of detecting and correcting for heteroscedasticity and autocorrelation in the next chapter.

We finished the chapter by considering nonlinear models that can be transformed into models that are linear in their parameters. Three of the more important of these are the semilog, double-log, and reciprocal models. Semilog models are especially useful in analyzing economic variables that tend to grow at a constant rate over time. Double-log models have the characteristic that the slope parameter measures the elasticity of Y with respect to X. Reciprocal models can be applied to variables that have a limiting or "asymptotic" value.

examples

example 1

A population consists of the four numbers 2, 4, 6, and 8. Show that $\bar{X}$ is an unbiased estimator of μ regardless of the sample size.

First we must list all the possible samples for $N = 1$, $N = 2$, $N = 3$, and $N = 4$. This is done in Table 3.21.

table 3.21. Sampling Distributions for $N = 1$, $N = 2$, $N = 3$, $N = 4$

$N = 1$	$\bar{X}$	$N = 2$	$\bar{X}$
2	2	2, 4	3
4	4	2, 6	4
6	6	2, 8	5
8	8	4, 6	5
Sum	20	4, 8	6
		6, 8	7
		Sum	30

$N = 3$	$\bar{X}$	$N = 4$	$\bar{X}$
2, 4, 6	4.00	2, 4, 6, 8	5
2, 4, 8	4.67	Sum	5
4, 6, 8	6.00		
2, 6, 8	5.33		
Sum	20.00		

The possible samples are

$N = 1$: 4
$N = 2$: 6
$N = 3$: 4
$N = 4$: 1

Dividing the above numbers into the sum for each sampling distribution:

$N = 1$: $20/4 = 5$
$N = 2$: $30/6 = 5$
$N = 3$: $20/4 = 5$
$N = 4$: $5/1 = 5$

Since $\mu = 5$, we have shown that $\bar{X}$ is an unbiased estimator:

$$5 - 5 = 0$$

example 2

Show that an alternative formula for calculating the correlation coefficient, R, is

$$R = B\left(\frac{S_X}{S_Y}\right) \tag{3.37}$$

From Equation (3.11):

$$B = \frac{\sum xy}{\sum x^2}$$

Also by definition:

$$S_X = \sqrt{\frac{\sum x^2}{N-1}}$$

$$S_Y = \sqrt{\frac{\sum y^2}{N-1}}$$

Note that these equations are expressed in deviations form. Therefore:

$$R = \frac{\sum xy}{\sum x^2}\left(\frac{\sqrt{\sum x^2}}{\sqrt{\sum y^2}}\right)$$

since the $N - 1$ term cancels.

$$R = \frac{\sum xy}{\sqrt{\sum x^2 \sum y^2}}$$

which is the same as Equation (3.20).

example 3

Suppose that a random sample is selected from the data in Table 3.10:

Consumption (Y)	Income (X)
$10,000	$10,000
13,000	15,000
8,000	20,000
9,250	25,000
15,000	30,000

Calculate A, B, and R^2 for a regression model in which consumption is the dependent variable (Y) and income the independent variable (X). Use Equation (3.20) to calculate R^2. Interpret the results.

$$\bar{Y} = \sum Y/N = 11{,}050$$

$$\bar{X} = \sum X/N = 20{,}000$$

x	y	xy	x^2	y^2
−10,000	−1,050	10,500,000	100,000,000	1,102,500
−5,000	1,950	−9,750,000	25,000,000	3,802,500
0	−3,050	0	0	9,302,500
5,000	−1,800	−9,000,000	25,000,000	3,240,000
10,000	3,950	39,500,000	100,000,000	15,602,500
		31,250,000	250,000,000	33,050,000

$$B = \frac{\sum xy}{\sum x^2} \qquad \text{from (3.11)}$$

$$= \frac{31{,}250{,}000}{250{,}000{,}000} = .125$$

$$A = \bar{Y} - B\bar{X} \qquad \text{from (3.12)}$$

$$= 11{,}050 - .125(20{,}000) = 8{,}550$$

$$R = \frac{\sum xy}{\sqrt{\sum x^2 \sum y^2}} \qquad \text{from (3.20)}$$

$$= \frac{31{,}250{,}000}{(15{,}811.388)(5{,}748.913)} = \frac{31{,}250{,}000}{90{,}898{,}294}$$

$$= .343$$

Therefore, $R^2 = (.343)^2 = .118$.

Since the percentage of the variation in consumption "explained" by income is only about 12 percent, income would not appear to be an important determinant of consumption. However, this conclusion is based upon a sample of only five families and therefore should not be taken seriously. Also, B, the marginal propensity to consume, is extremely low (.125) and therefore suspect. Only the value of A (positive) conforms to the expected result.

This example partially demonstrates the complexity of the calculations involved in regression analysis. The reader can easily imagine how difficult this problem would be for a sample size of 25, 100, or 1,000. The advantage of having a computer perform these calculations is obvious.

example 4

Test the null hypothesis, $\beta = 0$, at the .05 level of significance for the data in Example 3.

$$SE(B) = s/\sqrt{\sum x^2}$$

$$s = \sqrt{(\sum y^2 - B^2 \sum x^2)/N - 2}$$

Therefore:

$$s = \sqrt{[(33{,}050{,}000) - (.125)^2(250{,}000{,}000)]/3}$$

$$= \sqrt{9{,}714{,}583.3} = 3{,}116.82$$

$$SE(B) = 3{,}116.82/15{,}811.388$$

$$= .197$$

$$T = .125/.197 = .63$$

The critical T value at the .05 level with 3 degrees of freedom (df) is 3.182. Since .63 is less than 3.182, the null hypothesis is accepted: $\beta = 0$; therefore, this confirms our finding in the preceding example that income is not an important determinant of consumption.

example 5

Construct a confidence interval for β at the .95 level for Example 4. Interpret your result.

The critical T value is 3.182. Multiplying this by the standard error:

$$3.182(.197) = .627$$

Adding and subtracting this result from B:

$$.125 + .627 = .752$$

$$.125 - .627 = -.502$$

The confidence interval is

$$-.502 < \beta < .752$$

This means that the true population parameter, β, lies within this interval with a .95 probability or level of confidence. Since 0 lies within this interval, the null hypothesis is accepted. This is expected because the T and confidence-interval methods of testing the null hypothesis are equivalent.

exercises

1. Let B_1 and B_2 be two estimators of β. Suppose that $E(B_1)$ and $E(B_2)$ are equal to each other, and both estimators have the same variance. Is there any reason to prefer B_1 over B_2?

2. Show that S_1 (Equation (3.4)) is a biased estimator of σ if the variable X takes on the values 2, 4, 6, and 8.

3. You have the following data on stock market prices and dividends for eight quarters (2-74 to 1-76). Stock market prices are measured by the Standard and Poor's Index. Dividends are total corporate dividends in billions of dollars. Calculate A, B, R^2, the standard errors, and the T values where stock prices are the dependent variable. Test the null hypotheses at the .05 level.

Stock Prices	Dividends
\$90.64	\$30.9
75.66	31.7
69.42	31.7
78.81	32.1
89.07	32.6
87.62	33.5
89.11	33.1
99.53	33.3

4. Calculate 95-percent confidence intervals for α and β for the stock-price model in Exercise 3. Are the null hypotheses accepted on the basis of these confidence intervals?

5. Calculate 90-, 95-, and 99-percent confidence intervals for α using the first sample ($K = 1$) in Demo 3.2.

6. Using the data in Exercise 3, calculate A, B, and R^2 where dividends are the dependent variable. Are your results the same? Let B_1 equal the slope of the regression with stock prices as the dependent variable, and B_2 the slope with dividends as the dependent variable. Does $B_1 = 1/B_2$? Does $B_1 \times B_2 = R^2$? Under what conditions will $B_1 = 1/B_2$?

7. Suppose the stock-price index was divided by 10 (e.g., the first value is now 9.064). Reestimate the regression of stock prices on dividends. How are your results different?

8. Select any sample other than the first one in Demo 3.3. Demonstrate the consequences of heteroscedasticity.

9. Select any sample in Demo 3.4. Demonstrate the consequences of autocorrelation.

10. How is the $\sum e^2$ affected in the presence of autocorrelation and heteroscedasticity? What effect does this have on the R^2?

11. You have the following demand data. Determine whether Model I or Model II fits the data better. Interpret your results.

Model I: $Q = \alpha + \beta P + \epsilon$
Model II: $ln\, Q = \alpha + \beta\, ln\, P + \epsilon$

Quantity (Q)	Price (P)	*ln Q*	*ln P*
1	$7.39	0.00	2.00
2	3.69	0.69	1.31
3	2.46	1.10	0.90
4	1.85	1.39	0.61
5	1.48	1.61	0.39
6	1.23	1.79	0.21
7	1.06	1.95	0.05
8	.92	2.08	−0.08
9	.82	2.20	−0.20
10	.74	2.30	−0.30

12. You have the following quarterly data (4-73 to 1-76) on government spending ($billions). Determine whether Model I or Model II fits the data better. Interpret your results.

Model I: $Y = \alpha + \beta X + \epsilon$
Model II: $ln\, Y = \alpha + \beta X + \epsilon$

Time (X)	Government Spending (Y)	*Ln Y*
1	285.6	5.65
2	297.8	5.69
3	304.4	5.71
4	312.3	5.74
5	323.8	5.78
6	331.6	5.80
7	338.1	5.82
8	343.1	5.83
9	344.8	5.84
10	349.2	5.85

13. Show that Assumption 6 of the regression model is a corollary to Assumptions 2 and 3.

computer exercises

1. Run the following program several times. This program was used to generate the random sample in Demo 3.1. Select any particular X (e.g., $X = 2$). Do the errors for that particular X appear to sum to zero?

```
10RANDOM
20DIM A(10,3)
30LET K=1.1
40LET C=-.045
50FOR I=1 TO 10
60LET A(I,1)=I
70LET K=K-.1
80LET C=C+.1
90LET A(I,2)=.09*RND+(1-K)+.01
100LET A(I,3)=A(I,2)-C
110LET S=S+A(I,3)
120NEXT I
130MAT PRINT A;
140PRINT "SUM OF ERROR=";S
150END
```

demo 3.5. Program That Demonstrates Stochastic Nature of Regression Model

2. You have the following data for thirty quarters (4-68 to 1-76) on stock market prices and dividends. Use the program in Demo 3.6 to fit a regression

```
5REM FIRST COLUMN IS Y
6REM SECOND COLUMN IS X
10REM S1=YBAR
20REM S2=XBAR
30REM S3=SUMXY
50REM S5=SUMX2
60REM S6=SUMY2
65DIM A(100,2)
70READ N
75FOR I=1 TO N
80READ A(I,1)
85NEXT I
90FOR I=1 TO N
95READ A(I,2)
100LET X=X+A(I,2)**2
105NEXT I
110FOR I=1 TO N
```

demo 3.6. Two-Variable Regression Program Run on Income-IQ Data. Statement 65 Is Dimensioned for Up to 100 Observations.

```
120LET S1=S1+A(I,1)
130LET S2=S2+A(I,2)
140NEXT I
150LET S1=S1/N
160LET S2=S2/N
170PRINT "YBAR=";S1
180PRINT "XBAR=";S2
190FOR I=1 TO N
200LET S3=S3+(A(I,2)-S2)*(A(I,1)-S1)
220LET S5=S5+(A(I,2)-S2)**2
230LET S6=S6+(A(I,1)-S1)**2
240NEXT I
250LET B=S3/S5
255LET A1=S1-B*S2
260PRINT "B=";B
270PRINT "A=";A1
296LET R2=B**2*S5/S6
297PRINT "R2=";R2
298LET E2=-R2*S6+S6
314LET S9=SQR(E2/(N-2))
320LET E3=S9/SQR(S5)
325LET E4=S9*SQR(X/(N*S5))
330PRINT "SE OF B=";E3
335PRINT "T(B)=";ABS(B/E3)
340PRINT "SE OF A=";E4
345PRINT "T(A)=";ABS(A1/E4)
347DATA 10
350DATA 5000,6000,7000,8000,9000,10000,11000,12000,13000,14000
360DATA 80,95,100,101,103,115,105,116,120,110
370END
RUN
YBAR= 9500
XBAR= 104.5
B= 221.639
A=-13661.3
R2= .737454
SE OF B= 46.756
T(B)= 4.74034
SE OF A=4913.63
T(A)= 2.78029
```

demo 3.6. Continued

line to the data where stock market price is the dependent variable. Test the null hypotheses at any desired level of significance. What do you conclude? (This program is dimensioned to run on up to one hundred observations. For larger N, Statement 65 must be changed. For example, for two hundred observations: 65DIM A(200, 2). Statement 347 contains the exact number of observations. The first series of data statements starting at 350 contain the dependent variable, and the second series the independent variable.)

Stock Prices	Dividends ($billions)
105.2	23.8
100.9	24.1
101.7	25.4
94.5	25
94.3	25.2
88.7	25
79.2	24.9
78.7	25.2
86.2	25
96.7	25.6
101.5	25.4
98.55	25.2
96.41	24.9
105.41	25.7
108.16	25.9
109.2	26.2
114.02	28.2
115	28.7
107.41	29.1
105.08	29.8
102.22	30.7
95.67	30
90.64	30.9
75.66	31.7
69.42	31.7
78.81	32.1
89.07	32.6
87.62	33.5
89.11	33.1
99.53	33.3

3. By changing Statements 80 and 95 as follows, the two-variable regression program can be rerun with dividends as the dependent variable. Work Exercise 6 with the thirty quarters of data.

```
80READ A(I,2)
95READ A(I,1)
```

4. The program in Demo 3.7 constructs a confidence interval given the critical T value, the value of the regression coefficient, and the standard error of the regression coefficient. Use this program to construct 95-percent confidence intervals for α and β in Computer Exercise 2.

```
10PRINT "CRITICAL VALUE"
20INPUT C
30PRINT "VALUE OF REGRESSION COEFFICIENT"
40INPUT A
50PRINT "SE OF REGRESSION COEFFICIENT"
60INPUT S
70LET U=A+C*S
80LET L=A-C*S
90PRINT L;"<POPULATION PARAMETER<";U
100END

RUN
CRITICAL VALUE
? 1.86
VALUE OF REGRESSION COEFFICIENT
? .104
SE OF REGRESSION COEFFICIENT
? .0025
 .09935<POPULATION PARAMETER< .10865

RUN
CRITICAL VALUE
? 2.306
VALUE OF REGRESSION COEFFICIENT
? .104
SE OF REGRESSION COEFFICIENT
? .0025
 .098235<POPULATION PARAMETER< .109765

RUN
CRITICAL VALUE
? 3.355
VALUE OF REGRESSION COEFFICIENT
? .104
SE OF REGRESSION COEFFICIENT
? .0025
 .956125E-1<POPULATION PARAMETER< .112388
```

demo 3.7. Confidence-Interval Program Run on First Sample ($K = 1$) in Demo 3.2.

5. Work Exercise 11 with the two-variable regression program in Demo 3.6. You need to type in only the quantity and price data, not the *ln Q* or the *ln P* data. When testing Model II, add the Statements

```
83LET A(I,1)=LOG(A(I,1))
97LET A(I,2)=LOG(A(I,2))
```

6. Work Exercise 12 with the following thirty quarters of data (instead of the ten quarters) using the two-variable regression program in Demo 3.6. You need to type in only the government-spending (Y) data. The data on time (X) may be added to the program with the Statement: 95LET A(I,2)=I. When testing Model II, add the Statement: 83LET A(I,1)=LOG(A(I,1)).

Government Spending
206.7
210.0
212.9
214.1
216.3
219.6
218.4
220.1
223.7
228.2
230.2
233.8
240.8
249.6
254.2
254.7
260.7
269.6
275.0
279.0
285.6
297.8
304.4
312.3
323.8
331.6
338.1
343.1
344.8
349.2

appendix 3.1

derivation of OLS estimators and proof of Gauss-Markov theorem

Equation (3.9) may be minimized by taking partial derivatives with respect to A and B. Note that (3.9) is also equal to

$$\sum_{I=1}^{N} (Y_I - A - BX_I)^2 = \sum e^2 \tag{1}$$

by Equation (3.10).

$$\frac{\partial \sum e^2}{\partial A} = -2 \sum (Y_I - A - BX_I) \tag{2}$$

$$\frac{\partial \sum e^2}{\partial B} = -2 \sum (Y_I - A - BX_I)X_I \tag{3}$$

Setting these derivatives to zero and dividing by -2:

$$\sum (Y_I - A - BX_I) = 0 \tag{4}$$

$$\sum (Y_I - A - BX_I)X_I = 0 \tag{5}$$

Equations (4) and (5) can be rewritten as

$$\sum Y_I - NA - B \sum X_I = 0 \tag{6}$$

$$\sum Y_I X_I - A \sum X_I - B \sum X_I^2 = 0 \tag{7}$$

where N is the number of observations. Equations (6) and (7) are termed the *normal equations* and can be solved simultaneously. From Equation (6):

$$NA = \sum Y_I - B \sum X_I \tag{8}$$

$$A = \frac{\sum Y_I}{N} - \frac{B \sum X_I}{N} \tag{9}$$

$$= \bar{Y} - B\bar{X} \tag{3.12}$$

Substituting Equation (9) into Equation (7):

$$\sum Y_I X_I - \left(\frac{\sum Y_I}{N} - \frac{B \sum X_I}{N}\right) \sum X_I - B \sum X_I^2 = 0 \tag{10}$$

$$B \sum X_I^2 = -\left(\frac{\sum Y_I}{N} - \frac{B \sum X_I}{N}\right) \sum X_I + \sum Y_I X_I \tag{11}$$

$$B \sum X_I^2 = \frac{-\sum Y_I \sum X_I}{N} + \frac{B(\sum X_I)^2}{N} + \sum Y_I X_I \tag{12}$$

$$B \sum X_I^2 - \frac{B(\sum X_I^2)}{N} = \sum Y_I X_I - \frac{\sum Y_I \sum X_I}{N} \tag{13}$$

$$B\left[\sum X_I^2 - \frac{(\sum X_I)^2}{N}\right] = \sum Y_I X_I - \frac{\sum Y_I \sum X_I}{N} \tag{14}$$

$$B = \frac{\sum Y_I X_I - \frac{\sum Y_I \sum X_I}{N}}{\sum X_I^2 - \frac{(\sum X_I)^2}{N}} \tag{15}$$

$$= \frac{\sum Y_I X_I - \bar{Y} \sum X_I}{\sum X_I^2 - \bar{X} \sum X_I} \tag{16}$$

$$= \frac{\sum Y_I X_I - \bar{Y} N \bar{X}}{\sum X_I^2 - N\bar{X}^2} \tag{17}$$

since $\sum X_I = N\bar{X}$ and $\sum Y_I = N\bar{Y}$. But note that

$$\sum Y_I X_I - N\bar{Y}\bar{X} = \sum (Y_I - \bar{Y})(X_I - \bar{X}) \tag{18}$$

$$\sum X_I^2 - N\bar{X}^2 = \sum (X_I - \bar{X})^2 \tag{19}$$

Therefore (dropping the I subscript):

$$B = \frac{\sum (X - \bar{X})(Y - \bar{Y})}{\sum (X - \bar{X})^2} \tag{3.11}$$

We have thus completed the derivation of the OLS estimators given by Equations (3.11) and (3.12). It now remains to be proven that they are BLUE (Gauss-Markov theorem). We will prove the theorem for B and allow the interested reader to follow the same thought process in proving the theorem for A.

The X term in Equation (3.11) can be expressed in deviations form (see Equations (3.21) and (3.22)):

$$B = \frac{\sum x_i(Y_i - \bar{Y})}{\sum x_i^2} \tag{20}$$

$$= \frac{\sum x_i Y_i - \bar{Y} \sum x_i}{\sum x_i^2} \tag{21}$$

$$= \frac{\sum x_i Y}{\sum x_i^2} \tag{22}$$

since

$$\sum x_i = 0$$

Let

$$c_i = \frac{x_i}{\sum x_i^2} \tag{23}$$

Therefore:

$$B = \sum c_i Y_i \tag{24}$$

Equation (24) shows that B is a linear estimator because c_i is not raised to a power. To show that B is an unbiased estimator of β, we must show that $E(B) = \beta$. Substituting Equation (3.25) into Equation (24):

$$B = \sum c_i(\alpha + \beta X_i + \epsilon_i) \tag{25}$$

$$= \alpha \sum c_i + \beta \sum c_i X_i + \sum c_i \epsilon_i \tag{26}$$

But $\sum c_i = 0$, $\sum c_i X_i = 1$ by definition. Therefore:

$$B = \beta + \sum c_i \epsilon_i \tag{27}$$

$$E(B) = \beta + E(\textstyle\sum c_i \epsilon_i) \tag{28}$$

$$= \beta + \sum c_i E(\epsilon_i) = \beta \tag{29}$$

since $E(\epsilon_i) = 0 = \sum c_i$.

We have proven that B is an unbiased linear estimator of β. It remains to be proven that B has minimum variance in comparison with all other unbiased linear estimators. Suppose that the form of Equation (24) is used to define another linear estimator:

$$D = \sum k_i Y_i \tag{30}$$

where $k_i \neq c_i$.

$$D = \sum k_i(\alpha + \beta X_i + \epsilon_i) \tag{31}$$

$$= \alpha \sum k_i + \beta \sum k_i X_i + \sum k_i \epsilon_i \tag{32}$$

$E(D) = \beta$ only if

$$\sum k_i = 0 \tag{33}$$

$$\sum k_i X_i = 1 \tag{34}$$

For the proof that follows, it should be noted that

$$\sum k_i X_i = \sum k_i x_i \qquad (35)^*$$

$$\text{Var } D = \text{Var} \sum k_i Y_i \tag{36}$$

$$= \text{Var}\,(k_1 Y_1 + k_2 Y_2 + \cdots + k_N Y_N) \tag{37}$$

$$= \text{Var } k_1 Y_1 + \text{Var } k_2 Y_2 + \cdots + \text{Var } k_N Y_N \tag{38}$$

Since the variance of a constant multiplied by a variable is equal to the square of the constant multiplied by the variance of a variable, Equation (38) is equal to

$$\text{Var } D = k_1^2 \text{ Var } Y_1 + k_2^2 \text{ Var } Y_2 + \cdots + k_N^2 \text{ Var } Y_N \tag{39}$$

$$= \sum k_i^2 \text{ Var } Y_i \tag{40}$$

The most difficult part of the proof involves rewriting Equation (40) as

$$\text{Var } D = \text{Var } Y_i \sum \left[k_i^2 - \frac{2k_i x_i}{\sum x_i^2} + \frac{x_i^2}{(\sum x_i^2)^2} + \frac{x_i^2}{(\sum x_i^2)^2} + \frac{2w_i x_i}{\sum x_i^2} - \frac{2x_i^2}{(\sum x_i^2)^2} \right] \tag{41}$$

The last two terms in Equation (41) are equal to (applying the summation):

$$\frac{2 \sum w_i x_i \sum x_i^2 - 2 \sum x_i^2}{(\sum x_i^2)^2} = \frac{2 \sum x_i^2 - 2 \sum x_i^2}{(\sum x_i^2)^2} = 0$$

since

$$\sum w_i x_i = 1$$

Therefore, Equation (41) can be written as

$$\text{Var } D = \text{Var } Y_i \sum \left(k_i - \frac{x_i}{(\sum x_i^2)} \right)^2 + \frac{\text{Var } Y_i}{(\sum x_i^2)} \tag{42}$$

$^*x_i = X_i - \bar{X}$
or $X_i = x_i + \bar{X}$
$\sum w_i(x_i + \bar{X}) = 1$
$\sum w_i x_i + \sum w_i \bar{X} = 1$
$\sum w_i x_i + \bar{X} \sum w_i = 1$
since $\sum w_i = 0$:
$\sum w_i x_i = 1$

From Equation (3.27):

$$\text{Var } B = \frac{\text{Var } Y_i}{\sum x_i^2} \tag{43}$$

Var D is not greater than Var B only if

$$k_i = \frac{x_i}{\sum x_i^2} \tag{44}$$

But

$$\frac{x_i}{\sum x_i^2} = c_i$$

and thus we have proven the Gauss-Markov theorem.

4

the multiple regression model

The two-variable model studied in the preceding chapter is greatly limited in practical application. Often an economist has a strong theoretical basis for including more than one explanatory variable in an econometric model. For example, in a model that attempts to explain the earnings of individuals, it is too simplistic to include a variable measuring IQ without also considering the effects of education and family background on earnings. Similarly, it is unrealistic to ignore the effect of wealth on family consumption expenditure, even though income may be more important than wealth in determining consumption expenditures.

Fortunately, the two-variable regression model can easily be extended to more than two variables by way of *multiple regression.* Instead of assuming that Y is a linear function of only one independent variable, we assume that Y is a linear function of $K - 1$ independent variables plus an error term:

$$Y = \beta_1 X_1 + \beta_2 X_2 + \beta_3 X_3 + \cdots + \beta_K X_K + \epsilon \tag{4.1}$$

It should be noted that X_1 is equal to one, since β_1 is the constant term. Therefore, X_1 is not really a variable and the number of independent variables is $K - 1$. Later when we present the model in matrix notation, this convention of assigning one to X_1 will be necessary.

The assumptions of the multiple regression model are the same as those of the two-variable model except for one additional assumption necessitated by the inclusion of more than one independent variable in the model. The additional assumption is (remember that there were seven assumptions presented for the two-variable model):

8. *Perfect multicollinearity* or *perfect collinearity* does not exist among the independent variables. If one variable is a linear combination of another, then perfect multicollinearity exists. For example, if $X_2 = 5X_3$, then X_2 and X_3 are linear combinations of each other. As will be demonstrated later, the multiple regression equation cannot be estimated in the presence of perfect multicollinearity. What if $X_2 = X_3^2$? In this case, X_2 and X_3 are not linear combinations of each other, and estimation is possible. The problem of perfect multicollinearity can be solved by simply dropping one of the perfectly collinear variables from the model. Although perfect multicollinearity is rare, the problem of "imperfect multicollinearity" or just "multicollinearity" is often a serious problem in multiple regression models and will be discussed in a later section.

As with the two-variable case, the problem is to estimate the parameters ($\beta_1 \ldots \beta_K$) so as to minimize the error sum of squares. Before the invention of the computer this problem would have been practically unsolvable, for as the number of variables and observations increases, the calculations become more and more complicated. The calculations for the three-variable case are within reason, but beyond this, they become incredibly difficult. First we will present the "simple" mathematics of the three-variable model in both algebraic and matrix form. In order to solve multiple regression models of more than three variables on the computer, the matrix form is normally used. Next we discuss the interpretation of the multiple regression model and the problems of multicollinearity, autocorrelation, and heteroscedasticity. The remainder of the chapter considers the topic of "dummy" variables.

the mathematics of the three-variable model in algebraic form

The three-variable model can be expressed as

$$Y = \beta_1 + \beta_2 X_2 + \beta_3 X_3 + \epsilon \tag{4.2}$$

where β_1 is the constant term (note the omission of X_1, which is equal to one). β_2, β_3 = parameters of the independent variables, X_2 and X_3. We desire to minimize the error sum of squares:

$$\min \sum e^2 = \sum (Y - \beta_1 - \beta_2 X_2 - \beta_3 X_3)^2 \tag{4.3}$$

where β_1, β_2 and β_3 are regression coefficients, the sample estimates of the population parameters. The following equations were obtained using differential calculus, the derivations of which are similar to those presented for the two-variable model (see Appendix 3.1).

$$\beta_2 = \frac{(\sum yx_2)(\sum x_3^2) - (\sum yx_3)(\sum x_2x_3)}{D} \tag{4.4}$$

$$\beta_3 = \frac{(\sum yx_3)(\sum x_2^2) - (\sum yx_2)(\sum x_2x_3)}{D} \tag{4.5}$$

$$\beta_1 = \bar{Y} - \beta_2\bar{X}_2 - \beta_3\bar{X}_3 \tag{4.6}$$

where

$$D \text{ (for denominator)} = (\sum x_2^2)(\sum x_3^2) - (\sum x_2x_3)^2 \tag{4.7}$$

As an example, suppose an economist specifies a "human capital" model in which earnings or income is the dependent variable, and years of education and IQ are the independent variables. Income is represented by Y, IQ by X_2, and years of education by X_3. The underlying theory behind this model is that IQ and education should both have an impact on the earnings of individuals. The data (hypothetical) available to test this theory are presented in Table 4.1. Note

table 4.1. Income-IQ-Education Data

Income (Y)	IQ (X_2)	Education (X_3)
$5,000	80	9
6,000	95	8
7,000	100	10
8,000	101	10
9,000	103	11
10,000	115	14
11,000	105	15
12,000	116	13
13,000	120	16
14,000	110	17

that the observations on income and IQ are the same as those for the income-IQ model discussed in the preceding chapter.

The calculations are presented in Demo 4.1. Following the convention established earlier, the small letters in Equations (4.4), (4.5), and (4.7) refer to deviations from the mean. Thus, $\sum yx_2 = 274{,}500$; $\sum yx_3 = 80{,}500$; $\sum x_2^2 = 1{,}238.5$; $\sum x_3^2 = 88.1$; $\sum x_2x_3 = 252.5$; and $D = 45{,}355.6$. Therefore:

$$B_2 = \frac{(274{,}500)(88.1) - (80{,}500)(252.5)}{45{,}355.6} = 85.044$$

$$B_3 = \frac{(80{,}500)(1{,}238.5) - (274{,}500)(252.5)}{45{,}355.6} = 669.992$$

$$B_1 = 9{,}500 - 85.044(104.5) - 669.992(12.3) = -7{,}628.13$$

yx_2	yx_3	x_2^2	x_3^2	x_2x_3
110250	14850	600.25	10.89	80.85
33250	15050	90.25	18.49	40.85
11250	5750	20.25	5.29	10.35
5250	3450	12.25	5.29	8.05
750	650	2.25	1.69	1.95
5250	850	110.25	2.89	17.85
750	4050	.25	7.29	1.35
28750	1750	132.25	.49	8.05
54250	12950	240.25	13.69	57.35
24750	21150	30.25	22.09	25.85
274500=SUM	80500=SUM	1238.5=SUM	88.1=SUM	252.5=SUM
45355.6=D				

demo 4.1. Calculations for Three-Variable Model in Algebraic Form

The standard errors of B_2 and B_3 can be obtained from the following equations. Because the equation for the standard error of the constant term (B_1) is rather complex, we will derive its value in the next section, which presents the model in matrix form. In any event, testing for the significance of the constant term is often not crucial in econometric work.

$$SE(B_2) = s\sqrt{\frac{\sum x_3^2}{D}} \tag{4.8}$$

$$SE(B_3) = s\sqrt{\frac{\sum x_2^2}{D}} \tag{4.9}$$

where

$$s = \sqrt{\frac{\sum e^2}{N-3}} \tag{4.10}$$

$$\sum e^2 = \sum y^2 - B_2 \sum yx_2 - B_3 \sum yx_3 \tag{4.11}$$

Equation (4.10) is used to calculate the "standard error of estimate (s)," the square of which is an estimate of the "variance" of the regression line. The standard error of estimate will prove to be extremely important in the next chapter when we discuss forecasting. Substituting into Equations (4.11) and (4.10), the standard error of estimate is equal to 863.63. The standard errors of B_2 and B_3 obtained from Equations (4.8) and (4.9) are 38.06 and 142.71, respectively.

The "multiple coefficient of determination" can be derived from the formula

$$R^2 = \frac{B_2 \sum yx_2 + B_3 \sum yx_3}{\sum y^2} \tag{4.12}$$

Note that $\sum y^2$ was calculated in Chapter 3 and is equal to 82,500,000. Therefore:

$$R^2 = \frac{(85.04)(274{,}500) + (669.99)(80{,}500)}{82{,}500{,}000} = .937$$

Before going on to an interpretation of the above regression statistics, we will present the mathematics of the model in matrix notation.

the multiple regression model in matrix form

A *matrix* is simply a rectangular array of numbers composed of a certain number of rows and columns. The dimension of a matrix is denoted by (I, J), where I refers to the number of rows and J to the number of columns. Thus, $A(5, 3)$ is a 5-row-by-3-column matrix named A. Each number or element of A is denoted as follows:

$$A(5, 3) = \begin{matrix} A_{11} & A_{12} & A_{13} \\ A_{21} & A_{22} & A_{23} \\ A_{31} & A_{32} & A_{33} \\ A_{41} & A_{42} & A_{43} \\ A_{51} & A_{52} & A_{53} \end{matrix}$$

Thus, A_{51} is the value of the number in the fifth row, first column; A_{ij} the value of the i row, j column.

Before generalizing the model to any number of variables and observations, let us present the income-IQ-education example in matrix form. A 10-row-by-1-column matrix $Y(10, 1)$ can represent the dependent variable (income):

$$Y = \begin{matrix} 5000 \\ 6000 \\ 7000 \\ 8000 \\ 9000 \\ 10000 \\ 11000 \\ 12000 \\ 13000 \\ 14000 \end{matrix}$$

Thus, the first observation (Y_1) on Y is \$5,000, and the tenth observation (Y_{10}) is \$14,000.

The independent variables can be represented by a 10-row-by-3-column matrix $X(10, 3)$, where the first column contains the observations on X_1 (all ones because this is the constant term), the second column is X_2 (IQ), and the third column is X_3 (education):

$$X = \begin{matrix} 1 & 80 & 9 \\ 1 & 95 & 8 \\ 1 & 100 & 10 \\ 1 & 101 & 10 \\ 1 & 103 & 11 \\ 1 & 115 & 14 \\ 1 & 105 & 15 \\ 1 & 116 & 13 \\ 1 & 120 & 16 \\ 1 & 110 & 17 \end{matrix}$$

Thus, the IQ of the person with the \$5,000 income is 80 and that person's years of education is 9; for the tenth observation (\$14,000 income), IQ is 110 and years of education is 17.

The regression coefficients (B_1, B_2, B_3) can be represented by a 3-row-by-1-column matrix $B(3, 1)$:

$$B = \begin{matrix} B_1 \\ B_2 \\ B_3 \end{matrix}$$

The values for B can be obtained by the following equation. The reader should refer to a more advanced book for proof.

$$B = (X'X)^{-1}X'Y \tag{4.13}$$

The prime on X indicates the transpose matrix in which the first row becomes the first column, the second row is now the second column, and the third row is the third column.

$$X' = \begin{matrix} 1 & 1 & 1 & 1 & 1 & 1 & 1 & 1 & 1 & 1 \\ 80 & 95 & 100 & 101 & 103 & 115 & 105 & 116 & 120 & 110 \\ 9 & 8 & 10 & 10 & 11 & 14 & 15 & 13 & 16 & 17 \end{matrix}$$

When any two matrices are multiplied, the resulting matrix has the same number of rows as the first matrix and the same number of columns as the second matrix. Since X' is (3, 10) and X is (10, 3), $X'X$ is (3, 3). Two matrices can be multiplied only if the inner dimension (10) is equal; that is, the first matrix's number of columns must equal the second matrix's number of rows.

Letting (1, 1) denote the first row, first column of $X'X$, (1, 1) is calculated by multiplying the respective elements in the first row of X' by those in the first column of X and then summing the result:

$$(1, 1) = 1(1) + 1(1) + 1(1) + 1(1) + 1(1) + 1(1) + 1(1) + 1(1) + 1(1) \\ + 1(1) = 10$$

Similarly, (1, 2) is obtained by multiplying the first row of X' by the second column of X. $X'X$ is calculated as follows:

$$(1, 2) = 1(80) + 1(95) + 1(100) + 1(101) + 1(103) + 1(115) + 1(105) \\ + 1(116) + 1(120) + 1(110) = 1{,}045$$

$$(1, 3) = 1(9) + 1(8) + 1(10) + 1(10) + 1(11) + 1(14) + 1(15) + 1(13) \\ + 1(16) + 1(17) = 123$$

$$(2, 1) = 80(1) + 95(1) + 100(1) + 101(1) + 103(1) + 115(1) + 105(1) \\ + 116(1) + 120(1) + 110(1) = 1{,}045$$

$$(2, 2) = 80(80) + 95(95) + 100(100) + 101(101) + 103(103) + 115(115) \\ + 105(105) + 116(116) + 120(120) + 110(110) = 110{,}441$$

$$(2, 3) = 80(9) + 95(8) + 100(10) + 101(10) + 103(11) + 115(14) \\ + 105(15) + 116(13) + 120(16) + 110(17) = 13{,}106$$

$$(3, 1) = 9(1) + 8(1) + 10(1) + 10(1) + 11(1) + 14(1) + 15(1) + 13(1) \\ + 16(1) + 17(1) = 123$$

$$(3, 2) = 9(80) + 8(95) + 10(100) + 10(101) + 11(103) + 14(115) \\ + 15(105) + 13(116) + 16(120) + 17(110) = 13{,}106$$

$$(3, 3) = 9(9) + 8(8) + 10(10) + 10(10) + 11(11) + 14(14) + 15(15) \\ + 13(13) + 16(16) + 17(17) = 1{,}601$$

Therefore, $X'X$ is equal to

$$\begin{matrix} 10 & 1045 & 123 \\ 1045 & 110441 & 13106 \\ 123 & 13106 & 1601 \end{matrix}$$

The "inverse" of $X'X$, $(X'X)^{-1}$, is a matrix such that $(X'X)^{-1}X'X$ is an identity matrix (ones down the diagonal and zeros elsewhere):

$$\text{Idn}\,(3, 3) = \begin{matrix} 1 & 0 & 0 \\ 0 & 1 & 0 \\ 0 & 0 & 1 \end{matrix}$$

The inverse of a matrix has the same dimension (only square matrices have inverses) as the original matrix and therefore $(X'X)^{-1}$ is (3, 3). The calculation of an inverse matrix is extremely complicated, and therefore we give only the result. The reader is encouraged to check to see if $X'X(X'X)^{-1}$ is the identity matrix. $(X'X)^{-1}$ is equal to (accuracy requires eight significant figures past the decimal point):

$$(X'X)^{-1} = \begin{matrix} 11.13160227 & -.13450820 & .24589466 \\ -.13450820 & .00194243 & -.00556712 \\ .24589466 & -.00556712 & .02730644 \end{matrix}$$

$X'Y$ is calculated in the same manner as $X'X$:

$$X'Y = \begin{matrix} 95000 \\ 10202000 \\ 1249000 \end{matrix}$$

Multiplying $(X'X)^{-1}$ by $X'Y$, our B matrix is obtained:

$$B = \begin{matrix} -7628.13 \\ 85.04 \\ 669.99 \end{matrix}$$

In Chapter 3 the R^2 for this same model except with education excluded was calculated (Table 3.9). The procedure is still the same. First Yc is calculated: $Yc = -7{,}628.13 + 85.04X_2 + 669.99X_3$. Then $\sum e^2$ is calculated and divided by the total sum of squares, $\sum y^2$. This latter ratio is then subtracted from one to get the R^2. The calculations are shown in Table 4.2.

table 4.2. Calculation of R^2 and the Error Matrix (E)

Y	Yc	$(Y - Yc) = E$	$(Y - Yc)^2$
\$5,000	5,205.45	−205.45	42,209.70
6,000	5,811.11	188.89	35,679.43
7,000	7,576.31	−576.31	332,133.21
8,000	7,661.36	338.64	114,677.04
9,000	8,501.44	498.56	248,562.07
10,000	11,531.94	−1,531.94	2,346,840.10
11,000	11,351.51	−351.51	123,559.28
12,000	10,947.00	1,053.00	1,108,809.00
13,000	13,297.15	−297.15	88,298.12
14,000	13,116.72	883.28	780,183.55
			5,220,951.30 $= \sum e^2$

$$R^2 = 1 - \frac{\sum e^2}{\sum y^2} = 1 - \frac{5{,}220{,}951.3}{82{,}500{,}000} = .937$$

The standard error of estimate can now be calculated directly from Equation (4.10) without the use of Equation (4.11):

$$s = \sqrt{\frac{\sum e^2}{N-3}} = \sqrt{\frac{5{,}220{,}951.3}{7}} = 863.63$$

The standard errors of the regression coefficients can be obtained by multiplying the standard error of estimate by the square root of the corresponding principle (left-to-right) diagonal elements of $(X'X)^{-1}$:

$$SE(B_1) = 863.63\sqrt{11.1316} = 2{,}881.42$$
$$SE(B_2) = 863.63\sqrt{.0019} = 38.06$$
$$SE(B_3) = 863.63\sqrt{.0273} = 142.71$$

The regression model in matrix form can be generalized for any number of variables and observations by simply specifying the dimensions of each matrix. Letting N stand for the number of observations and K for the number of variables (dependent plus independent), the multiple regression model specified in Equation (4.1) can be written in matrix notation:

$$Y = X\beta + \epsilon \tag{4.14}$$

where Y is $(N, 1)$; X is (N, K); β is $(K, 1)$; and ϵ is $(N, 1)$:

$$Y = \begin{matrix} Y_1 \\ Y_2 \\ \vdots \\ \cdot \\ Y_N \end{matrix} \qquad X = \begin{matrix} 1 & X_{21} \ldots X_{K1} \\ 1 & X_{22} \ldots X_{K2} \\ \vdots & \vdots \qquad \vdots \\ \cdot & \cdot \qquad \cdot \\ 1 & X_{2N} \ldots X_{KN} \end{matrix} \qquad \beta = \begin{matrix} \beta_1 \\ \beta_2 \\ \vdots \\ \cdot \\ \beta_K \end{matrix} \qquad \epsilon = \begin{matrix} \epsilon_1 \\ \epsilon_2 \\ \vdots \\ \cdot \\ \epsilon_N \end{matrix}$$

The least squares estimators of β and ϵ are

$$B = \begin{matrix} B_1 \\ B_2 \\ \vdots \\ \cdot \\ B_K \end{matrix} = (X'X)^{-1}X'Y$$

$$E = \begin{matrix} e_1 \\ e_2 \\ \vdots \\ \cdot \\ e_N \end{matrix} = Y - XB$$

$$s = \sqrt{\frac{\sum e^2}{N-K}}$$

partial regression coefficients

Demo 4.2 presents a computer printout of the regression coefficients, the standard error of estimate, and the standard errors for each regression coefficient, along with their T values, the R^2, adjusted R^2, the F value for the entire regression, the degrees of freedom, the Durbin-Watson Statistic and the correlation matrix. In this section we discuss the interpretation of the regression coefficients. The other statistics are explained in following sections.

```
REGRESSION COEFFICIENTS
-7628.13
85.044
669.992
STD. ERROR OF ESTIMATE= 863.63
SE(B1)= 2881.42                    T 1=-2.64735
SE(B2)= 38.0628                    T 2 = 2.23431
SE(B3)= 142.712                    T 3 = 4.69471
R SQUARED= .936715
ADJUSTED R SQUARED= .918634
F= 51.8055
DEGREES OF FREEDOM= 7
DW= 2.35762
CORRELATION MATRIX
 1  .858751  .944237
 .858751  1  .764408
 .944237  .764408  1
```

demo 4.2. Regression of Income on IQ and Education

How do we interpret the multiple regression equation $Y = -7{,}628.13 + 85.04X_2 + 669.99X_3$? Given two individuals with the same education (X_3 held constant), a one-point difference in IQ is associated with an \$85.04 difference in income on the average. Likewise, a one-year difference in education, holding IQ (X_2) constant, is associated with a \$669.99 difference in income on the average. Thus, the regression coefficient on X_2 represents the change in income that can be expected if X_3 is held constant or controlled for, and the coefficient on X_3 indicates the change in income if X_2 is held constant. These coefficients are termed *partial regression coefficients*. Multiple regression analysis is a powerful statistical tool because it allows us to answer the question: How important is IQ or education in explaining income after controlling for other variables?

In the two-variable model, the coefficient on IQ was 221.64 (Table 3.8). After controlling for education, the value is only 85.04. What this suggests is that the size of the contribution of IQ in explaining income is much smaller after controlling for education. Are there other variables important in explaining income? For example, women might be discriminated against. After controlling for education, this hypothesis could be tested by examining the regression coefficient on the variable sex.[1] If it were negative and significantly different from zero, then the hypothesis of sex discrimination would be supported. However, if the coefficient were insignificant, then any differences in income between the sexes might be due solely to differences in education. Of course, in testing this hypothesis, we must be confident that all important income-determining variables have been included in our model. This is obviously a problem in model specification.

hypothesis tests

To test for the statistical significance of the regression coefficients, a T test can be applied with $N - K$ degrees of freedom, where N is the number of observations (10) and K is the number of variables (3).

$$T(B_1) = \frac{B_1}{SE(B_1)} = \frac{7{,}628.13}{2{,}881.42} = 2.647$$

$$T(B_2) = \frac{B_2}{SE(B_2)} = \frac{85.04}{38.06} = 2.234$$

$$T(B_3) = \frac{B_3}{SE(B_3)} = \frac{669.99}{142.71} = 4.695$$

Although the computer may not print out the absolute values of T (Demo 4.2), only the absolute values should be used in testing the null hypotheses. Table 4.3 presents the critical values of T at various probability levels given seven

table 4.3. Critical Values of T Given Seven Degrees of Freedom

Probability	.2	.1	.05	.02	.01	.001
T value	1.415	1.895	2.365	2.998	3.499	5.405

degrees of freedom. Since $T(B_1)$ is greater than 2.365, the constant term is significant at the .05 level. Similarly, 2.234 is greater than 1.895 (but not 2.365) and therefore IQ is significant at the .1 level, but not at the .05 level. Because 4.695 is greater than 3.499, education is significant at the .01 level.

[1] Variables that take on discrete values such as sex require the use of "dummy" variables, a topic that is covered in a later section.

adjusted R^2

R^2 measures the proportion of the variation in the dependent variable explained by the independent variables. However, there are two major problems in using R^2 for the purpose of "explaining" the dependent variable. First, we can never be certain that the model has been correctly specified, and therefore the use of R^2 to compare alternative models can lead to the erroneous conclusion that one model is better than another. Second, R^2 is a function of the number of independent variables in the model; R^2 is never reduced and is usually increased by adding independent variables to the model. To demonstrate the latter problem, we have used the random number function on the computer to generate a third independent variable, which in theory should not add to the explanatory power of the model. As can be seen in Demo 4.3, this random variable is statistically insignificant ($T = .68$), but the R^2 (.941) is higher than that of the three-variable model (.937).

```
REGRESSION COEFFICIENTS
-8028.44
 88.8863
 709.574
-902.453
STD. ERROR OF ESTIMATE = 898.388
SE(B 1)= 3053.87                  T 1 =-2.62894
SE(B 2)= 39.9901                  T 2 = 2.22271
SE(B 3)= 159.312                  T 3 = 4.454
SE(B 4)= 1318.01                  T 4 =-.684711
R SQUARED= .941302
ADJUSTED R SQUARED= .911953
F= 32.0725
DEGREES OF FREEDOM= 6
DW= 2.61276
CORRELATION MATRIX
   1  .858751  .944237  .543762
  .858751  1  .764408  .536025
  .944237  .764408  1  .607221
  .543762  .536025  .607221  1
```

demo 4.3. Multiple Regression Model Containing Random Variable

To correct for the problem of the R^2 increasing as more variables are added to a multiple regression model, an "adjusted" R^2, $\bar{R}^2$, can be calculated that accounts for the number of variables in the model:

$$\bar{R}^2 = 1 - (1 - R^2)\frac{N - 1}{N - K} \tag{4.15}$$

The adjusted $\bar{R}^2$ in Demo 4.3 is .912, which is slightly less than the adjusted $\bar{R}^2$ of the original model in Demo 4.2.[2] Comparing the adjusted $\bar{R}^2$ between any two models is valid only if the dependent variable is the same. It should also be pointed out that the adjusted $\bar{R}^2$ can be negative. For example, if $R^2 = .18$, $K = 3$, and $N = 10$, then $\bar{R}^2 = -.05$, a meaningless value.

F test and analysis of variance

The F statistic printed out by the regression program allows us to test the null hypothesis that $\beta_2 = \beta_3 = \cdots = \beta_K = 0$. If the null hypothesis is true, then the overall model is not significant in explaining the dependent variable, and the R^2 is not significantly different from zero. The degrees of freedom for the numerator are $K - 1$; and for the denominator, $N - K$:

$$F_{K-1,N-K} = \frac{R^2(N-K)}{(1-R^2)(K-1)} \tag{4.16}$$

Substituting into Equation (4.16) for the regression in Demo 4.2:

$$F = \frac{.9367(7)}{.0633(2)} = 51.81$$

The critical value for F at the .01 level of significance with (2, 7) degrees of freedom is 9.55. Since 51.81 is greater than 9.55, the null hypothesis is rejected.

Frequently, computer regression programs also print out an F statistic in addition to or in place of the T statistic for the individual regression coefficients. The F and T statistics are related by the formula $F = T^2$. Table 4.4 shows how the F statistics are calculated for B_2 and B_3 of the three-variable model. This is also termed an *analysis of variance* test. X_2 (without X_3) means that the regression is run with two variables only—Y and X_2. The explained sum of squares (ESS) is equal to 60,839,927 in this example. Then the regression is run with both X_2 and X_3 in the equation, and the ESS increases by 16,439,122. Similarly, the addition of X_2 adds 3,723,430 to ESS in comparison to the model with Y regressed on X_3 only. The residual sum of squares (RSS) is $\sum e^2$ for the three-variable model. The equation for F is

$$F(B_K) = \frac{(\text{Increase in ESS by adding } X_K)(N-K)}{\text{RSS}} \tag{4.17}$$

The F values can be compared with an F table with one and seven degrees of

[2]If one is simply interested in maximizing $\bar{R}^2$, the rule to follow is to leave all variables in the model for which the T statistics are greater than one, and drop all the others. Since this would leave insignificant variables in a model, this is an absurd rule. This rule also violates the purpose of regression analysis, which is to test a previously specified model.

table 4.4. Analysis of Variance, F Test

	Sum of Squares
Variation in Y Caused by:	
X_2 (without X_3)	60,839,927
Addition of X_3	16,439,122
Residual or error	5,220,951
Total	82,500,000
Variation in Y Caused by:	
X_3 (without X_2)	73,555,619
Addition of X_2	3,723,430
Residual or error	5,220,951
Total	82,500,000

$$F(B_2) = \frac{(3{,}723{,}430)(7)}{5{,}220{,}951} = 4.99 \qquad T^2 = (2.234)^2 = 4.99$$

$$F(B_3) = \frac{(16{,}439{,}122)(7)}{5{,}220{,}951} = 22.04 \qquad T^2 = (4.695)^2 = 22.04$$

freedom. Note that in the T test there are $N - K$ degrees of freedom, while with the F test there is one degree of freedom for the numerator and $N - K$ degrees of freedom for the denominator. Table 4.5 presents the critical F values for one and seven degrees of freedom. The conclusions regarding significance of the regression coefficients are exactly the same as those derived from the T test.

table 4.5. Critical F Values for One and Seven Degrees of Freedom

.05 Level =	5.59
.01 Level =	12.25

correlation matrix

The correlation matrix printed out by the regression program contains the R ("simple" correlation) for each two-variable regression as defined in Chapter 3. For example, the first row and first column (1, 1) of the matrix is the correlation of the dependent variable with itself. Obviously this must equal one, as do the other diagonal elements (2, 2) and (3, 3), which represent the correlations of each independent variable with itself. The first row and second column (1, 2) contains the correlation of the dependent variable Y with X_2 (.858751), and the (1, 3) element is the correlation of Y with X_3 (.944237). The (2, 3) element is the correlation of X_2 with X_3 (.764408), which obviously must equal the (3, 2) element, the correlation of X_3 with X_2. Similarly, the other elements of the matrix are duplicated; for example, (1, 2) = (2, 1).

multicollinearity

The only additional assumption of the multiple regression model is that no perfect multicollinearity exists. As an example, suppose we add a third independent variable to the model—months of education (X_4). Obviously X_4 equals twelve times X_3, which is years of education (Table 4.6).

table 4.6. Data Demonstrating Perfect Multicollinearity

Years of Education (X_3)	Months of Education (X_4)
9	108
8	96
10	120
10	120
11	132
14	168
15	180
13	156
16	192
17	204

Demo 4.4 presents a computer regression run with income as the dependent variable and IQ, years of education, and months of education as the independent variables. The computer prints out that the matrix $(X'X)$ cannot be inverted. Consequently, all the output is meaningless except for the degrees of freedom and the correlation matrix, which contains a one for the correlation of X_3 with X_4. Thus, when two or more independent variables are perfectly correlated or collinear, the method of ordinary least squares is not applicable. This conclusion makes sense, since if we could obtain estimates of the regression parameters with ordinary least squares, how could they be interpreted? The regression coefficient on years of education measures the change in income per one-year change in education, holding months of education and IQ constant. But months of education cannot be held constant as years of education change! Estimation of the regression parameters in the presence of perfect multicollinearity is therefore absurd.

In practice, perfect multicollinearity occurs only from an error in model specification. This error is easy to detect by simply examining the correlation

```
CAN'T INVERT MATRIX AT LINE 390
REGRESSION COEFFICIENTS
-.179605E 9
-148229
 7916.67
 .125331E 8
STD. ERROR OF ESTIMATE= .221239E 10
SE(B 1)= .105537E 9                T 1 =-1.70182
SE(B 2)= .97507E 8                 T 2 =-.152019E-2
DIVISION BY 0 AT LINE 660
SE(B 3)= 0         T 3 = 0
DIVISION BY 0 AT LINE 660
SE(B 4)= 0         T 4 = 0
R SQUARED=-.355977E 12
ADJUSTED R SQUARED=-.533965E 12
F=-2
DEGREES OF FREEDOM= 6
DW= .231045E-1
CORRELATION MATRIX
   1  .858751  .944237   .944237
   .858751  1   .764408   .764408
   .944237 .764408  1   1
   .944237 .764408  1   1
```

demo 4.4. Regression with Perfect Multicollinearity

matrix. Then one of the variables that is perfectly collinear with another can be dropped from the model. More generally, two or more of the independent variables are highly correlated with each other, giving rise to *imperfect multicollinearity* or simply *multicollinearity.* As one variable moves, so moves the other, making it very difficult to interpret the regression coefficients in terms of holding other variables constant. To demonstrate the consequences of multicollinearity, consider a model in which Y is income, X_2 is IQ, and X_3 is a random variable created to have a high degree of correlation (.98) with X_2. When this regression is run (Demo 4.5), the standard error of B_2 is so large that it is impossible to reject the null hypothesis. The standard error of B_2 is 246.28 in comparison to 38.06 when years of education is the other independent variable (Demo 4.2). Consequently, the values of the population coefficients cannot be precisely estimated in the presence of multicollinearity.

Detecting and correcting for multicollinearity can be an extremely difficult problem. The problem of detection is not difficult in the case of two independent variables, as the simple correlation can be examined. But for more than two independent variables, the simple correlations do not provide information on the existence of more complex relationships between or among the independent variables. These relationships are measured by the *partial correlation coefficients,* which measure the correlation between two variables after holding the others constant.

```
REGRESSION COEFFICIENTS
-13696.7
 392.844
-162.687
STD. ERROR OF ESTIMATE= 1699.1
SE(B 1)= 5074.08              T 1 =-2.69935
SE(B 2)= 246.277              T 2 =  1.59513
SE(B 3)= 229.469              T 3 =-.708974
R SQUARED= .755047
ADJUSTED R SQUARED= .68506
F= 10.7884
DEGREES OF FREEDOM= 7
DW= 1.25335
CORRELATION MATRIX
1   .858751   .81609
.858751   1   .980599
.81609   .980599   1
```

demo 4.5. Regression in Presence of Multicollinearity

As an example, consider the regression of income (Y) on IQ (X_2) and education (X_3) in Demo 4.2. The simple correlation of income with IQ is .86 and with education .94; the simple correlation of IQ with education is .76:

$$R_{YX_2} = .86$$
$$R_{YX_3} = .94$$
$$R_{X_2X_3} = .76$$

But how is Y correlated with X_2, holding X_3 constant? How is Y correlated with X_3, holding X_2 constant? How is X_2 correlated with X_3 holding Y constant? These questions are not answered by examining the simple correlation coefficients, but rather by calculating the partial correlation coefficients.

Suppose that the following two regressions were run:

$$Y = \beta_1 + \beta_2 X_3 + \epsilon \tag{4.18}$$
$$X_2 = \beta_1 + \beta_2 X_3 + \epsilon \tag{4.19}$$

Equation (4.18) measures the effect of X_3 on Y, ignoring X_2. Similarly, Equation (4.19) measures the effect of X_3 on X_2, ignoring Y. Therefore, the residuals of Equation (4.18) include the effect of X_2, and the residuals of Equation (4.19) include the effect of Y. The partial correlation of Y with X_2, holding X_3 constant, is defined as the simple correlation of the residuals from both equations. In effect, the residuals net out the effect of X_3, since X_3 is included in both equations. Following the same line of reasoning, the calculation of the partial correlation of Y with X_3, holding X_2 constant, involves estimating the following two equations and calculating the simple correlation of the residuals from both equations:

$$Y = \beta_1 + \beta_2 X_2 + \epsilon \tag{4.20}$$

$$X_3 = \beta_1 + \beta_2 X_2 + \epsilon \tag{4.21}$$

And the partial correlation of X_2 with X_3 can be obtained by calculating the simple correlation of the residuals from

$$X_2 = \beta_1 + \beta_2 Y + \epsilon \tag{4.22}$$

$$X_3 = \beta_1 + \beta_2 Y + \epsilon \tag{4.23}$$

For the three-variable case, the following equations can be used to calculate the respective partial correlation coefficients:

$$r_{YX_2} = \frac{R_{YX_2} - R_{YX_3}R_{X_2X_3}}{\sqrt{(1 - R^2_{YX_3})(1 - R^2_{X_2X_3})}} \tag{4.24}$$

$$r_{YX_3} = \frac{R_{YX_3} - R_{YX_2}R_{X_2X_3}}{\sqrt{(1 - R^2_{YX_2})(1 - R^2_{X_2X_3})}} \tag{4.25}$$

$$r_{X_2X_3} = \frac{R_{X_2X_3} - R_{YX_2}R_{YX_3}}{\sqrt{(1 - R^2_{YX_2})(1 - R^2_{YX_3})}} \tag{4.26}$$

Therefore:

$$r_{YX_2} = .657$$

$$r_{YX_3} = .864$$

$$r_{X_2X_3} = -.278$$

It is interesting to compare the partial with the simple correlation coefficients. In all three cases, the respective partial correlations are less than the simple correlations, demonstrating the importance of controlling for other variables. In one case (IQ with education), the partial correlation is negative in sign.

In addition to calculating the partial correlations, there are some obvious indications of multicollinearity. If the R^2 is significant (F test), but the regression coefficients are insignificant (T or F test), then multicollinearity is often the problem. Also, if the sign of a coefficient is the opposite of what is expected, then multicollinearity should be suspected. If these problems are corrected by dropping one of the highly collinear variables from the model, then multicollinearity is probably the culprit.

Correcting for multicollinearity is unfortunately much more difficult than detecting it. One common procedure is to simply drop one of the independent variables from the model. Although this usually corrects the problem, the cure may be worse than the disease. If there is strong justification for including a variable in a model, then dropping it is an error in model specification. However, if the variable in question is similar to another variable in the model, the model may be improved by dropping one of the collinear variables. For example, consumption is a function of income. The inclusion of both personal income and disposable income in a model to explain consumption is an error in model specification. Since personal income and disposable income are highly collinear, multicollinearity would be present in such a model.

Often multicollinearity is a consequence of the sample's being too small. Collecting additional data may solve the problem. Other techniques, such as pooling cross-section and time-series data, first differencing the data, ridge regression, and factor analysis, are covered in more-advanced books. The reader can refer to the Bibliography for sources dealing with these topics.

autocorrelation

In Chapter 3 we discussed the causes and consequences of autocorrelation. In this section we are concerned with detecting and correcting for autocorrelation. At the minimum, we must know whether or not autocorrelation exists in our model. If autocorrelation does exist, then we can state that our estimates of the population parameters are less precise than they would appear to be from examining the confidence intervals constructed from the biased standard errors. Since autocorrelation is frequently a serious problem in econometric work, it is extremely important to test for its existence.

One of the most important relationships in economics is that between consumption (Y) and disposable income (X_2). Using the years 1951 to 1970, the least squares regression equation is $Y = 5.17 + .90X_2$. The data are presented in Table 4.7, and the regression results in Demo 4.6.[3] It would appear that the relationship between consumption and income is almost perfect, as the R^2 is .999, $T(B_2)$ is 170.07, and the F is 28922.1. But could it be possible that autocorrelation is responsible for these spectacular results? As was demonstrated in Chapter 3, autocorrelation may lead to an underestimate of the standard error of a regression coefficient, and consequently greater precision than would exist without autocorrelation.

There are several techniques for detecting autocorrelation. One technique is to examine the residuals (ERROR MATRIX in Demo 4.6) for evidence of any persistent trend in the sign of the error term. Thus, the residuals are $+ + + + - + + + - - - - - - - - - + + - +$. Given the string of positive values followed by negative values, it would appear that autocorrelation exists. But could this pattern have occurred by chance? Swed and Eisenhart have developed a special technique and table to answer this question.[4] In their framework, *run* is defined as an uninterrupted sequence of one symbol ($+$ or $-$).

[3]It is assumed that income is uncorrelated with the error term. If this is not the case, a simultaneous model should be specified (see Chapter 7).

[4]Frieda S. Swed and C. Eisenhart, "Tables for Testing Randomness of Grouping in a Sequence of Alternatives," *Annals of Mathematical Statistics*, Vol. 14, 1943.

table 4.7. Disposable Income (X_2) and Consumption (Y) in Current Dollars (Billions)

	X_2	Y
1951	226.6	206.3
1952	238.3	216.7
1953	252.6	230.0
1954	257.4	236.5
1955	275.3	254.4
1956	293.2	266.7
1957	308.5	281.4
1958	318.8	290.1
1959	337.3	311.2
1960	350.0	325.2
1961	364.4	335.2
1962	385.3	355.1
1963	404.6	375.0
1964	438.1	401.2
1965	473.2	432.8
1966	511.9	466.3
1967	546.3	492.1
1968	591.2	535.8
1969	631.6	577.5
1970	684.7	616.8

```
REGRESSION COEFFICIENTS
 5.16797
 .900325

STD. ERROR OF ESTIMATE= 3.17411
SE(B 1) = 2.20555          T 1 = 2.34317
SE(B 2) = .529382E-2       T 2 = 170.071
R SQUARED= .999378
ADJUSTED R SQUARED= .999344
F= 28922.1
DEGREES OF FREEDOM= 18
DW= 1.22551
CORRELATION MATRIX
 1   .999689
 .999689   1

ERROR MATRIX
 2.88168    3.01549    2.59015    .411697   -1.37247    2.44336
 1.51834    2.09167   -2.3523    -4.91818   -1.95352   -3.03668
-5.56043   -1.59952   -1.59811   -.255524    4.91565    1.64032
-3.68652    4.82074
```

demo 4.6. Regression of Consumption on Income

Thus, there are seven runs in the consumption-income model for the years 1951 to 1970. A very small number of runs—i.e., infrequent sign change—would support the hypothesis of positive autocorrelation. Letting N_1 equal the number of + signs, N_2 the number of − signs, and n the number of runs, the null hypothesis (no autocorrelation) can be tested at the .05 level using Statistical Table 4. For example, in the consumption-income model, $N_1 = 10$, $N_2 = 10$, and $n = 7$. The critical value for positive autocorrelation given in the table is 6 and that for negative autocorrelation is 16. Since n is greater than 6 and less than 16, it is not possible to conclude on the basis of the Swed and Eisenhart test that autocorrelation exists. However, this is a borderline case; for example, if the sign of the fifth residual (−) were a +, then the number of runs would only be 6.

The most commonly used test for autocorrelation is the Durbin-Watson (DW, or d). The Durbin-Watson statistic is powerful against errors that follow a *first order autoregressive* process (defined below when discussing the problem of correcting for autocorrelation), provided the regression equation does not contain a lagged dependent variable. The d statistic is defined as

$$d = \frac{\sum_{t=2}^{N} (e_t - e_{t-1})^2}{\sum_{t=1}^{N} e_t^2} \tag{4.27}$$

As will be demonstrated in one of the exercises, when the error terms are uncorrelated with each other, the value of d is about two. The range of d is from zero to four, with a value under two suggesting positive autocorrelation, and a value over two negative autocorrelation. Statistical Tables 5A and 5B define a d_L and a d_U for any sample size (N) and for up to five explanatory variables (k' = number of independent variables).

The Durbin-Watson statistic is illustrated in Figure 4.1. Between 0 and d_L the hypothesis of positive autocorrelation is supported, while a value of d greater than $4 - d_L$ would lead us to accept the hypothesis of negative autocorrelation. A value of d between d_U and $4 - d_U$ supports the null hypothesis of no autocorrelation. For our consumption-income model, $d = 1.226$, $N = 20$, $k' = 1$, $d_L = 1.20$, and $d_U = 1.41$ at the .05 level of significance. If d were less than d_L, the null hypothesis would be rejected; we would conclude that positive autocorrelation existed in our model. The ranges between d_L and d_U and $4 - d_U$ and $4 - d_L$ are the "indeterminant" areas. Since 1.226 is in the zone of indeterminancy (1.20 to 1.41), we can neither accept nor reject the null hypothesis.

Because the estimated standard errors of the regression coefficients are biased downward in the presence of autocorrelation, the conclusions drawn from hypothesis tests and confidence intervals can be erroneous, although the coefficients themselves are unbiased estimators of the population parameters. Consequently, we will have greater confidence in our estimates than might be

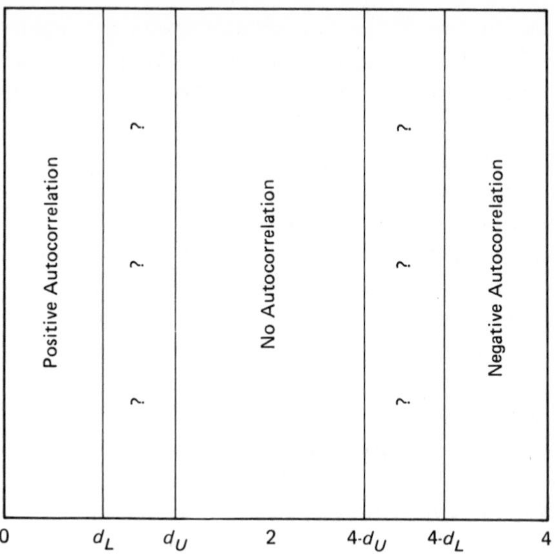

figure 4.1. Durbin-Watson Statistic

warranted in comparison to a model in which better information on the magnitude of the estimated standard errors was known. We now consider two commonly used techniques for correcting for autocorrelation, both of which attempt to obtain better information: *generalized difference* and *first difference* equation models. It can be shown that the first difference method is actually a special case of the generalized difference model.

The major assumption of these techniques is that the error term follows a first-order autoregressive scheme: $\epsilon_{t+1} = \rho\epsilon_t + u_t$, where ρ is termed the *coefficient of autocorrelation*, the absolute value of which is less than one. Since u_t is nonautocorrelated by the assumptions of the classical linear regression model, we desire to derive an equation that contains the u_t but not the autocorrelated ϵ_t. To demonstrate this derivation, we will use the two-variable model.

$$Y_t = \beta_1 + \beta_2 X_t + \epsilon_t \tag{4.28}$$

or

$$Y_{t+1} = \beta_1 + \beta_2 X_{t+1} + \epsilon_{t+1} \tag{4.29}$$

Multiplying Equation (4.28) by ρ:

$$\rho Y_t = \rho\beta_1 + \rho\beta_2 X_t + \rho\epsilon_t \tag{4.30}$$

And subtracting Equation (4.30) from Equation (4.29):

$$Y_{t+1} - \rho Y_t = \beta_1 - \rho\beta_1 + \beta_2 X_{t+1} - \rho\beta_2 X_t + \epsilon_{t+1} - \rho\epsilon_t \tag{4.31}$$

Collecting terms and noting that $\epsilon_{t+1} = \rho\epsilon_t + u_t$:

$$Y_{t+1} - \rho Y_t = \beta_1(1 - \rho) + \beta_2(X_{t+1} - \rho X_t) + u_t \tag{4.32}$$

If ρ were known, it would be a rather simple process to estimate Equation (4.32), which is the "generalized difference" equation. All that is required is to subtract a certain portion (ρ) of the variable in the present time period from the following period. In practice, there is no way of knowing ρ for certain, and therefore an educated guess must be made as to its value.

One possible guess is that $\rho = 1$. This is known as the "first difference" method. When ρ is equal to one, the intercept term (β_1) in Equation (4.32) vanishes and the regression line is through the origin. In estimating this model, it is therefore necessary to constrain the constant term to zero. This problem is solved by eliminating the column of ones in the X matrix (the X matrix for the two-variable model is now dimensioned N by one instead of N by two). The first difference equation is

$$Y_{t+1} - Y_t = \beta_2(X_{t+1} - X_t) + u_t \tag{4.33}$$

or

$$\Delta Y_t = \beta_2(\Delta X_t) + u_t \tag{4.34}$$

As an example, reconsider the consumption-income regression in Demo 4.6.[5] In terms of Equation (4.34), ΔY_t is the change in consumption from one period to the next, and ΔX_t is the change in income. β_2 has the same interpretation as the coefficient on X in the original model, as it is the marginal propensity to consume (MPC), $\Delta Y/\Delta X$. Our estimate of β_2 in the original model is .90, and its standard error is .005; B_1 is 5.17, and its standard error is 2.21. As was mentioned earlier, the Durbin-Watson statistic (1.23) is suggestive of positive autocorrelation but is in the indeterminant zone (see Figure 4.1).

The data used to estimate the original model (Table 4.7) may be transformed into first difference form by simply subtracting successive values, as specified in Equation (4.33). The transformed data are presented in Table 4.8. Note that one observation is lost in the first differencing process, and therefore $N = 19$.

The regression results for the first difference model are given in Demo 4.7. B_2 is equal to .88, which is very close to the value of the original model (.90). However, the T, R^2, and F level are considerably lower, but the Durbin-Watson statistic (2.20) leads us to accept the null hypothesis of no autocorrelation. The estimated standard error of B_2 is about six times that of the original model (.029 versus .005). This illustrates the potential danger of attempting to test hypotheses in the presence of autocorrelation.

[5]As the reader may remember, it is implicitly assumed that income is uncorrelated with the error term. If this is not the case, a simultaneous model should be specified (see Chapter 7). In any event, this model is given for illustrative purposes only.

table 4.8. X and Y Data in First Difference Form

ΔX	ΔY
11.7	10.4
14.3	13.3
4.8	6.5
17.9	17.9
17.9	12.3
15.3	14.7
10.3	8.7
18.5	21.1
12.7	14.0
14.4	10.0
20.9	19.9
19.3	19.9
33.5	26.2
35.1	31.6
38.7	33.5
34.4	25.8
44.9	43.7
40.4	41.7
53.1	39.3

```
REGRESSION COEFFICIENTS
 .877933

STD. ERROR OF ESTIMATE= 3.45641
SE( B 2) = .288348E-1                    T 2 = 30.447
R SQUARED= .911177
ADJUSTED R SQUARED= .911177
F= 174.391
DEGREES OF FREEDOM= 17
DW= 2.20053
```

demo 4.7. Regression of ΔY on ΔX—First Difference Model

An interesting aspect of the first difference model emerges when time (T) is included as one of the independent variables:

$$Y_t = \beta_1 + \beta_2 X_t + \beta_3 T + \epsilon_t \tag{4.35}$$

Since the first difference of time is equal to one (e.g., 1970 − 1969 = 1), the first difference equation of (4.35) is equivalent to

$$\Delta Y_t = \beta_2(\Delta X_t) + \beta_3 + u_t \tag{4.36}$$

Thus, Equation (4.36) is estimated with an intercept term (β_3), which measures the change in Y resulting from a one-period change in time.

Although the derivation of the following equation is beyond the scope of this book, another estimate of ρ can be obtained by noting an approximate relationship between the Durbin-Watson statistic and ρ:

$$d \cong 2(1 - \rho) \tag{4.37}$$

Thus, when ρ is one, as in the first difference model, the Durbin-Watson statistic is approximately equal to zero. Therefore, the first difference model represents one extreme and is not necessarily a good estimate of ρ. Solving Equation (4.37) for ρ:

$$\rho \cong (2 - d)/2 \tag{4.38}$$

The use of Equation (4.38) to estimate ρ has two major advantages over the first difference method. First, it is not necessary to constrain the constant term to zero. Second, it utilizes the Durbin-Watson statistic in order to obtain a more precise estimate of ρ.

Substituting the Durbin-Watson statistic (1.226) from the original model into Equation (4.38), ρ is equal to .387. This value is then used to transform the data as specified in Equation (4.32), the generalized difference equation. The transformed data are given in Table 4.9, where $Y^* = Y_{t+1} - \rho Y_t$ and $X^* = X_{t+1} - \rho X_t$.

table 4.9. Transformed Data for Estimating Generalized Difference Model

X^*	Y^*
150.606	136.901
160.378	146.137
159.644	147.490
175.686	162.875
186.659	168.247
195.032	178.187
199.411	181.198
213.924	198.931
219.465	204.766
228.950	209.348
244.277	225.378
255.489	237.576
281.520	256.075
303.655	277.536
328.772	298.806
348.195	311.642
379.782	345.357
402.806	370.145
440.271	393.308

The regression results for the generalized difference model are shown in Demo 4.8. It is interesting that the $T(B_2)$, R^2, and F level are considerably above those for the first difference model, approaching those of the original model. But in contrast to the original model, the null hypothesis of no autocorrelation (DW $= 1.89$) is accepted. Thus, the generalized difference model appears to be a better method for correcting for autocorrelation than the first difference model. Since the first difference model is a special case of the generalized difference model, this conclusion is not surprising. Of course, Equation (4.38) is not the only way to estimate ρ; the interested reader can refer to the Bibliography for discussions of other methods.

```
REGRESSION COEFFICIENTS
 4.64668
 .894778

STD. ERROR OF ESTIMATE= 2.97133
SE(B 1 )= 2.1537                T 1  = 2.15754
SE(B 2 )= .796313E-2            T 2  = 112.365
R SQUARED= .998655
ADJUSTED R SQUARED= .998576
F= 12625.9
DEGREES OF FREEDOM= 17
DW= 1.88508
```

demo 4.8. Regression Results for Generalized Difference Model

Table 4.10 summarizes the regression results of the three different models. Consistently, the estimate of β_2 obtained from these models is about .9, but its

table 4.10. Summary of Three Different Estimation Techniques for Consumption-Income Model

	Original Model	**First Difference**	**Generalized Difference**
B_1	5.17	0*	7.59**
B_2	.90	.88	.89
$SE(B_2)$	.005	.029	.008
$T(B_2)$	170.07	30.45	112.36
$\bar{R}^2$	.999	.911	.999
F	28922.1	174.4	12625.9
DW	1.23	2.20	1.89

*Constant term constrained to zero.
**$B_1(1-\rho) = 4.65$; since $\rho = .387$, $B_1 = 7.59$.

estimated standard error varies widely from model to model. To show the significance of this, consider the 95 percent confidence intervals for β_2 for each model:

Original model:	$.89 < \beta_2 < .91$
First difference model:	$.82 < \beta_2 < .94$
Generalized difference model:	$.87 < \beta_2 < .91$

The width of the confidence interval of the original model is one-sixth that of the first difference model and one-half that of the generalized difference model. Correcting for the problem of autocorrelation clearly makes a big difference in the precision of the parameter estimates.

heteroscedasticity

As with autocorrelation, the estimating equations for calculating the standard errors of the regression coefficients lead to an overestimate of the precision of a model if estimated with data in which heteroscedasticity is present. Unfortunately, there is no easy way to detect heteroscedasticity similar to the Durbin-Watson statistic in the case of autocorrelation. One of the most commonly used tests for heteroscedasticity is that developed by Goldfeld and Quandt, and we will demonstrate how to apply this test.[6] Because the Goldfeld-Quandt test requires the separation of the data into two ordered sets, it is not routinely calculated by standard computer packages. An alternative to the Goldfeld-Quandt test is that developed by Park.[7] The advantage of the Park over the Goldfeld-Quandt test is that the data need not be separated or ordered in any way. We will compare the Park with the Goldfeld-Quandt test.

If the pattern of heteroscedasticity is approximately known, the generally preferred method to correct for heteroscedasticity is *weighted least squares*. Alternatively, some guess must be made as to the pattern in order to correct for the problem of heteroscedasticity. We will discuss both of these methods.

To facilitate our discussion, consider the hypothetical cross-section data in Table 4.11. These data are divided into five income groups, and the variance of consumption for each income group is presented. Clearly, the variance of consumption increases as income increases, suggesting that heteroscedasticity might be a problem in a model in which consumption was the dependent and income the independent variable. The data in Table 4.11 are very realistic in

[6] S. M. Goldfeld and R. E. Quandt, "Some Tests for Homoscedasticity," *Journal of the American Statistical Society*, 60 (1965), 539–47.

[7] R. E. Park, "Estimation with Heteroscedastic Error Terms," *Econometrica*, 34 (October 1966), 888.

table 4.11. Hypothetical Consumption-Income Data

Income ($000)	Consumption ($000)	
10	8.0	
10	8.2	
10	8.3	VAR = .073
10	8.1	
10	8.7	
15	12.3	
15	9.4	
15	11.6	VAR = 2.473
15	12.0	
15	8.9	
20	15.0	
20	16.0	
20	12.0	VAR = 9.997
20	11.3	
20	19.1	
25	19.1	
25	18.6	
25	22.4	VAR = 10.393
25	23.1	
25	15.1	
30	24.2	
30	16.7	
30	27.0	VAR = 16.685
30	26.0	
30	22.1	

the sense that budget studies have often found heteroscedasticity to be a problem.[8]

The regression results for this model are presented in Demo 4.9. The constant term (—.152) is not significantly different from zero, but the T value for B_2 (.774) is equal to 10.2, suggesting a very precise estimate for the marginal propensity to consume. Given our expectation that heteroscedasticity is likely to exist, with the consequence that this precision may be illusory (although the regression coefficient itself is unbiased), how can we detect the problem of heteroscedasticity?

The Goldfeld-Quandt test is a useful indicator of heteroscedasticity and involves the following steps: (1) Order the observations on the basis of the X

[8]See S. J. Prais and H. S. Houthakker, *The Analysis of Family Budgets* (New York: Cambridge University Press, 1955).

```
REGRESSION COEFFICIENTS
-.152
 .774

STD. ERROR OF ESTIMATE= 2.68575
SE(B 1 )= 1.61145              T 1 =-.943248E-1
SE(B 2 )= .759646E-1           T 2 = 10.189
R SQUARED= .818633
ADJUSTED R SQUARED= .810748
F= 103.815
DEGREES OF FREEDOM= 23
DW= 2.45264
```

demo 4.9. Regression of Consumption on Income

variable from smallest to largest. Of course, the test can be performed on any X variable in a multiple regression model, depending on which independent variable(s) is (are) believed to be associated with a heteroscedastic error term. (2) Exclude a certain portion of the middle (M) observations. (3) Reestimate the model separately with each of the two remaining sets of data and have the computer print out the error sum of squares for each of the two regressions. (4) Calculate the F statistic:

$$F = \frac{\sum e_2^2}{\sum e_1^2} \tag{4.39}$$

where $\sum e_2^2$ is the error sum of squares from the regression estimated with the higher X's; and $\sum e_1^2$ with the lower X's. The degrees of freedom for Equation (4.39) are

$$df = \frac{N - M - 2K}{2} \tag{4.40}$$

where N is the number of observations (25), K is the number of variables in the model (2), and M is the number of excluded observations (we exclude the middle five observations in calculating the Goldfeld-Quandt test below). Therefore, df is equal to eight: $(25 - 5 - 4)/2 = 8$; this value is the same for both the numerator and the denominator.

The regression results for the two separate regressions, excluding the observations in the $20,000 income group, are presented in Demos 4.10 and 4.11.[9]

[9]The error sum of squares may be printed out by the multiple regression program presented in this chapter by adding the statement:

```
595 PRINT "ERROR SUM OF SQU ARES="; S
```

```
REGRESSION COEFFICIENTS
 3.1
 .516

ERROR SUM OF SQUARES= 10.184
STD. ERROR OF ESTIMATE= 1.12827
SE(B 1 )= 1.81929                T 1 = 1.70397
SE(B 2 )= .142717                T 2 = 3.61556
R SQUARED= .620354
ADJUSTED R SQUARED= .572898
F= 13.0723
DEGREES OF FREEDOM= 8
```

demo 4.10. Regression on Smaller X's

```
REGRESSION COEFFICIENTS
 1.96
 .708

ERROR SUM OF SQUARES= 108.312
STD. ERROR OF ESTIMATE= 3.67954
SE(B 1 )= 12.8521                T 1 = .152505
SE(B 2 )= .465429                T 2 = 1.52118
R SQUARED= .224354
ADJUSTED R SQUARED= .127398
F= 2.31398
DEGREES OF FREEDOM= 8
```

demo 4.11. Regression on Larger X's

The error sum of squares for the lower X's is 10.18, and for the higher X's, 108.31. The resulting F statistic is

$$F = \frac{108.31}{10.18} = 10.64$$

The critical F value at the .01 level with eight degrees of freedom for both the numerator and the denominator is 6.03. Therefore, the null hypothesis is rejected in favor of the alternate hypothesis of heteroscedasticity.

The Park test involves estimating the equation

$$ln\ e^2 = \beta_1 + \beta_2\ ln\ X + v \tag{4.41}$$

where e^2 is obtained from the original regression presented in Demo 4.9.[10] The values for $ln\ e^2$ and $ln\ X$ are given in Table 4.12. Park suggests that if B_2 is significantly different from zero, the null hypothesis should be rejected.

[10]The error for each observation may be printed out by the multiple regression program presented in this chapter by responding yes(1) to the question, "Do you want residuals printed?" This will result in a row-by-row printing of the unsquared errors (ERROR MATRIX).

table 4.12

Ln e^2	*Ln X*
−1.77	2.30
−0.98	2.30
−0.68	2.30
−1.34	2.30
0.21	2.30
−0.34	2.71
1.44	2.71
−3.90	2.71
−1.22	2.71
1.88	2.71
−2.23	3.00
−0.79	3.00
2.40	3.00
2.79	3.00
2.66	3.00
−4.65	3.22
−1.03	3.22
2.33	3.22
2.72	3.22
2.82	3.22
0.25	3.40
3.70	3.40
2.74	3.40
2.15	3.40
−0.07	3.40

When Equation (4.41) is fitted to the data in Table 4.12, the results are as reported in Demo 4.12. B_2 is significantly different from zero ($T = 2.07$) at the .05 level, but not at the .01 level. Thus, the Park test is less suggestive of heteroscedasticity than the Goldfeld-Quandt test in this particular example.

```
REGRESSION  COEFFICIENTS
-6.21412
 2.24857

STD. ERROR OF ESTIMATE= 2.10645
SE(B 1 )= 3.20434                  T 1  =-1.93928
SE(B 2 )= 1.08589                  T 2  = 2.07073
R SQUARED= .157136
ADJUSTED R SQUARED= .120489
F=4.28791
DEGREES OF FREEDOM= 23
```

demo 4.12. Park Test

Because the technique of ordinary least squares gives too much weight to the observations with large error variances, an appropriate technique for correcting for the problem of heteroscedasticity is to weight the observations in inverse proportion to their error variances. Unfortunately, we rarely know the pattern of the true error term, and therefore this procedure of *weighted least squares* must be an approximate one at best.

As an example, suppose we use the square root of the variance of consumption (see Table 4.11) as weights. These weights are presented in Table 4.13 for each income group. The data can then be divided by these weights, and the model can be reestimated with these transformed data, which are presented in Table 4.14.

table 4.13. Weights

Income	Weight (w_i)
\$10,000	$0.27 = w_1$
15,000	$1.57 = w_2$
20,000	$3.16 = w_3$
25,000	$3.22 = w_4$
30,000	$4.08 = w_5$

The transformed model is of the form

$$Y^* = \beta_2 X^* + \epsilon^* \tag{4.42}$$

where ϵ^* is homoscedastic (assuming the weights are approximately correct). Note that this model is estimated without an intercept term because the column of ones in the X matrix is divided by a nonconstant term (the weights). The results of estimating this model with the weighted data are given in Demo 4.13. The precision of this model is even greater than that of the original model, thereby demonstrating the problem of estimating the appropriate weights.

```
REGRESSION COEFFICIENTS
 .814008

STD. ERROR OF ESTIMATE= 1.05755
SE(B 2 )= .117635E-1              T 2 = 69.198
R SQUARED= .989173
F= 2277
DEGREES OF FREEDOM= 23
```

demo 4.13. Weighted Least Squares

table 4.14. Weighted Data

X^*	Y^*
37.0	29.6
37.0	30.3
37.0	30.7
37.0	30.0
37.0	32.2
9.6	7.8
9.6	6.0
9.6	7.4
9.6	7.6
9.6	5.7
6.3	4.7
6.3	5.1
6.3	3.8
6.3	3.6
6.3	6.0
7.8	5.9
7.8	5.8
7.8	6.9
7.8	7.2
7.8	4.7
7.4	5.9
7.4	4.1
7.4	6.6
7.4	6.4
7.4	5.4

$X^* = X_i/w_i$
$Y^* = Y_i/w_i$

The difficulty of applying weighted least squares in practice has led to the development of second-best techniques, which involve making an educated guess as to the pattern of the heteroscedastic error term. We will complete our discussion by considering one of these techniques.

Suppose we believe the error term is related to the square of the independent variable. Then it can be proven that the heteroscedastic model (e.g., the two-variable model) can be transformed into a homoscedastic one by dividing through by X:

$$Y = \beta_1 + \beta_2 X_2 + \epsilon \tag{4.43}$$

Dividing Equation (4.43) by X_2:

$$\frac{Y}{X_2} = \beta_1 \frac{1}{X_2} + \beta_2 + \frac{\epsilon}{X_2} \tag{4.44}$$

Note that β_2 is now the constant term, and therefore the first regression coefficient (.73) printed out in Demo 4.14 is the estimated marginal propensity to consume. The transformed data are given in Table 4.15.

The regression results suggest that the slope coefficient (.73) is highly signif-

```
REGRESSION COEFFICIENTS
 .730591
 .65326

STD. ERROR OF ESTIMATE= .117247
SE(B 1 )= .617386E-1            T 1  =  11.8336
SE(B 2 )= .984689               T 2  =  .663418
R SQUARED= .187765E-1
ADJUSTED R SQUARED=-.238854E-1
F= .440123
DEGREES OF FREEDOM= 23
```

demo 4.14. Correcting for Heteroscedasticity by Way of Equation (4.44)

table 4.15. Transformed Data for Estimating Equation (4.44)

$\frac{Y}{X_2}$	$\frac{1}{X_2}$
.80	.10
.82	.10
.83	.10
.81	.10
.87	.10
.82	.07
.63	.07
.77	.07
.80	.07
.59	.07
.75	.05
.80	.05
.60	.05
.56	.05
.96	.05
.76	.04
.74	.04
.90	.04
.92	.04
.60	.04
.81	.03
.56	.03
.90	.03
.87	.03
.74	.03

icant ($T = 11.8$), a conclusion not markedly different from that of the original model. Such a precise estimate implies that we have still not corrected for the problem of heteroscedasticity. The interested reader may wish to refer to some of the more-advanced books in the Bibliography for a description of some of the other techniques for correcting for heteroscedasticity.

regression on dummy independent variables

So far, the independent variables in the regression equation have taken on values over a continuous range. However, in econometric research it is frequently desirable to use a variable that is restricted to two or more integer values. For example, suppose that it is hypothesized that women might be discriminated against in earnings after controlling for IQ and education. If we create a new variable, X_4, and assign to it a one if female and zero otherwise, then the coefficient on X_4 represents how much (more or less) females make in comparison to males, controlling for the other variables. If the coefficient on X_4 is negative and significantly different from zero, the hypothesis of discrimination against women would be supported. It is of course unimportant whether the zero is assigned to a male or a female. If, instead, the zero is assigned to a female, then the coefficient on X_4 indicates how much (more or less) males make in comparison to females. Let us define X_4 as

$$X_4 = \begin{cases} 1 \text{ if female} \\ 0 \text{ if male} \end{cases}$$

And suppose X_4 takes on the following values:

Sex (X_4)
0
1
0
1
0
1
0
1
0
1

Since the T value on X_4 is only .706 (Demo 4.15), the null hypothesis is not rejected—sex discrimination does not appear to exist. Alternatively, if the first seven observations on X_4 are women and the last three are men, then the regression coefficient on X_4 is significantly different from zero (as can be seen in Demo 4.16). After controlling for IQ and education, women make about

```
REGRESSION COEFFICIENTS
-7056.84
 74.1213
 698.858
 430.316

STD. ERROR OF ESTIMATE= 896.288
SE( B 1)= 3097.75                 T 1 =-2.27806
SE( B 2)= 42.4194                 T 2 =  1.74735
SE( B 3)= 153.639                 T 3 =  4.5487
SE( B 4)= 609.072                 T 4 =  .706512
R SQUARED= .941576
ADJUSTED R SQUARED= .912364
F= 32.2324
DEGREES OF FREEDOM= 6
DW= 2.357
CORRELATION MATRIX
1  .858751  .944237  .174078

.858751  1  .764408  .260585

.944237  .764408  1  .336909E-1

.174078  .260585  .336909E-1  1
```

demo 4.15. Regression of Income-IQ-Education-Sex Model, Sex Insignificant

```
REGRESSION COEFFICIENTS
-3327.53
 66.124
 567.467
-1517.61

STD. ERROR OF ESTIMATE= 674.943
SE(B 1)= 2908.32                  T 1 =-1.14414
SE(B 2)= 30.8292                  T 2 =  2.14485
SE(B 3)= 119.852                  T 3 =  4.73473
SE(B 4)= 649.46                   T 4 =-2.33673
R SQUARED= .966869
ADJUSTED R SQUARED= .950304
F= 58.3669
DEGREES OF FREEDOM= 6
DW= 2.59311
CORRELATION MATRIX
 1  .858751  .944237  -.797724

 .858751  1  .764408  -.637273

 .944237  .764408  1  -.669027

-.797724  -.637273  -.669027  1
```

demo 4.16. Regression of Income-IQ-Education-Sex Model, Sex Significant

$1,518 less than men. However, the reader should be warned that any conclusions made from small samples are suspect. We are using small samples for expositional purposes only.

In general, if there are N distinct classes, $N - 1$ dummy variables have to be included in the regression. Thus, for the sex variable, there are two classes and one dummy variable is needed. Whichever class is assigned zeros for all the dummy variables is the reference group and is excluded from the regression. The regression coefficients measure the differential impact between the included and the excluded class. As an example of the use of more than one dummy variable, consider the following model:

$$Y = \beta_1 + \beta_2 X_2 + \beta_3 X_3 + \epsilon$$

where Y is income, and X_2 and X_3 are dummy variables that represent, respectively, the Ph.D. and M.A. degrees. The reference group is those with a B.A. degree. X_2 and X_3 are defined as follows:

	X_2	X_3
Ph.D.	1	0
M.A.	0	1
B.A.	0	0

Suppose X_2 and X_3 take on the following values:

X_2	X_3
0	0
0	0
0	0
0	1
0	1
0	1
0	0
1	0
1	0
1	0

Thus, the first three observations are B.A. degrees, the next three are M.A.'s, the seventh observation is a B.A., and the last three are Ph.D.'s. The results of this regression are reported in Demo 4.17. Only the coefficient on the Ph.D. degree (5750) is significantly different from zero. Ph.D.'s make about $5,750 more than B.A.'s, but M.A.'s do not make significantly more (statistically speaking) than B.A.'s. Because there are no other variables included in this

```
REGRESSION COEFFICIENTS
 7250
 5750
 1750
STD. ERROR OF ESTIMATE= 1880.35
SE(B 1)= 940.175                    T 1 = 7.71133
SE(B 2)= 1436.14                    T 2 = 4.00379
SE(B 3)= 1436.14                    T 3 = 1.21854
R SQUARED= .7
ADJUSTED R SQUARED= .614286
F= 8.16667
DEGREES OF FREEDOM= 7
DW=1.48232
CORRELATION MATRIX
 1  .797724 -.113961

 .797724  1 -.428572

-.113961 -.428572  1
```

demo 4.17. Regression of Income-Degree Model

model, the constant term can be interpreted as the average income that B.A.'s earn (X_2 and X_3 are set at zero). For Ph.D.'s ($X_2 = 1$, $X_3 = 0$), $B_1 + B_2$ is their average income; for M.A.'s ($X_2 = 0$, $X_3 = 1$), $B_1 + B_3$ is their average income. However, if other variables are included in the regression, it would obviously be necessary to add the effects of these variables, and the intercept term would not have such a neat interpretation.

regression on dummy dependent variables

Occasionally in economic research the dependent variable is dichotomous, or a dummy variable. In this section we briefly discuss the estimation and interpretation of regression models in which the dependent variable takes on a value of zero or one. As an example, consider the hypothetical data in Table 4.16. The dependent variable is whether or not family income is below the poverty line (1 = poverty, 0 = otherwise). Hypothesizing that sex and race might help to explain poverty, the independent variables are coded: sex (1 = female, 0 = male), and race (1 = nonwhite, 0 = white). Normally, in models with a dummy dependent variable, the independent variables are also dummies because of the difficulty of interpreting the coefficients on a continuous independent variable.

The regression of poverty on sex and race is presented in Demo 4.18. How are the results interpreted? The coefficient on sex, .55, means that females have a .55 higher probability than males of being in poverty. Similarly, nonwhites have a .35 higher probability than whites. The overall regression equation,

table 4.16. Hypothetical Data on Poverty, Sex, and Race of 30 Families

Poverty (Y)	Sex (X_2)	Race (X_3)
1 = *poverty* 0 = *otherwise*	1 = *female* 0 = *male*	1 = *nonwhite* 0 = *white*
1	1	0
1	1	1
1	1	1
0	0	0
0	0	0
0	0	0
0	0	0
1	1	1
0	0	1
0	0	1
0	1	0
0	0	0
1	1	1
1	1	1
0	0	0
0	0	0
0	0	1
0	0	0
0	1	0
0	0	0
1	1	1
1	0	1
0	0	0
1	1	1
1	1	0
1	1	1
1	0	1
0	0	1
1	0	0
0	0	0

Poverty = .05 + .55 Sex + .35 Race, is termed a *linear probability model.* For example, the probability of a family headed by a white male of being in poverty is .05 + .55(0) + .35(0) = .05. The same probability for a family headed by a white female is .05 + .55(1) + .35(0) = .60. This probability for a nonwhite female is .95.

It can be proven that the assumption of homoscedasticity does not hold for linear probability models. Correcting for heteroscedasticity may therefore be necessary. Another problem with linear probability models is that there is no guarantee that the probability obtained from the regression equation will lie between zero and one. One solution is to automatically assign a zero to prob-

```
REGRESSION COEFFICIENTS
 .500001E-1
 .55
 .35

STD. ERROR OF ESTIMATE= .352242
SE(B 1 )= .946621E-1            T 1  = .528196
SE(B 2 )= .138926               T 2  = 3.95894
SE(B 3 )= .136423               T 3  = 2.56556
R SQUARED= .545249
ADJUSTED R SQUARED= .511564
F= 16.1866
DEGREES OF FREEDOM= 27
DW= 1.99179
CORRELATION MATRIX

 1   .659082   .530349

 .659082   1   .327327

 .530349   .327327   1
```

demo 4.18. Regression of Dummy Dependent Variable, Poverty, on Sex and Race

abilities less than zero, and a one to probabilities greater than one. Alternatively, a log ("logit") model can be used which ensures that the probabilities will lie between zero and one. The reader should refer to a more-advanced book for an explanation of logit models.

summary

The two-variable regression model presented in the preceding chapter allowed us to begin our discussion of econometric theory without resort to difficult mathematical calculations. However, the two-variable model is an oversimplification of reality. In contrast, the multiple regression model is general and therefore more in line with reality. Unfortunately, the calculations are difficult, thereby requiring the computer for most practical applications. Consequently, we have relied upon the three-variable model for expositional purposes. Although the calculations are difficult for the three-variable model, they are not beyond reason. If there are more than three variables, the matrix form is normally used in order to organize the data for computer solution.

The coefficients of the multiple regression model are *partial regression coefficients* in the sense that any particular coefficient measures the change in the dependent variable that can be expected from a one-unit change in the independent variable, holding the other variables constant. This interpretation is the same as in the two-variable model except that there are of course no variables being held constant. Because economists often wish to control for the influence of other variables, multiple regression analysis can be an extremely useful and powerful statistical tool.

The methodology for testing the null hypotheses with respect to each individual regression coefficient is essentially the same as in the two-variable model. A T test or confidence interval can be constructed to test the null hypotheses. The degrees of freedom are $N - K$ (number of observations minus number of variables). Alternatively, an F test can be applied with one degree of freedom for the numerator and $N - K$ degrees of freedom for the denominator.

The overall significance of the multiple regression model can be tested by applying an F test with $K - 1$ degrees of freedom for the numerator and $N - K$ degrees of freedom for the denominator. The null hypothesis is that all of the regression coefficients are equal to zero. If the null hypothesis is true, then the R^2 is not significantly different from zero.

Multicollinearity is often a serious problem in multiple regression models. Thus, if one independent variable is highly correlated with another, it is difficult to interpret the partial regression coefficients because one of the variables cannot be held constant while the other one is varied. The result is large standard errors and imprecise estimates of the population parameters. Multicollinearity may be detected in three-variable models by examining the simple correlation coefficients, although this is not foolproof. A better clue can be gained by examining the *partial correlation coefficients* and by examining the significance of the regression coefficients. If the coefficients are insignificant, but the R^2 is significant, multicollinearity may be a problem. As discussed above, correcting for multicollinearity can be a monumental task.

Autocorrelation and heteroscedasticity are two other problems common to regression models. As demonstrated in Chapter 3, the consequences of autocorrelation and heteroscedasticity are the same: The estimated standard errors of the regression coefficients are biased downward, thereby making it difficult to test the null hypotheses. Because of the existence of the Durbin-Watson test, the detection of autocorrelation is not necessarily difficult. In contrast, correcting for autocorrelation is often difficult, but not impossible. One commonly used procedure for correcting for autocorrelation is the "generalized difference" equation. Commonly used tests for heteroscedasticity are the Goldfeld-Quandt and the Park tests. *Weighted least squares* is an accepted procedure for correcting for the problem of heteroscedasticity.

We ended the chapter by discussing dummy variables. Because economists often use variables that must be discretely measured, the defining of dummy variables in a regression model is common. Usually the dummies are independent variables, but occasionally a dependent dummy variable is defined. In the case of dummy independent variables, the regression coefficients are interpreted with reference to an excluded class. In the case of a dummy dependent variable, several models are possible. We discussed *linear probability* models in which the regression coefficients are interpreted as probabilities.

As mentioned in Chapter 1, a regression model may be used for purposes of forecasting. This topic is considered in the next chapter.

examples

The examples are based upon the following set of hypothetical data containing five observations on three variables. For expositional purposes, the number of observations and variables is necessarily small. All numbers are in thousands of dollars.

Consumption (Y)	Income (X_2)	Wealth (X_3)
10	20	30
9	17	35
15	25	28
12	19	50
18	30	29

example 1

Suppose that a multiple regression model is specified in which consumption is the dependent variable (Y) and income (X_2) and wealth (X_3) are the independent variables. Estimate the parameters of the model

$$Y = \beta_1 + \beta_2 X_2 + \beta_3 X_3 + \epsilon$$

$$\bar{Y} = 12.8 \quad \bar{X}_2 = 22.2 \quad \bar{X}_3 = 34.4$$

y	y^2	x_2	x_3	yx_2	yx_3	x_2^2	x_3^2	x_2x_3
−2.8	7.84	−2.2	−4.4	6.16	12.32	4.84	19.36	9.68
−3.8	14.44	−5.2	0.6	19.76	−2.28	27.04	0.36	−3.12
2.2	4.84	2.8	−6.4	6.16	−14.08	7.84	40.96	−17.92
−0.8	0.64	−3.2	15.6	2.56	−12.48	10.24	243.36	−49.92
5.2	27.04	7.8	−5.4	40.56	−28.08	60.84	29.16	−42.12
	54.80			75.20	−44.60	110.80	333.20	−103.40

$$D = (110.8)(333.2) - (-103.4)^2 = 26{,}227.0$$

$$B_2 = \frac{(75.2)(333.2) - (-44.6)(-103.4)}{26{,}227} = .78$$

$$B_3 = \frac{(-44.6)(110.8) - (75.2)(-103.4)}{26{,}227} = .11$$

$$B_1 = 12.8 - (.78)(22.2) - (.11)(34.4) = -8.3$$

Therefore, the estimated equation is

$$Y = -8.3 + .78X_2 + .11X_3$$

example 2

Calculate the standard errors of B_2 and B_3.

$$\sum e^2 = 54.8 - (.78)(75.2) - (.11)(-44.6) = 1.05$$

$$s = \sqrt{\frac{1.05}{2}} = .725$$

$$SE(B_2) = .725\sqrt{\frac{(333.2)}{26{,}227}} = .08$$

$$SE(B_3) = .725\sqrt{\frac{(110.8)}{26{,}227}} = .05$$

example 3

Test the null hypotheses

$$\beta_2 = 0$$

$$\beta_3 = 0$$

at the .05 level of significance.

$$T(B_2) = \frac{.78}{.08} = 9.75$$

$$T(B_3) = \frac{.11}{.05} = 2.20$$

The critical T value at the .05 level with two degrees of freedom ($N - K = 5 - 3$) is 4.303. Therefore, the null hypothesis $\beta_2 = 0$ is rejected; the null hypothesis $\beta_3 = 0$ is accepted. We can conclude that income is significant in explaining consumption, whereas wealth is not significant.

example 4

Calculate the R^2 and $\bar{R}^2$.

$$R^2 = \frac{(.78)(75.2) + (.11)(-44.6)}{54.8} = .98$$

$$\bar{R}^2 = 1 - (1) - (1 - .98)(4)/2 = .96$$

example 5

Test the null hypotheses as in Example 3 using the F test.

$$F(B_2) = (9.75)^2 = 95.06$$

$$F(B_3) = (2.2)^2 = 4.84$$

The critical F value at the .05 level with one degree of freedom for the numerator and two degrees of freedom for the denominator is 18.5. The conclusions are the same as before.

example 6

Test the overall significance of the model by way of the F test at the .01 level.

$$F = \frac{(.98)(2)}{(.02)(2)} = 49.0$$

The critical F value at the .01 level of significance with two degrees of freedom for the numerator ($K - 1 = 2$) and two degrees of freedom for the denominator ($N - K = 2$) is 99.0. The small sample size prevents us from concluding that the overall model is significant ($49 < 99$). Note that the critical T value at the .01 level with two degrees of freedom is 9.925. Since $9.75 < 9.925$, B_2 is not significantly different from zero at the .01 level (although significant at the .05 level).

example 7

What are the simple correlations between income and wealth, between consumption and income, and between consumption and wealth?

From Equation (3.20):

$$R = \frac{\sum x_2 x_3}{\sqrt{\sum x_2^2 \sum x_3^2}}$$

$$= \frac{-103.40}{\sqrt{(110.8)(333.2)}} = -.54$$

$$R = \frac{\sum y x_2}{\sqrt{\sum y^2 \sum x_2^2}}$$

$$= \frac{75.2}{\sqrt{(54.8)(110.8)}} = .96$$

$$R = \frac{\sum y x_3}{\sqrt{\sum y^2 \sum x_3^2}}$$

$$= \frac{-44.6}{\sqrt{(54.8)(333.2)}} = -.33$$

exercises

1. Suppose that you believe that stock market prices (Y) are affected by the overall levels of inflation and unemployment in the economy, and you attempt to estimate the parameters of the model

$$Y = \beta_1 + \beta_2 X_2 + \beta_3 X_3 + \epsilon$$

where X_2 is the change in the Consumer Price Index (ΔCPI) and X_3 is the unemployment rate. Calculate B_1, B_2, B_3, $SE(B_2)$, $SE(B_3)$, R^2, and the F statistic using the following set of data and interpret your results. Estimate this model where X_2 is the change in the Wholesale Price Index (ΔWPI), and compare the results of this model with the first.

Quarter	Stock Prices	ΔCPI	ΔWPI	Unemployment Rate
2–73	107.41	.020	.048	4.8
3–73	105.08	.023	.027	4.8
4–73	102.22	.022	.015	4.8
1–74	95.67	.033	.068	5.1
2–74	90.64	.027	.028	5.3
3–74	75.66	.033	.074	5.8
4–74	69.42	.024	.026	7.2
1–75	78.81	.015	−.006	8.7
2–75	89.07	.017	.019	8.6
3–75	87.62	.019	.023	8.3
4–75	89.11	.014	.006	8.3
1–76	99.53	−.003	.005	7.5

2. Suppose that the same model is specified as in the first part of Exercise 1, except that an additional independent variable is added: ΔWPI (change in the Wholesale Price Index). Do you think that multicollinearity would be a problem in such a model? If so, how would you solve the problem?

3. You suspect that there is a relationship between salary (Y) and years of experience. Given the following hypothetical set of data, which model fits the data better? Interpret your results. Is multicollinearity a problem in Model II?

Model I: $Y = \beta_1 + \beta_2 X_2 + \epsilon$

Model II: $Y = \beta_1 + \beta_2 X_2 + \beta_3 X_2^2$

Salary (Y)	Experience (X_2)	X_2^2
$14,780	1	1
15,300	2	4
15,620	3	9
15,840	4	16
16,020	5	25
16,160	6	36
16,280	7	49
16,400	8	64
16,500	9	81
16,580	10	100

4. Referring to Table 4.11, can you think of any other way of weighting the data in order to correct for the problem of heteroscedasticity?

5. Collect quarterly data and reestimate the consumption function (Demo 4.6).

Does autocorrelation exist? If so, correct for it. The regression in Demo 4.6 is based on yearly data. Does the use of quarterly data seem to make a difference?

6. Show that d, the Durbin-Watson statistic, is "close" to 2 if N is large.

7. In a study of the determinants of salaries of 596 professors, Katz[11] tested the following salary model and obtained the results shown in Table 4.17. Interpret the results.

The dependent variable is:

table 4.17. Dependent Variable Is 1969–70 Academic-Year Salary

Variable (name)	*B* (Standard Error)	*F*
Books (B)	230 (86)	7.21
Articles (A)	18 (8)	5.37
Excellent Articles (E)	102 (28)	13.43
Dissertations (F)	489 (60)	66.85
Public Service (P)	89 (38)	5.65
Committees (C)	156 (49)	10.02
Experience (Y)	189 (17)	126.92
Teaching Rating (T)[a]	53(370)	0.01
Physical and Laboratory Scientist (D_2)[b]	−791(435)	3.31
Humanities (D_3)[b]	−1181(594)	3.95
English Professors (D_4)[b]	−2293(529)	18.75
Groups 2, 3, 4, 5, of Undergraduate Schools (U_2)[c]	−474(364)	1.69
Group 6 (U_3)[c]	−2025(794)	6.50
Foreign and Other (U_4)[c]	27(478)	0.00
Groups 2, 3, 4 of Graduate Schools (G)[d]	−875(306)	8.15
Administrators (M)[e]	2557(641)	15.89
Female (X)[f]	−2410(528)	20.80
11-Month Appointment (N)[g]	1184(505)	5.50
Ph.D. Degree (R)[h]	1919(607)	10.01
Constant: 11,155		
Multiple $R = .82 (R^2 = .68)$		
$F = 50.05$ Standard Error $= 2946$		
Mean of Dependent Variable = 15,679		
Standard Deviation of Dependent Variable = 5093		

[a]Reference group is bottom 50 percent of teachers by vote of students.
[b]Reference group is Social Sciences.
[c]Reference group is top group of undergraduate school rankings.
[d]Reference group is top group of graduate school rankings.
[e]Reference group is those without administrative assignment.
[f]Reference group is male sex.
[g]Reference group is 9-month appointment type.
[h]Reference group is professor without Ph.D.

[11]David A. Katz, "Faculty Salaries, Promotions, and Productivity at a Large University," *American Economic Review*, June 1973.

S = 1969–70 academic-year salary corrected to a 100 percent departmental basis.

The independent variables are:

B = Number of books published, either authored or edited, lifetime.

A = Number of articles published, lifetime.

E = Number of articles published in the very best journals in a particular discipline ("excellent" articles).

T = A dummy indicating whether or not a professor is ranked in the top 50 percent of all instructors by vote of students.

F = Number of dissertations supervised since 1964, a measure of research and graduate teaching ability. Lifetime dissertations were not available.

P = Number of hours devoted per week to public service activities in 1970.

C = Number of hours devoted per week to committee assignments in 1970.

Y = Number of years since highest degree, a measure of experience.

D_1 = A dummy indicating whether or not a professor is a social scientist (economics, political science, or sociology).

D_2 = A dummy indicating whether or not a professor is a physical or laboratory scientist (electrical engineering, mathematics, physics, psychology, or zoology).

D_3 = A dummy indicating whether or not a professor is in the humanities (French or history).

D_4 = A dummy indicating whether or not a professor is in the English Department. D_1 to D_4 were included to measure possible differences in market supply and demand for the various major disciplines. D_3 and D_4 were not combined because of considerable salary differences found in previous regression runs.

U_1 = A dummy indicating whether or not a professor received his undergraduate degree from schools containing the top 10 percent of all faculty in the country.

U_2 = A dummy indicating whether or not a professor received his undergraduate degree from schools containing the next 70 percent of all faculty.

U_3 = A dummy indicating whether or not a professor received his undergraduate degree from schools containing the bottom 20 percent of all faculty.

U_4 = A dummy indicating whether or not a professor received his undergraduate degree from a foreign school or one that was not ranked.

G = A dummy indicating whether or not a professor received his highest graduate degree from the bottom groups of graduate school departments. U_1 through G were included to measure quality of education.

M = A dummy indicating whether or not a professor had an administrative assignment.

X = A dummy indicating whether or not a professor was a female. This was included to measure the extent of discrimination, if any.

N = A dummy indicating whether or not a professor was on an 11-month appointment.

R = A dummy indicating whether or not a professor possessed the Ph.D.

8. In connection with Exercise 7, one might wish to predict whether or not an assistant professor will be promoted to associate professor. What model would you use to predict promotion to associate professor?

computer exercises

1. Estimate the stock price model with the unemployment rate, ΔCPI, and ΔWPI included as independent variables (use the following 69 quarters of data) and interpret your results. The computer program in Demo 4.19 is a generalized regression program that will work on any number of observations and variables by following the directions in the remark (REM) Statements 1–15. Thus, for 69 observations and 3 variables, Statements 20, 25, 30, 35, 40, and 45 would read:

```
20DIM Y(69,1),Z(69,1),W(69,1)
25DIM X(69,3),B(3,69)
30DIM R(3),T(3),G(3),Q(3)
35DIM C(3,3),D(3,3),E(3,1),F(3,1),P(3,3)
40LET N=69
45LET A4=2
```

For 69 observations and 4 variables:

```
20DIM Y(69,1),Z(69,1),W(69,1)
25DIM X(69,4),B(4,69)
30DIM R(4),T(4),G(4),Q(4)
35DIM C(4,4),D(4,4),E(4,1),F(4,1),P(4,4)
40LET N=69
45LET A4=3
```

The data statements begin at 2000. The first series contains the observations on Y. Each succeeding series contains the observations on the independent variables.

Quarter Year	Stock Prices	Unemployment Rate	ΔCPI	ΔWPI
1–59	56.15	6.1	.0	.003
2–59	57.46	4.9	.006	.001
3–59	57.05	5.6	.006	0
4–59	59.06	5.5	.002	−.007
1–60	55.02	5.4	.002	.009
2–60	57.26	5.5	.006	−.004
3–60	54.81	5.7	.002	−.003
4–60	56.8	6.8	.006	.003
1–61	64.12	6.9	0	.003
2–61	65.62	6.8	.001	−.014
3–61	67.26	6.8	.005	.005
4–61	71.74	6	−.001	.003
1–62	70.29	5.5	.001	−.002
2–62	55.63	5.5	.003	−.007
3–62	58	5.8	.008	.012
4–62	62.64	5.6	−.003	−.008
1–63	65.67	5.6	.004	−.005
2–63	70.11	5.7	.004	.004
3–63	72.85	5.5	.005	0
4–63	74.17	5.5	.005	0
1–64	78.8	5.4	.001	.001
2–64	80.24	4.9	.003	−.004
3–64	83.41	5.1	.004	.007
4–64	83.96	5	.004	0
1–65	86.83	4.7	.002	.006
2–65	85.04	4.5	.01	.015
3–65	89.38	4.4	.001	.002
4–65	91.73	4.1	.007	.011
1–66	88.88	3.8	.009	.012
2–66	86.06	4	.008	.003
3–66	77.81	3.8	.011	.01
4–66	81.33	3.8	.005	−.008
1–67	89.42	3.6	.003	−.002
2–67	91.43	4	.009	.006
3–67	95.81	4.1	.009	−.001
4–67	95.3	3.7	.009	.006
1–68	90.75	3.6	.011	.013
2–68	98	3.8	.012	.005
3–68	99.9	3.6	.011	.004
4–68	105.2	3.3	.012	.006
1–69	100.9	3.4	.015	.017
2–69	101.7	3.4	.016	.013
3–69	94.5	4	.013	.004
4–69	94.3	3.5	.014	.013
1–70	88.7	4.4	.016	.013
2–70	79.2	5	.013	.01
3–70	78.7	5.6	.01	.006
4–70	86.2	6.2	.014	0

Quarter Year	Stock Prices	Unemployment Rate	ΔCPI	ΔWPI
1–71	96.7	6	.006	.018
2–71	101.5	5.6	.014	.012
3–71	98.55	6	.007	.002
4–71	96.41	6	.006	.008
1–72	105.41	5.9	.007	.017
2–72	108.16	5.5	.008	.012
3–72	109.2	5.5	.01	.012
4–72	114.04	5.1	.009	.022
1–73	115	5	.02	.056
2–73	107.41	4.8	.02	.048
3–73	105.08	4.8	.023	.027
4–73	102.22	4.8	.022	.015
1–74	95.67	5.1	.033	.068
2–74	90.64	5.3	.027	.028
3–74	75.66	5.8	.033	.074
4–74	69.42	7.2	.024	.026
1–75	78.81	8.7	.015	−.006
2–75	89.07	8.6	.017	.019
3–75	87.62	8.3	.019	.023
4–75	89.11	8.3	.014	.006
1–76	99.53	7.5	−.003	.005

```
1 REM N IS NUMBER OF OBSERVATIONS
3 REM K IS NUMBER OF VARIABLES (DEPENDENT + INDEPENDENT)
5 REM AT ST.20 IS DIM Y(N,1),Z(N,1),W(N,1)
7 REM AT ST.25 IS DIM X(N,K),B(K,N)
9 REM AT ST.30 IS DIM R(K),T(K),G(K),Q(K)
11 REM AT ST.35 IS DIM C(K,K),D(K,K),E(K,1),F(K,1),P(K,K)
13 REM AT ST. 40 IS N=NUMBER OF OBSERVATIONS
15 REM AT ST.45 IS A4=NUMBER OF INDEPENDENT VARIABLES
20 DIM Y(10,1),Z(10,1),W(10,1)
25 DIM X(10,3),B(3,10)
30 DIM R(3),T(3),G(3),Q(3)
35 DIM C(3,3),D(3,3),E(3,1),F(3,1),P(3,3)
40 LET N=10
45 LET A4=2
50 PRINT "DO YOU WANT RESIDUALS PRINTED? (1=YES,0=NO)"
55 INPUT W1
70 FOR I=1 TO N
90 LET X(I,1)=1
100 NEXT I
110 FOR I=1 TO N
120 READ Y(I,1)
130 NEXT I
140 FOR J=2 TO A4+1
```

demo 4.19. Multiple Regression Program Run on Income-IQ-Education Model

```
150 FOR I=1 TO N
160 READ X(I,J)
170 NEXT I
180 NEXT J
376 MAT B=TRN(X)
380 MAT C=B*X
390 MAT D=INV(C)
400 MAT E=B*Y
410 MAT F=D*E
420 PRINT "REGRESSION COEFFICIENTS"
430 MAT PRINT F
440 REM CALC Y CALC
450 FOR I=1 TO N
460 FOR J=1 TO A4+1
470 LET Z(I,1)=Z(I,1)+X(I,J)*F(J,1)
480 NEXT J
490 NEXT I
500 FOR I=1 TO N
510 REM W = ERROR MATRIX
520 LET W(I,1)=Z(I,1)-Y(I,1)
530 REM CALC SUM OF Y
540 LET S2=S2+Y(I,1)
550 REM CALC SUM OF ERROR SQUARED
560 LET S=S+(Y(I,1)-Z(I,1))**2
570 REM S1=SUM OF ERROR SQUARED
580 LET S1=S
590 NEXT I
600 REM CALC STD. ERROR OF ESTIMATE
610 LET S=SQR(S/(N-A4-1))
620 PRINT "STD. ERROR OF ESTIMATE=";S
630 REM CALC STD. ERRORS OF REGRESSION COEF.
640 FOR J=1 TO A4+1
650 LET R(J)=SQR((S**2)*(D(J,J)))
660 LET T(J)=F(J,1)/R(J)
670 PRINT "SE(B";J;")=";R(J);"T";J;"=";T(J)
680 NEXT J
690 REM CALC MEAN OF Y
700 LET S2=S2/N
710 REM CALC TOTAL VARIATION
720 FOR I=1 TO N
730 LET S3=S3+(Y(I,1)-S2)**2
740 NEXT I
750 REM CALC R SQUARED
760 LET R2=1-(S1/S3)
770 PRINT "R SQUARED = ";R2
775 PRINT "ADJUSTED R SQUARED= ";1-(1-R2)*(N-1)/(N-A4-1)
777 PRINT "F = ";R2*(N-A4-1)/((1-R2)*A4)
779 PRINT "DEGREES OF FREEDOM = ";N-A4-1
780 REM CALC DURBIN WATSON
790 FOR J=2 TO N
```

demo 4.19. Continued

```
 800 LET S4=S4+(W(J,1)-W(J-1,1))**2
 810 NEXT J
 820 PRINT "DW = ";S4/S1
 830 REM CALC CORRELATION MATRIX
 840 FOR J=2 TO A4+1
 850 FOR I=1 TO N
 860 LET Q(J)=Q(J)+X(I,J)
 865 REM Q CONTAINS SUM OF EACH INDEPENDENT VARIABLE
 870 NEXT I
 880 NEXT J
 890 FOR I=1 TO N
 900 LET X(I,1)=Y(I,1)-S2
 905 NEXT I
 910 FOR I=1 TO N
 912 FOR J=2 TO A4+1
 915 LET X(I,J)=X(I,J)-Q(J)/N
 917 REM X CONTAINS (Y-YBAR)*(X-XBAR) AND IS OF ORDER N BY A4+1
 919 NEXT J
 920 NEXT I
 930 FOR J=1 TO A4+1
 940 FOR I=1 TO N
 950 LET G(J)=G(J)+X(I,J)*X(I,J)
 960 REM G CONTAINS SUM OF EACH COLUMN SQUARED OF X
 970 NEXT I
 980 NEXT J
 990 MAT B=TRN(X)
1000 MAT P=B*X
1010 REM P CONTAINS SUM OF XY
1020 FOR I=1 TO A4+1
1030 FOR J=1 TO A4+1
1040 LET P(I,J)=P(I,J)/SQR(G(I)*G(J))
1050 NEXT J
1060 NEXT I
1070PRINT "CORRELATION MATRIX"
1080MAT PRINT P;
1085IF W1=0 THEN 3000
1090PRINT "ERROR MATRIX"
1100MAT PRINT W;
2000DATA 5000,6000,7000,8000,9000,10000,11000,12000,13000,14000
2010DATA 80,95,100,101,103,115,105,116,120,110
2020DATA 9,8,10,10,11,14,15,13,16,17
3000END
RUN
DO YOU WANT RESIDUALS PRINTED? (1=YES,0=NO)
? 1
REGRESSION COEFFICIENTS
-7628.13
 85.044
 669.992
```

demo 4.19. Continued

```
STD. ERROR OF ESTIMATE= 863.63
SE(B 1 )= 2881.42                    T 1  =-2.64735
SE(B 2 )= 38.0628                    T 2  =  2.23431
SE(B 3 )= 142.712                    T 3  =  4.69471
R SQUARED= .936715
ADJUSTED R SQUARED= .918634
F= 51.8055
DEGREES OF FREEDOM= 7
DW= 2.35762
 CORRELATION MATRIX
 1   .858751   .944237

 .858751   1   .764408

 .944237   .764408   1

ERROR MATRIX
  205.32 -189.013 576.191 -338.765 -498.685 1531.82 351.372 -1053.13
  297.023 -883.424
```

demo 4.19. Continued

2. Work Exercise 3 with the program in Demo 4.19.

5

forecasting

As explained in Chapter 1, once an econometric model has been specified, estimated, and verified, it may be used for purposes of *prediction* (cross-section) or *projection* (time-series). In this book we classify both prediction and projection under the general heading of *forecasting*. Forecasting means that the parameter estimates are used to predict or project the value (or a range of values) of the dependent variable given information on the independent variable(s).

The forecasting aspect of econometric work is important because of its applied, or policy-oriented, nature. For example, what is the likely effect of a change in monetary policy on inflation and unemployment? What is the probable impact of a change in fiscal policy? To what extent can an individual expect his or her income to increase by going to school for an additional year? If disposable income is increased by cutting taxes, how will this policy affect consumption expenditures? These questions can be addressed within a forecasting context, and they involve estimation of a *forecast error*.

Forecasting involves error because the linear regression model underlying a forecast is probabilistic, as explained in Chapter 3. Thus, we rarely know the population parameters with certainty and therefore cannot forecast the dependent variable without error. But even if we knew the population parameters with certainty, the stochastic error term would ensure a nonzero forecast error.[1] In this chapter we will demonstrate how to estimate the forecast error for both

[1]For example, not all relevant variables can be included in a model.

the two-variable and multiple regression models. The estimation of the forecast error for the multiple regression model requires matrix notation. The reader may wish to review the section on matrix notation in Chapter 4.

types of forecasts

We distinguish between two types of forecasts: Type I, in which the values for all the independent variables are known with certainty; and Type II, in which the values for at least one of the independent variables are not known with certainty. A Type I forecast is sometimes termed an *unconditional forecast*; Type II, a *conditional forecast*. Estimation of the error of a Type II forecast is extremely difficult and beyond the scope of this book. Consequently, we will only demonstrate how to calculate the error associated with a Type I forecast.

To further understand the distinction between a Type I and a Type II forecast, consider the following two models:

$$Y(T) = \beta_1 + \beta_2 X_2(T) + \epsilon \tag{5.1}$$

$$Y(T) = \beta_1 + \beta_2 X_2(T-1) + \epsilon \tag{5.2}$$

where Y is stock prices and X_2 is corporate profits. The T (in parentheses) refers to the present time period. In Equation (5.1) corporate profits in the current period are used to project stock prices in the same period. In Equation (5.2) corporate profits in the *preceding* period are used to project stock prices in the current period.

Now suppose we used Equation (5.1) to project stock prices in the $(T + 1)$ period. In order to do so, we would have to know the value for corporate profits in the $(T + 1)$ period. Obviously, we would have to guess or estimate corporate profits in the $(T + 1)$ period, and this would be an example of a Type II forecast.

Alternatively, we could use Equation (5.2) to project stock prices in the $(T + 1)$ period:

$$Y(T+1) = \beta_1 + \beta_2 X_2(T) + \epsilon$$

Since corporate profits are known with certainty in today's period (T), this would be a Type I forecast. Because values for the independent variable(s) must be estimated, the error associated with a Type II forecast is considerably greater than that of a Type I forecast. For this reason, it is often desirable to specify models with lags, as in Equation (5.2). We will further discuss regression models with lags in the next chapter.

It is frequently useful to test a model's ability to forecast by comparing the actual values of the dependent variable with the forecasted values. To do so, we must know the actual values in the forecast period. Such a forecast period is termed *ex post*. This is illustrated in Figure 5.1. $T(1)$ to $T(2)$ is the period

$T(1)$ to $T(2)$	Model Estimation Period
$T(2)$ to $T(3)$ Present	Ex Post Forecast
$T(3)$ to $T(4)$ Future	Ex Ante Forecast

figure 5.1. Ex Post Versus Ex Ante Forecast

over which the model is estimated, and $T(3)$ is the present time period. The *ex post* forecast period is from $T(2)$ to $T(3)$. An *ex post* may be distinguished from an *ex ante* forecast in that the latter is a forecast to some future date from the present—$T(3)$ to $T(4)$ in Figure 5.1. The accuracy of an *ex post* forecast may be measured by calculating the *root-mean-square* (RMS) error. The RMS error will be discussed later in this chapter.

estimating the error of a Type I forecast—the two-variable case

Reconsider the model presented in the preceding chapter in which consumption is the dependent variable and disposable income the independent variable. This model was estimated using time-series data for the years 1951 to 1970 (see Table 4.7). The least squares regression equation is

$$Y(T) = 5.17 + .9X_2(T) \tag{5.3}$$

Since Equation (5.3) is of the form of Equation (5.1), we cannot use this model to make a Type I forecast. Alternatively, suppose the data are used to estimate a model of the form of Equation (5.2). Because disposable income is lagged (one year), we would be able to use this model to make a Type I forecast.

The lagged data are presented in Table 5.1 and the regression results in Demo 5.1. Note that one observation is lost in the lagging process.

The R^2 in Demo 5.1 is quite high (.999) and equal to that of the unlagged model. However, the estimated regression coefficients of the lagged model are markedly different from those of the unlagged model, suggesting that the relationship between lagged disposable income and consumption is also quite different from that of the unlagged model.

Now suppose we wish to use our lagged model to forecast consumption in the year 1971. Referring to Figure 5.1, it can be seen that this would be an *ex post* forecast, since 1971 is beyond the range of the estimation period (1951–70), but not into the future. In order to forecast consumption in 1971, we need to know the value for disposable income in 1970. From Table 4.7 this value is

table 5.1. Disposable Income (X_2) and Consumption Data (Y) Lagged One Year (Billions of Current Dollars)

$X_2(T-1)$	$Y(T)$
226.6	216.7
238.3	230.0
252.6	236.5
257.4	254.4
275.3	266.7
293.2	281.4
308.5	290.1
318.8	311.2
337.3	325.2
350.0	335.2
364.4	355.1
385.3	375.0
404.6	401.2
438.1	432.8
473.2	466.3
511.9	492.1
546.3	535.8
591.2	577.5
631.6	616.8

```
REGRESSION COEFFICIENTS
-7.54109
 .991489

STD. ERROR OF ESTIMATE= 4.70358
SE(B 1 )= 3.593               T 1 =-2.09883
SE(B 2 )= .903805E-2          T 2 =  109.702
R SQUARED= .998589
ADJUSTED R SQUARED= .998506
F= 12034.5
DEGREES OF FREEDOM= 17
DW= 2.13909
CORRELATION MATRIX
 1 .999294
 .999294 1
```

demo 5.1. Regression of Consumption on Disposable Income Lagged One Year

$684.7 billion. Our forecast can be calculated by using the estimated regression coefficients in Demo 5.1 and substituting into the equation

$$\hat{Y}(T+1) = B_1 + B_2 X_2(T) \tag{5.4}$$

where the hat over Y means "estimated." Therefore:

$$\hat{Y}(1971) = -7.54109 + .991489(684.7) = 671.33$$

Our forecast of $671.33 billions of consumption for 1971 is termed a "point forecast." As was done in the preceding chapter with respect to the individual regression coefficients, a confidence interval can be constructed around this point forecast and is termed an *interval forecast*. In order to construct an interval forecast, we must have knowledge of the forecast error (f), which is defined as

$$f(T+1) = \hat{Y}(T+1) - Y(T+1) \tag{5.5}$$

where $Y(T+1)$ is the actual value of Y in the $(T+1)$ period.

It can be proven that the expected value of the forecast error, f, is equal to zero:

$$E(f) = 0 \tag{5.6}$$

Thus, our point forecast is an unbiased estimator of the actual value, $Y(T+1)$. Equation (5.6) holds regardless of whether the population parameters, β_1 and β_2, are known with certainty.

However, the variance of the forecast error, $\sigma_f{}^2$, depends on whether or not β_1 and β_2 are known with certainty. If β_1 and β_2 are known with certainty, it can be proven that the forecast error variance is equal to the variance of the disturbance term of the regression equation:

$$\sigma_f{}^2 = \sigma^2 \tag{5.7}$$

You may remember from the preceding chapter that the estimator of σ^2 is s^2, where s is the "standard error of estimate." Therefore:

$$\hat{\sigma}_f{}^2 = s^2 \tag{5.8}$$

It can be proven that the estimator, $\hat{\sigma}_f{}^2$, of the forecast error variance is the minimum possible among all linear estimators.

From Demo 5.1 the standard error of estimate, s, is equal to 4.70. The critical T value at the .05 level for seventeen degrees of freedom is 2.11. A .95 interval forecast may be constructed by multiplying 2.11 by 4.70, and then adding and subtracting this result from the point forecast of 671.33:

$$4.70 \times 2.11 = 9.92$$

$$671.33 - 9.92 = 661.41$$

$$671.33 + 9.92 = 681.25$$

Therefore:

$$661.41 < Y(T+1) < 681.25 \tag{5.9}$$

The interpretation of the interval in Equation (5.9) is that there is a .95 probability that the actual Y value (when observed) will lie within the interval of \$661.41 to \$681.25 billion. This concept is illustrated in Figure 5.2.

Only rarely are β_1 and β_2 known with certainty. Equation (5.8) can be adjusted to account for the fact that β_1 and β_2 normally must be estimated:

$$\hat{\sigma}_f^2 = s^2\left[1 + \frac{1}{N} + \frac{(X_T - \bar{X})^2}{\sum x^2}\right] \tag{5.10}$$

where N is the number of observations in the estimated period (19 in the above example), X_T is the particular value used to predict Y (684.7), and $\sum x^2$ is the sum of the squared deviations of X about the mean $\bar{X}$ in the estimated period. Although $\sum x^2$ is not printed out in Demo 5.1, this value is 270,837, $\bar{X}$ is equal to 379.189. One of the computer exercises presents a program that calculates the forecast error for both the two-variable and multiple regression models.

Examination of Equation (5.10) reveals that the variance of the forecast error, when β_1 and β_2 are not known with certainty, is affected by three factors in addition to s^2:

1. N, the number of observations in the estimated period. The larger the sample size in the estimated period, the smaller the variance of the forecast error, and consequently our forecast becomes more precise. Thus, as N approaches infinity, the $1/N$ term approaches zero or vanishes.
2. The distance X_T is from $\bar{X}$. The closer X_T is to $\bar{X}$, the smaller the variance of the forecast error. If X_T is equal to $\bar{X}$, the $(X_T - \bar{X})^2$ term is equal to zero. Intuitively, this means that the closer the forecast period is to our immediate experience (the estimated period), the more precise our forecast will be. Thus, large error can result by attempting to forecast too far into the future.

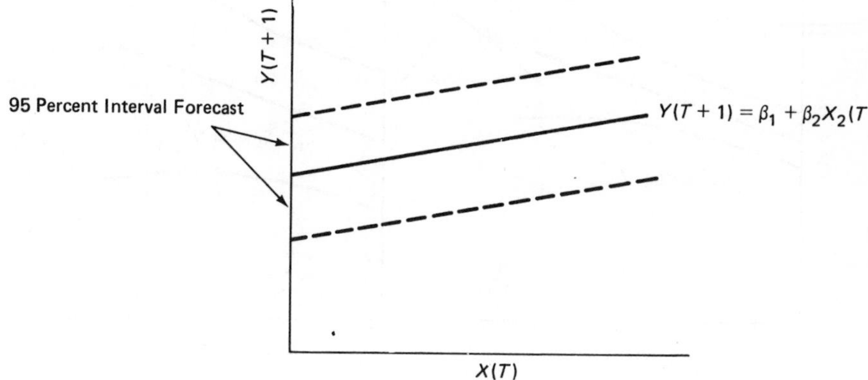

figure 5.2. Forecast Interval When Parameters Are Known with Certainty

3. The variance of X. In the extreme case in which X does not vary at all ($\sum x^2 = 0$), the forecast error variance is infinite. Intuitively, this means that since X does not change, X cannot be used to forecast a changing Y.

The first two factors are illustrated in Figure 5.3. The top half of the figure shows that the width of the forecast interval increases as X_T lies farther from $\bar{X}$. The bottom half shows that the width of the forecast interval decreases as N increases. The fact that the forecast interval widens the farther X_T lies from $\bar{X}$ can also be seen from the data presented in Table 5.2. For example, given an X_T value for disposable income of $700 billion, the forecast error variance

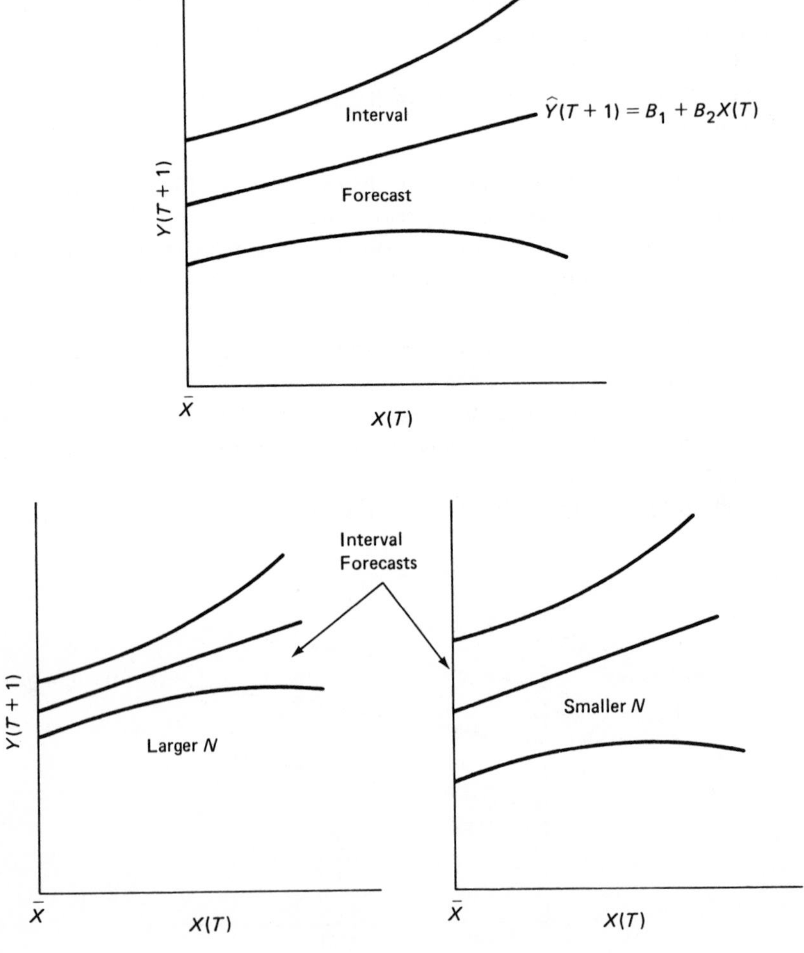

figure 5.3. Illustration of Equation (5.10)

table 5.2. Forecast Error Variance for Particular Values of X_T from \$700 to \$900 Billion

X_T	$\hat{\sigma}_f^2$
\$700	31.70
720	32.78
740	33.92
760	35.13
780	36.41
800	37.75
820	39.16
840	40.63
860	42.17
880	43.78
900	45.44

is 31.70, while an X_T value of \$900 billion leads to a forecast error variance of 45.44. The reader is encouraged to check on the accuracy of the numbers presented in this table by substituting the given values into Equation (5.10). It should also be pointed out that the same principle applies if we are attempting to forecast a value of less than $\bar{X}$. In Figure 5.4 the forecast interval is at its narrowest where $X_T = \bar{X}$.

We are now prepared to construct a forecast interval around our point forecast of \$671.33 billion. Substituting into Equation (5.10):

$$\hat{\sigma}_f^2 = (4.7)^2\left[1 + \frac{1}{19} + \frac{(684.7 - 379.189)^2}{270{,}837}\right] = 30.86$$

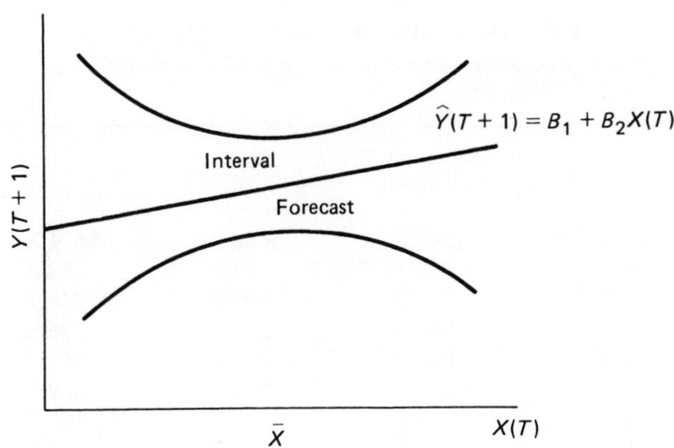

figure 5.4. Interval Forecast over Entire Range of $X(T)$

Therefore:

$$\hat{\sigma}_f = \sqrt{30.86} = 5.55$$

and

$$5.55 \times 2.11 = 11.71$$
$$671.33 - 11.71 = 659.62$$
$$671.33 + 11.71 = 683.04$$

The forecast interval (.95 probability level) is

$$659.62 < Y(T + 1) < 683.04 \tag{5.11}$$

Comparing this forecast interval with that in Equation (5.9), we see that the use of Equation (5.10) instead of (5.8) has added about \$4 billion to the width of the interval. Except in the rare circumstance when β_1 and β_2 are known with certainty, Equation (5.10) should be used in calculating the error of a Type I forecast.

RMS error

Suppose that we use our model to forecast consumption for each year over the period 1971–78. Referring to Figure 5.1, it can be seen that this is an *ex post* forecast, since the 1971–78 time period is beyond the estimation period but not into the future. By comparing the actual (Y) with the forecasted values ($\hat{Y}$), some notion of the reliability of the model can be gained. For example, our point forecast of \$671.3 billion (rounded) for the year 1971 can be compared with an actual value of \$668.2 billion (Table 5.3). This represents an error of \$3.1 billion, or only about 0.5 percent.

table 5.3. Disposable Income, Consumption (Y), and Forecasted Consumption ($\hat{Y}$) for the Period 1971–78 (Billions)

	Disposable Income	Y	$\hat{Y}$
1971	\$742.8	\$668.2	\$671.3
1972	801.3	733.0	728.9
1973	901.7	809.9	786.9
1974	984.6	889.6	886.5
1975	1,086.7	979.1	968.7
1976	1,184.5	1,089.9	1,069.9
1977	1,305.1	1,210.0	1,166.9
1978	1,458.4	1,350.8	1,286.5

A commonly used measure of the accuracy of an *ex post* forecast is the root-mean-square (RMS) error, which is defined by the equation

$$\text{RMS error} = \sqrt{\frac{1}{N}\Sigma(\hat{Y} - Y)^2} \tag{5.12}$$

where N is the number of periods in the *ex post* forecast period. N is equal to eight in the example given in Table 5.3. The RMS error is an absolute measure. A useful relative measure is the *RMS proportional error*, which is defined as

$$\text{RMS proportional error} = \sqrt{\frac{1}{N}\Sigma\left(\frac{\hat{Y} - Y}{Y}\right)^2} \tag{5.13}$$

If the RMS porportional error is multiplied by 100, the result is the *RMS percent error*. These various error concepts are calculated in Table 5.4. Thus, the RMS error is \$29.7 billion, the RMS proportional error is .025, and the RMS percent error is 2.5. It is interesting that the error (—64.3) is greatest for the 1978 forecast, the period furthest away from the estimation period. This is in accordance with Equation (5.10).

table 5.4. Calculation of RMS Error

	$\hat{Y} - Y$	$(\hat{Y} - Y)^2$	$\left(\frac{\hat{Y} - Y}{Y}\right)^2$
1971	3.1	9.61	.00002
1972	−4.1	16.81	.00003
1973	−23.0	529.00	.00080
1974	−3.1	9.61	.00001
1975	−10.4	108.16	.00011
1976	−20.0	400.00	.00034
1977	−43.1	1,857.61	.00127
1978	−64.3	4,134.49	.00227
		7,065.29	.00485

$$\text{RMS error} = \sqrt{7{,}065.29/8} = \$29.7 \text{ billion}$$

$$\text{RMS proportional error} = \sqrt{.00485/8} = .025$$

$$\text{RMS percent error} = .025 \times 100 = 2.5\%$$

estimating the error of a Type I forecast—the general case

Because the same principles apply in the two-variable case as in the general case of multiple regression, the two-variable case is convenient for expositional purposes. However, as explained in the preceding chapter, the two-variable case is too limited for most practical applications. Consequently, we extend our analysis to multiple regression in this section. In doing so, we make use of the matrix notation developed in Chapter 4.

Reconsider the human capital model presented in Chapter 4:

$$Y = \beta_1 + \beta_2 X_2 + \beta_3 X_3 + \epsilon \tag{5.14}$$

where Y is income, X_2 is IQ, and X_3 is years of education. The estimating equation is

$$\hat{Y} = -7628.13 + 85.04X_2 + 669.99X_3 \tag{5.15}$$

Suppose we wish to use Equation (5.15) to predict the income of a particular individual given his IQ and education. Because IQ and education are known and need not be estimated (the model was estimated with cross-section, not time-series, data), Equation (5.15) can be used to make a Type I forecast. For example, if an individual has an IQ of 140 and twenty years of education, the point forecast of income is

$$\hat{Y} = -7628.13 + 85.04(140) + 669.99(20) = \$17{,}677$$

In order to construct an interval forecast around this point forecast, the forecast error variance, σ_f^2, must be estimated. In the two-variable case, Equation (5.10) served this purpose. The following equation provides an estimate of σ_f^2 in the general case of any number of variables:

$$\hat{\sigma}_f^2 = s^2(1 + \tilde{X}(X'X)^{-1}\tilde{X}') \tag{5.16}$$

where $\tilde{X}$, $(X'X)^{-1}$, and $\tilde{X}'$ are matrices as defined below. The proof of Equation (5.16) can be found in more-advanced textbooks.[2]

The expression $(X'X)^{-1}$ was presented in Chapter 4:

$$(X'X)^{-1} = \begin{matrix} 11.13160227 & -.13450820 & .24589466 \\ -.13450820 & .00194243 & -.00556712 \\ .24589466 & -.00556712 & .02730644 \end{matrix}$$

$\tilde{X}$ is a one-row-by-K-column matrix in which the first element is one (representing the constant term) and the other elements are the observations on the independent variables. Remember that K is equal to the number of variables in the model. Therefore, $\tilde{X}$ is

$$\tilde{X} = 1 \quad 140 \quad 20$$

$\tilde{X}'$ is the transpose matrix:

[2]See R. S. Pindyck and D. L. Rubinfeld, *Econometric Models and Econometric Forecasts* (New York: McGraw-Hill, 1976), pp. 181–85.

$$\begin{matrix} 1 \\ 140 \\ 20 \end{matrix}$$

Multiplying these three matrices as specified in Equation (5.16), the result is a scalar or single number:

$$\tilde{X}(X'X)^{-1}\tilde{X}' = .1076$$

Therefore:

$$\hat{\sigma}_f^2 = (863.63)^2(1 + .1076) = 826{,}111$$

or

$$\hat{\sigma}_f = \sqrt{826{,}111} = 908.91$$

The critical T value at the .05 level with $N - K(7)$ degrees of freedom is 2.365. We can now construct the desired forecast interval around the point forecast of \$17,677:

$$908.91 \times 2.365 = 2{,}150$$
$$17{,}677 - 2{,}150 = 15{,}527$$
$$17{,}677 + 2{,}150 = 19{,}827$$

The forecast interval is therefore:

$$\$15{,}527 < Y < \$19{,}827 \tag{5.17}$$

Given an individual with an IQ of 140 and twenty years of education, we are 95 percent confident that this person's income will lie between \$15,527 and \$19,827.

It is interesting to examine how the square root of the forecast error variance ($\hat{\sigma}_f$) differs as the values of X lie farther and farther from their means. We know from Chapter 4 that the mean of IQ is 104.5 and the mean of education is 12.3. The square root of the forecast error variance is presented for selected X values in Table 5.5. As can easily be seen, the minimum variance for these selected

table 5.5. $\hat{\sigma}_f$ for Selected X Values

	X_2 (IQ)	X_3 (Education)	$\hat{\sigma}_f$
	80	9	1001.62
	90	10	809.97
	100	11	682.60
Mean:	104.5	12.3	642.24
	120	14	686.36
	130	15	842.25
	135	17	859.48
	140	20	908.91

X values occurs at the mean values of X: $\hat{\sigma}_f = 642.24$. Thus, the closer the X values to their means, the greater the confidence we can have in our forecast.

summary

Possibly the most important practical application of econometric theory is forecasting. Confronted with uncertainty, policy makers can make decisions using the forecasting techniques discussed in this chapter. *Uncertainty* is defined in terms of the *forecast error*, or the difference between the forecasted and the actual value of the dependent variable.

By substituting the given values of the independent variables into the estimated regression equation, a *point forecast* can be constructed. The estimated forecast error variance can then be used to calculate a *forecast interval* around this point forecast. Examination of the point and forecast intervals allows policy makers to determine the likely impact of alternative courses of action.

If the independent variables are known with certainty (Type I forecast), estimation of the forecast error variance, σ_f^2, is a straightforward procedure. In contrast, estimation of σ_f^2 when the independent variables are not known with certainty (Type II forecast) is difficult, if not impossible. Consequently, specification of time-series models that contain lags is often advantageous if these models are to be later used for purposes of forecasting. The subject of lags is considered in the next chapter.

If the population parameters are known with certainty, the estimator of σ_f^2 is s^2, the square of the standard error of estimate. But in the more usual case in which the parameters are estimated, s^2 is adjusted by certain factors: (1) the number of observations in the estimated period, (2) the distances the values of the independent variables are from their means, and (3) the variances of the independent variables. The result is an estimated forecast error variance greater than s^2, the difference depending on the magnitude of these factors.

The reliability of a forecasting model may be judged by comparing the forecasted with the actual values. A useful absolute measure is the *RMS error*, which indicates how well a model performs during an *ex post* time period. A relative measure is the *RMS proportional* or *RMS percent* error.

We closed the chapter by demonstrating how the forecast error variance is calculated in the general case, and noting that the same principles apply as in the two-variable case. For example, the farther the values of the independent variables from their means, the larger the forecast error. Consequently, we cannot have much confidence in forecasts that are far into the future. Nor can we have much confidence in forecasts based on models estimated with small samples. If policy makers carefully consider its inherent errors, forecasting can be a valuable tool in making decisions.

examples

example 1

From Table 5.3 the point forecast of consumption for 1978 is $1,286.5 billion. The 1977 value for disposable income which was used to make this forecast is $1,305.1 billion. Calculate the forecast error variance, $\hat{\sigma}_f^2$.

From Equation (5.10):

$$\hat{\sigma}_f^2 = (4.7)^2\left[1 + \frac{1}{19} + \frac{(1305.1 - 379.189)^2}{270{,}837}\right]$$

$$= 93.16$$

or

$$\hat{\sigma}_f = 9.65$$

example 2

$(X'X)^{-1}$ for the consumption-income (lagged) model is

$$(X'X)^{-1} = \begin{matrix} .58352200 & -.00140007 \\ -.00140007 & .00000369 \end{matrix}$$

(Note that the inverse matrix is accurate to eight digits because rounding can lead to a big error when matrices are multiplied by each other.) Use Equation (5.16) to derive the result in Example 1.

$$\tilde{X}(X'X)^{-1} = -1.2437094 \quad .00341575$$

$$\tilde{X}(X'X)^{-1}\tilde{X}' = 3.214$$

$$\hat{\sigma}_f^2 = (4.7)^2(1 + 3.214) = 93.09$$

or

$$\hat{\sigma}_f = 9.65$$

example 3

Construct an interval forecast around the point forecast of $1,286.5 billion of consumption for the year 1978. Do so for both the .95 and .99 probability levels and interpret your results.

The critical T value with 17 degrees of freedom at the .95 level is 2.11, and the value at the .99 level is 2.898.

$$2.11 \times 9.65 = 20.4$$

$$1{,}286.5 - 20.4 = 1{,}266.1$$

$$1{,}286.5 + 20.4 = 1{,}306.9$$

Therefore, the forecast interval at the .95 level is

$$1{,}266.1 < Y(1978) < 1{,}306.9$$

$$2.898 \times 9.65 = 28.0$$

$$1{,}286.5 - 28.0 = 1{,}258.5$$

$$1{,}286.5 + 28.0 = 1{,}314.5$$

Therefore, the forecast interval at the .99 level is

$$1{,}258.5 < Y(1978) < 1{,}314.5$$

We are 95 percent confident that the interval of $1,266.1 to $1,306.9 billion contains the actual Y value, and 99 percent confident that the interval of $1,258.5 to $1,314.5 billion contains the actual Y value. Note that the interval at the .99 level is wider. Since we have greater confidence at this level, this is the expected result. From Table 5.3 it can be seen that the actual Y value is $1,350.8 billion, which does not lie in either of the intervals constructed. It appears that 1978 may lie too far from the estimation period (1951–70) to use our forecasting model with any degree of accuracy.

exercises

1. Many economists theorize that inflation is caused by excess money creation. Although there is wide disagreement as to the length of the lag, the following model might be used to test this theory:

$$\text{Model I:} \quad Y(T) = \beta_1 + \beta_2 X_2(T-1) + \epsilon$$

where Y = Consumer Price Index (CPI)

X_2 = money supply (M_1)

Estimate this model with the following monthly data for 1976, and interpret your results.

Month/Year	CPI (1967 = 100)	M_1 (billions)
1/76	166.7	$301.0
2/76	167.1	292.9
3/76	167.5	295.3
4/76	168.2	303.5
5/76	169.2	298.5
6/76	170.1	302.5
7/76	171.1	305.2
8/76	171.9	303.1
9/76	172.6	304.4
10/76	173.3	309.3
11/76	173.8	312.3
12/76	174.3	321.3

2. An alternative to Model I is one that puts the emphasis on government budget policy, as opposed to monetary policy:

$$\text{Model II:}\quad Y(T) = \beta_1 + \beta_2 X_2(T-1) + \epsilon$$

where Y = CPI (same as Model I)

X_2 = government budget surplus or deficit

Estimate this model with data on the government deficit or surplus, and interpret your results.

Month/Year	Deficit or Surplus (millions)
1/76	\$−5,091
2/76	−8,987
3/76	−8,623
4/76	872
5/76	−5,731
6/76	7,048
7/76	−11,247
8/76	−2,211
9/76	757
10/76	−12,981
11/76	−7,385
12/76	−2,419

3. One test of a model is its ability to forecast. Using both Models I and II, forecast the CPI for January 1977. Construct .95 confidence intervals around your point forecasts. Interpret your results.

4. You have the following monthly data for 1977. Calculate the RMS error, RMS proportional error, and RMS percent error for both Models I and II. Use the parameter estimates obtained from Exercises 1 and 2. Interpret your results.

Month/Year	CPI	M_1 (billions)	Deficit or Surplus (millions)
1/77	175.3	319.7	\$−2,664
2/77	177.1	309.9	−6,554
3/77	178.2	312.4	−9,475
4/77	179.6	322.3	4,469
5/77	180.6	315.5	−6,043
6/77	181.8	321.4	10,194
7/77	182.6	372.2	−8,678
8/77	183.3	325.2	−5,044
9/77	184.0	328.2	1,545
10/77	184.5	332.5	−14,663
11/77	185.4	335.3	−9,269
12/77	186.1	344.9	−4,852

computer exercises

1. You theorize that both the money supply and government budget policy may have an impact on inflation, and you decide to test the model:

$$\text{Model III:}\quad Y = \beta_1 + \beta_2 X_2(T-1) + \beta_3 X_3(T-1) + \epsilon$$

where Y = Consumer Price Index (CPI)

X_2 = money supply (M_1)

X_3 = government deficit or surplus

Estimate this model with the 1976 data presented in Exercises 1 and 2, and interpret the results. The computer program presented in Chapter 4 for the solution of a multiple regression equation should be used. Because you will need the inverse matrix, $(X'X)^{-1}$, for a later exercise, the following two statements should be added to this program:

```
413 PRINT "INVERSE MATRIX"
415 MAT PRINT D;
```

2. Calculate a point forecast for the CPI for January 1977 (Model III) and construct a forecast interval around this point forecast at the .95 level. The program in Demo 5.2 will calculate the forecast error variance and its square root. At Statement 230 the inverse matrix is input row by row. More than one DATA statement may be used if needed. Statements 10 and 20 explain how to dimension Statement 30. This program is run on the income-IQ-education example presented in this chapter. Note that the standard error of estimate, the number of variables, and the values of X are input (after the question marks) while the program is running.

```
 10 REM K=NUMBER OF VARIABLES
 20 REM AT ST.30 IS DIM D(K,K),F(1,K),G(K,1),H(1,K)
 30 DIM D(3,3),F(1,3),G(3,1),H(1,3)
 35 DIM T(1,1)
 40 PRINT "STD. ERROR OF ESTIMATE"
 50 INPUT S
 60 PRINT "NUMBER OF VARIABLES"
 70 INPUT K
 80 FOR I=1 TO K
 90 FOR J=1 TO K
100 READ D(I,J)
110 NEXT J
120 NEXT I
130 LET F(1,1)=1
135 PRINT "VALUES OF X"
140 FOR I=2 TO K
150 INPUT F(1,I)
```

demo 5.2. Program for Calculating Forecast Error Variance

```
160 NEXT I
170 MAT G=TRN(F)
180 MAT H=F*D
190 MAT T=H*G
200 LET X=T(1,1)
205 LET V=(S**2)*(1+X)
210 PRINT "FORECAST ERROR VARIANCE=";V
220 PRINT "SQUARE ROOT OF ERROR VARIANCE=";SQR(V)
230 DATA 11.1316,-.1345,.2459,-.1345,.0019,-.0056,.2459,-.0056,.0273
250 END

RUN
STD. ERROR OF ESTIMATE
? 863.63
NUMBER OF VARIABLES
? 3
VALUES OF X
? 140
? 20
FORECAST ERROR VARIANCE= 826111
SQUARE ROOT OF ERROR VARIANCE= 908.906
```

demo 5.2 Continued

3. The inverse matrix was rounded in Demo 5.2. Does it make a difference if the inverse matrix is not rounded?

4. With the 1977 set of data presented in Exercise 4 above, calculate the RMS error for Model III. Demo 5.3 may be used for this purpose. The forecasted and actual values for each time period are input into the program at Statements 140 and 150 (see Table 5.3). The number of time periods in the *ex post* forecast period is input after the first question mark. The error for each time period, along with the RMS error, RMS proportional error, and RMS percent error, is output by the program.

```
5REM Y=ACTUAL, F=FORECASTED
10PRINT "N="
20INPUT N
30DIM Y(100),F(100)
35PRINT "ERROR FOR EACH TIME PERIOD"
40FOR I=1 TO N
50READ Y(I),F(I)
60LET S=S+(Y(I)-F(I))**2
70PRINT F(I)- Y(I)
80LET S1=S1+((F(I)-Y(I))/Y(I))**2
90NEXT I
100LET R=SQR(S/N)
110LET R1=SQR(S1/N)
120PRINT "RMS ERROR=";R
```

demo 5.3. Program for Calculating RMS Error

```
125PRINT "RMS PROPORTIONAL ERROR=";R1
130PRINT "RMS PERCENT ERROR=";R1*100
140DATA 668.2,671.3,733,728.9,809.9,786.9,889.6,886.5,979.1,968.7
150DATA 1089.9,1069.9,1210,1166.9,1350.8,1286.5
160END
RUN
N=
? 8
ERROR FOR EACH TIME PERIOD
 3.1
-4.1
-23
-3.1
-10.4
-20
-43.1
-64.3
RMS ERROR= 29.718
RMS PROPORTIONAL ERROR= .246365E-1
RMS PERCENT ERROR= 2.46365
```

demo 5.3 Continued

6

the importance of time and lags in a regression model

dynamic relationships

The real world is very different from the static models presented in introductory economics textbooks. Since many, if not most, economic relationships are dynamic—that is, they involve time—it is important to understand how economists take account of the time factor in their models. In this chapter we discuss two types of dynamic models—distributed lag and autoregressive, and in Chapter 8 we examine simulation models.

Even in introductory economics, although not explicitly, students learn of the importance of lags when studying the multiplier concept with respect to the two-variable consumption-income model: $Y = \alpha + \beta X + \epsilon$, where Y is consumption and X is income. The multiplier measures the impact of a change in investment or government spending on income and is derived from the marginal propensity to consume (MPC), which measures the change in consumption resulting from a one-dollar change in income. For example, if the MPC is .75, a once and for all change in investment of \$1.00 can have a multiplier impact on income equal to as much as \$4.00. But it is never assumed that this change of \$4.00 occurs instantaneously, and therefore the concept of a time lag is implicit. Consequently, in the first period, income rises by \$1.00; in the second, by \$0.75 ($.75 \times 1$); in the third, by \$0.56 ($.75 \times .75$); in the fourth, by \$0.42 ($.75 \times .56$); and so on. The sum of the changes for all the periods is equal to \$4.00. The changes in income in each time period given an MPC of .5 and .9 are shown in Demo 6.1. The multiplier process is carried out over twenty-five time periods

```
         1 TIME= 1
         .5 TIME= 2
         .25 TIME= 3
         .125 TIME= 4
         .0625 TIME= 5
         .03125 TIME= 6
         .015625 TIME= 7
         .78125E-2 TIME= 8
         .390625E-2 TIME= 9
         .195313E-2 TIME= 10
         .976563E-3 TIME= 11
         .488281E-3 TIME= 12
MPC=.5   .244141E-3 TIME= 13
         .12207E-3 TIME= 14
         .610352E-4 TIME= 15
         .305176E-4 TIME= 16
         .152588E-4 TIME= 17
         .762939E-5 TIME= 18
         .38147E-5 TIME= 19
         .190735E-5 TIME= 20
         .953674E-6 TIME= 21
         .476837E-6 TIME= 22
         .238419E-6 TIME= 23
         .119209E-6 TIME= 24
         .596046E-7 TIME= 25
         TOTAL CHANGE IN INCOME= 2

         1 TIME= 1
         .9 TIME= 2
         .81 TIME= 3
         .729 TIME= 4
         .6561 TIME= 5
         .59049 TIME= 6
         .531441 TIME= 7
         .478297 TIME= 8
         .430467 TIME= 9
         .387421 TIME= 10
         .348679 TIME= 11
         .313811 TIME= 12
MPC=.9   .28243 TIME= 13
         .254187 TIME= 14
         .228768 TIME= 15
         .205891 TIME= 16
         .185302 TIME= 17
         .166772 TIME= 18
         .150095 TIME= 19
         .135085 TIME= 20
         .121577 TIME= 21
         .109419 TIME= 22
         .984772E-1 TIME= 23
         .886295E-1 TIME= 24
         .797665E-1 TIME= 25
         TOTAL CHANGE IN INCOME= 9.2821
```

demo 6.1. Demonstration of Importance of Time in Multiplier Process

and the total is printed out for each MPC. The equation for the multiplier that gives the maximum possible increase in income is 1/(1 − MPC).

As the MPC increases, the number of time periods required to reach the maximum possible change in income also increases because people are spending a higher portion of their income at each stage, thereby keeping the multiplier process going for a longer period of time. Thus, for an MPC of .9, one would expect a total increase in income of $10.00, but after twenty-five time periods, the increase is only $9.28. In contrast, for an MPC of .5, the multiplier process has completely worked itself out after twenty-five periods (total change in income = 2).

Since an infinite number of time periods might be required, it is unrealistic to assume that the multiplier process will reach its limit at 1/(1 − MPC). It is also unrealistic to assume, as many introductory textbooks do, that the multiplier impact in each period is equal. It therefore makes sense to introduce the concept of a time lag into the regression model. Economics is a social science, and as such it deals with human decisions that are often slow in the making. The concepts of *short run* and *long run* are at the heart of many economic theories. For example, an increase in the price of gasoline may have little effect on consumption of gasoline in the short run because people have committed themselves to a particular car and life style of driving to work separately. But in the long run they can buy a more efficient car and form car pools. Thus, the long-run price elasticity of demand for gasoline exceeds its short-run elasticity.

Business decisions are also characterized in terms of the short and long runs. Moore defines *short run* as ". . . the period of time long enough to permit suppliers to vary their output within limits of their existing capacity, but too short to permit them to vary the size of their plants or to enter or leave the industry," and he defines *long run* as ". . . a period of time long enough that firms are able to change the size of their existing plants and to enter or leave the industry. In the long run, supply is much more elastic than in the short run."[1] Implicit in this analysis is some notion of the dynamics of technological change. That is, a major determinant of the optimum plant size is the existing state of technology, and the desire to alter the production process in some way can lead to innovations and inventions.

distributed lag models

Accepting the importance of a time lag in economic theory, let us proceed to revise the consumption-income model so that it contains a time lag. Suppose that we have quarterly data (*I*–53 to *I*–70) on consumption and disposable income (deflated by a price index), and furthermore we hypothesize that an income change in this period will not have any impact on consumption beyond

[1] Basil J. Moore, *An Introduction to Modern Economic Theory* (New York: Free Press, 1973), pp. 160–61.

four quarters. Our model is then

$$Y_t = \alpha + \beta_0 X_t + \beta_1 X_{t-1} + \beta_2 X_{t-2} + \beta_3 X_{t-3} + \beta_4 X_{t-4} + \epsilon_t \qquad (6.1)$$

where Y_t is consumption in the present time period, α is the constant term, X_t is disposable income in the present period, X_{t-1} is disposable income in the previous period, and so forth. Equation (6.1) is termed a *distributed lag* model, since its independent variables represent only current and lagged values of the explanatory variable, income. The *short-run MPC* is defined as β_0, and the *long-run MPC* as the sum of the coefficients on the present and lagged values of the explanatory variable: $\beta_0 + \beta_1 + \beta_2 + \beta_3 + \beta_4$. The regression run for this equation is shown in Demo 6.2. Rounding off, the constant term is 54.62, and the MPCs with the associated time period in parentheses are .67(0), —.032(1), .025(2), —.060(3), and .036(4). The long-run impact on consumption of a $1 change in income is equal to the sum of these coefficients: $.639.

Only the constant term and B_0 are statistically significant, but the reader should be able to discover the problem immediately by examining the correlation matrix. The data used to estimate the model suffer from serious multi-

```
REGRESSION COEFFICIENTS
 54.6172
 .665955
-.322876E-1
 .246582E-1
-.595703E-1
 .361328E-1

STD. ERROR OF ESTIMATE= 5.62155
SE(A)= 3.41661              T(A)= 15.9858
SE(B0)= .160512             T(B0)= 4.14893
SE(B1)= .286941             T(B1)=-.112524
SE(B2)= .295196             T(B2)= .835315E-1
SE(B3)= .286985             T(B3)=-.207573
SE(B4)= .167124             T(B4)= .216203

R SQUARED= .993651
ADJUSTED R SQUARED= .993113
F= 1846.82
DEGREES OF FREEDOM= 59
DW= .22577
CORRELATION MATRIX

1        .997294  .996075  .993862  .991265  .988884
.997294  1        .998913  .996777  .994242  .991774
.996075  .998913  1        .99889   .996816  .994391
.993862  .996777  .99889   1        .998909  .996869
.991265  .994242  .996816  .998909  1        .99888
.988884  .991774  .994391  .996869  .99888   1
```

demo 6.2. Consumption-Income Distributed Lag Model

collinearity. Consequently, standard errors are large and T ratios small. Given such a situation, estimation of Equation (6.1) is impossible. Distributed lag models of this form also suffer from three other problems. First, there is no a priori way of knowing the maximum length of the lag. Second, as the length of the lag increases, the number of independent variables increases and the degrees of freedom are reduced. Finally, the creation of lagged variables reduces the number of observations available for estimation.

the Koyck model

One solution to the problem of estimating distributed lag models is to assume that the impact of the explanatory variable declines geometrically and the βs are all of the same sign:

$$\beta_K = \beta_0 L^K \qquad K = 0, 1, 2, 3, \ldots \quad 0 < L < 1 \tag{6.2}$$

Equation (6.2) is known as the *Koyck* model[2] and is illustrated in Figure 6.1. Thus, we need to know only β_0 and L in order to derive $\beta_1 \ldots \beta_K$. It can be proven that the following equation can be used to estimate β_0 and L. The derivation is given in Example 1.

$$Y_t = \alpha(1 - L) + \beta_0 X_t + LY_{t-1} + u_t \tag{6.3}$$

Equation (6.3) is termed an *autoregressive* model because a lagged value of the dependent variable (Y_{t-1}) appears on the right side of the equation. Note that

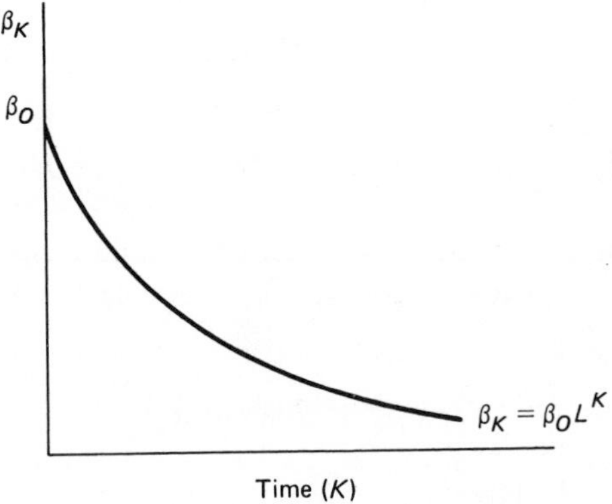

figure 6.1. Koyck Model

[2] L. M. Koyck, *Distributed Lags and Investment Analysis* (Amsterdam: North-Holland, 1954).

u_t is the error term. When this equation is estimated with the same consumption-income data as before (Demo 6.3), B_0 is equal to .078 and L is .889. L is sometimes termed the *rate of decline*, and $(1 - L)$, the *speed of adjustment*.

```
REGRESSION COEFFICIENTS
 5.25
 .778809E-1
 .88916

STD. ERROR OF ESTIMATE= 2.67364
SE(A)= 3.3709                 T(A)= 1.55745
SE(B0)= .374166E-1            T(B0)= 2.08145
SE(L)= .592824E-1             T(L)= 14.9987
R SQUARED= .998556
ADJUSTED R SQUARED= .998512
F= 22473.8
DEGREES OF FREEDOM= 65
DW= 1.56348
CORRELATION MATRIX
1   .996775   .99923
.996775   1   .996752
.99923   .996752   1
```

demo 6.3. Consumption-Income Autoregressive Model

The equation for the long-run impact or the sum of the Bs is given by

$$\sum_{K=0}^{\infty} B_K = B_0\left(\frac{1}{1-L}\right) \tag{6.4}$$

Substituting .078 (B_0) and .889 (L) into this equation, the long-run impact is equal to .7. The value of each B for twenty-five time periods is given in Demo 6.4.

the adaptive expectation model

The *adaptive expectation* model is another commonly used autoregressive model in which the independent variable takes on expected or optimum values. Consider the model

$$Y_t = \beta_0 + \beta_1 X_t^* + \epsilon_t \tag{6.5}$$

where Y = quantity demanded
X^* = expected price

Thus, people may buy more today if they expect prices to be higher in the future. Further suppose that expectations are a weighted average of present prices and

```
.078 TIME= 0
.069342 TIME= 1
.061645 TIME= 2
.548024E-1 TIME= 3
.487194E-1 TIME= 4
.433115E-1 TIME= 5
.385039E-1 TIME= 6
.03423 TIME= 7
.304305E-1 TIME= 8
.270527E-1 TIME= 9
.240498E-1 TIME= 10
.213830E-1 TIME= 11
.190071E-1 TIME= 12
.168973E-1 TIME= 13
.150217E-1 TIME= 14
.133543E-1 TIME= 15
.011872 TIME= 16
.105542E-1 TIME= 17
.938267E-2 TIME= 18
.834119E-2 TIME= 19
.741532E-2 TIME= 20
.659222E-2 TIME= 21
.586048E-2 TIME= 22
.520997E-2 TIME= 23
.463166E-2 TIME= 24
.411755E-2 TIME= 25

SUM OF B'S= .669725
```

demo 6.4. Koyck Model for $B_0 = .078$, $L = .889$

expectations in the previous period:

$$X_t^* = gX_t + (1 - g)X_{t-1}^* \tag{6.6}$$

where $0 \leq g \leq 1$. If $g = 0$, expectations do not change. If $g = 1$, expectations are always the same as present prices. Since these are extremes, one would expect g to lie between 0 and 1. As an example, the hypothetical data in Table 6.1 represent actual and expected prices for fifteen time periods where $g = .4$. The quantity demanded in each time period is also given.

Unfortunately, there is no way to observe the expected price data in Table 6.1; only actual prices are ever observed. Therefore, Equation (6.5) cannot be estimated in its present form. However, the following autoregressive equation can be used to estimate β_0, β_1, and g. The derivation is presented in Example 2.

$$Y_t = g\beta_0 + g\beta_1 X_t + (1 - g)Y_{t-1} + u_t \tag{6.7}$$

What is interesting about Equation (6.7) is that it has the same form as Equation (6.3), the equation for the Koyck model. When Equation (6.7) is estimated using

table 6.1. Hypothetical Price and Quantity Data

Time (t)	Price (X)	Expected Price (X^*)	Quantity (Y)
1	\$125	\$128	30.6
2	140	133	31.6
3	130	132	31.3
4	155	141	33.2
5	145	143	33.5
6	163	151	35.2
7	170	158	36.7
8	182	168	38.6
9	173	170	39.0
10	192	179	40.8
11	203	188	42.7
12	178	184	41.9
13	163	176	40.2
14	182	178	40.7
15	175	177	40.4

the data in Table 6.1 (Demo 6.5), $gB_0 = 1.96$, $gB_1 = .08$, and $(1 - g) = .60$. Therefore, $g = .4$, $B_0 = 4.9$, and $B_1 = .2$.

```
REGRESSION COEFFICIENTS
 1.95825
 .805855E-1
 .598679

STD. ERROR OF ESTIMATE= .347072E-1
SE(GB0)= .877992E-1          T 1 = 22.3038
SE(GB1)= .727918E-3          T 2 = 110.707
SE(1-G)= .348125E-2          T 3 = 171.972
R SQUARED= .999934
ADJUSTED R SQUARED= .999922
F= 83124.8
DEGREES OF FREEDOM= 11
DW= 2.96448
CORRELATION MATRIX
 1  .906692  .962411
 .906692  1  .758175
 .962411  .758175  1
```

demo 6.5. Adaptive Expectation Model

the stock adjustment model

In the adaptive expectation model, the independent variable takes on expected or optimum values. The reverse is true of the stock adjustment model. It is the dependent variable that takes on optimum values:

$$Y_t^* = \beta_0 + \beta_1 X_t + \epsilon \tag{6.8}$$

As an example, suppose that Y^* is the optimum level of capital, X is output, and today's capital stock is a weighted average of the desired capital stock and the capital stock in the previous period:

$$Y_t = pY_t^* + (1 - p)Y_{t-1} \tag{6.9}$$

where $0 \leq p \leq 1$. If $p = 0$, the capital stock never changes; and if $p = 1$, the capital stock always equals the desired capital stock—i.e., adjustment is immediate. As with the adaptive expectation model, p is expected to lie between these extremes. It can be proven that estimates of β_0, β_1, and p can be obtained by fitting the following equation. The derivation is given in Example 3.

$$Y_t = p\beta_0 + p\beta_1 X_t + (1 - p)Y_{t-1} + u_t \tag{6.10}$$

Thus, the stock adjustment model has the same mathematical form as the Koyck and adaptive expectation models.

There are serious statistical problems associated with the estimation of autoregressive models. One major assumption of the regression model is that the independent variables are nonstochastic and the dependent variable is stochastic. Obviously, Y_t (the dependent variable) and Y_{t-1} (an independent variable) represent the same variable. They cannot be both stochastic and nonstochastic.

Consequently, the autoregressive models discussed in this chapter contain a stochastic explanatory variable (Y_{t-1}). It can be proven that ordinary least squares (OLS) estimators are best linear unbiased estimators (BLUE) provided the stochastic explanatory variable is uncorrelated with the error term. Unfortunately, in both the Koyck and adaptive expectation models, Y_{t-1} is correlated with the error term. However, Y_{t-1} is not necessarily correlated with the error term in the stock adjustment model.

Autocorrelation can also be a serious problem in autoregressive models. It cannot be detected by the Durbin-Watson statistic (d) because the presence of Y_{t-1} as an explanatory variable causes d to be biased toward two. Durbin has developed a test for autocorrelation in autoregressive models, and the reader can refer to his article for an explanation.[3]

the Almon polynomial lag

The assumption of the Koyck model that the βs decline over time is overly restrictive and not necessarily realistic. An alternative developed by Almon[4] is to assume that the βs may follow patterns, as illustrated in Figure 6.2. Patterns

[3]J. Durbin, "Testing for Serial Correlation in Least-Squares Regression When Some of the Regressors Are Lagged Dependent Variables," *Econometrica*, 38 (1970), 410–21.

[4]S. Almon, "The Distributed Lag between Capital Appropriations and Expenditures," *Econometrica*, 33 (1965), 178–96.

such as those illustrated in this figure may be approximated by fitting a polynomial to these curves of the following form:

$$\beta_i = b_0 + b_1 i + b_2 i^2 + \cdots + b_p i^p \tag{6.11}$$

where p is the degree of the polynomial. The *length of the lag* may be defined as the number of βs excluding β_0 (see Equation (6.1)), and normally the degree of the polynomial is less than the length of the lag.

We will now demonstrate these concepts by using some concrete examples. Suppose that the lag is approximated by way of a second-degree polynomial ($p = 2$) and we have the following parameter estimates:

$$b_0 = 1.1$$
$$b_1 = 0.7$$
$$b_2 = -0.5$$

For a second-degree polynomial:

$$B_i = 1.1 + .7i - .5i^2 \tag{6.12}$$

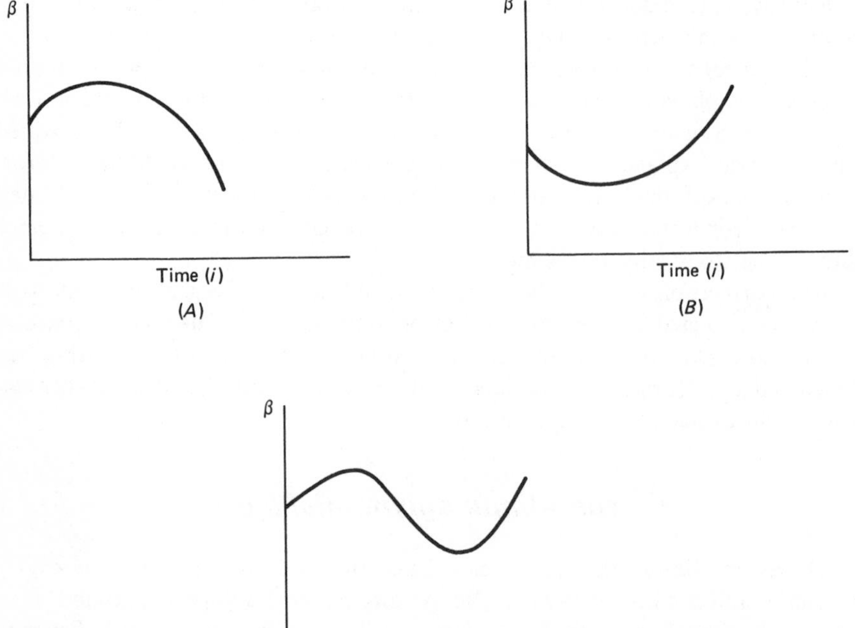

figure 6.2. Almon Polynomial Lag

where B is the estimate of β. If the length of the lag is four ($\beta_0, \beta_1, \beta_2, \beta_3, \beta_4$), then

$$B_0 = 1.1$$
$$B_1 = 1.1 + .7 - .5 = 1.3$$
$$B_2 = 1.1 + .7(2) - .5(4) = .5$$
$$B_3 = 1.1 + .7(3) - .5(9) = -1.3$$
$$B_4 = 1.1 + .7(4) - .5(16) = -4.1$$

Thus, the Bs increase for one time lag and decrease after that (Figure 6.2A). Alternatively, if

$$b_0 = 1.1$$
$$b_1 = -2.0$$
$$b_2 = 0.5$$

then

$$B_0 = 1.1$$
$$B_1 = 1.1 - 2 + .5 = -.4$$
$$B_2 = 1.1 - 2(2) + .5(4) = -.9$$
$$B_3 = 1.1 - 2(3) + .5(9) = -.4$$
$$B_4 = 1.1 - 2(4) + .5(16) = 1.1$$

The Bs decrease for two time lags and then increase (Figure 6.2B). If it is theorized that the pattern of the time lag might be cyclical (Figure 6.2C), then a higher-degree polynomial might be specified.

A major problem with the Almon approach is that the length of the lag must be specified. Unfortunately, there is no a priori way of knowing what the length is, and therefore a guess must be made. Nor is there any way of knowing the correct degree of the polynomial.

Once the length of the lag and the degree of the polynomial are specified, the next step is to estimate the parameters of Equation (6.11). To illustrate the estimation technique, suppose we specify the following model:

$$Y_t = \alpha + \beta_0 X_t + \beta_1 X_{t-1} + \beta_2 X_{t-2} + \epsilon_t \tag{6.13}$$

where Y is consumption and X is income. The length of the lag is two. Furthermore, the pattern of the lag is approximated by a second-degree polynomial. Therefore:

$$\beta_i = b_0 + b_1 i + b_2 i^2 \tag{6.14}$$

Rewriting Equation (6.13):

$$Y_t = \alpha + \sum_{i=0}^{j} \beta_i X_{t-i} + \epsilon_t \tag{6.15}$$

where j is the length of the lag (2), and substituting Equation (6.14) into Equation (6.15).

$$Y_t = \alpha + \sum_{i=0}^{j} (b_0 + b_1 i + b_2 i^2) X_{t-i} + \epsilon_t \tag{6.16}$$

or

$$Y_t = \alpha + b_0 \sum_{i=0}^{j} X_{t-i} + b_1 \sum_{i=0}^{j} iX_{t-i} + b_2 \sum_{i=0}^{j} i^2 X_{t-1} + \epsilon_t \tag{6.17}$$

If $j = 2$:

$$\sum_{i=0}^{j} X_{t-i} = X_t + X_{t-1} + X_{t-2}$$

$$\sum_{i=0}^{j} iX_{t-i} = X_{t-1} + 2X_{t-2}$$

$$\sum_{i=0}^{j} i^2 X_{t-i} = X_{t-1} + 4X_{t-2}$$

Thus, Equation (6.17) is equivalent to

$$Y_t = \alpha + b_0(X_t + X_{t-1} + X_{t-2}) + b_1(X_{t-1} + 2X_{t-2}) + b_2(X_{t-1} + 4X_{t-2}) + \epsilon_t \tag{6.18}$$

The parameters b_0, b_1, and b_2 can be estimated from Equation (6.18), and then the βs can be estimated by substituting these values into Equation (6.14).

Let us demonstrate the Almon approach by way of the data in Table 6.2.

table 6.2. Data for Demonstrating Almon Lag

Year	Y_t	X_t	$X_t + X_{t-1} + X_{t-2}$	$X_{t-1} + 2X_{t-2}$	$X_{t-1} + 4X_{t-2}$
1951	206.3	226.6	—	—	—
1952	216.7	238.3	—	—	—
1953	230.0	252.6	717.5	691.5	1144.7
1954	236.5	257.4	748.3	729.2	1205.8
1955	254.4	275.3	785.3	762.6	1267.8
1956	266.7	293.2	825.9	790.1	1304.9
1957	281.4	308.5	877.0	843.8	1394.4
1958	290.1	318.8	920.5	894.9	1481.3
1959	311.2	337.3	964.6	935.8	1552.8
1960	325.2	350.0	1006.1	974.9	1612.5
1961	335.2	364.4	1051.7	1024.6	1699.2
1962	355.1	385.3	1099.7	1064.4	1764.4
1963	375.0	404.6	1154.3	1114.1	1842.9
1964	401.2	438.1	1228.0	1175.2	1945.8
1965	432.8	473.2	1315.9	1247.3	2056.5
1966	466.3	511.9	1423.2	1349.4	2225.6
1967	492.1	546.3	1531.4	1458.3	2404.7
1968	535.8	591.2	1649.4	1570.1	2593.9
1969	577.5	631.6	1769.1	1683.8	2776.4
1970	616.8	684.7	1907.5	1814.0	2996.4

Y is consumption and X is disposable income in billions of current dollars. The constructed variables in the last three columns are used to predict Y for the years 1953–70 (two observations are lost because the length of the lag is two).

The regression results for Equation (6.18) are presented in Demo 6.6. The parameter estimates (T values in parentheses) are

$$\alpha = 1.55(0.39)$$
$$b_0 = 0.72(4.94)$$
$$b_1 = -1.10(1.70)$$
$$b_2 = 0.42(1.30)$$

```
REGRESSION COEFFICIENTS
 1.55471
  .715046
-1.09681
  .415665
STD. ERROR OF ESTIMATE= 3.0641
SE(B 1 )= 4.00226                  T 1  =  .388458
SE(B 2 )= .144634                  T 2  =  4.94383
SE(B 3 )= .644648                  T 3  =-1.70141
SE(B 4 )= .319288                  T 4  =  1.30185
R SQUARED= .999458
ADJUSTED R SQUARED= .999341
F= 8598.7
DEGREES OF FREEDOM= 14
DW= 1.75721
CORRELATION MATRIX
 1   .999577  .999062  .998927
 .999577   1  .999797  .999694
 .999062   .999797  1  .999982
 .998927   .999694  .999982  1
```

demo 6.6. Regression Results for Equation (6.18)

These parameter estimates can be substituted into Equation (6.14) in order to obtain estimates of the βs:

$$B_0 = b_0 = 0.72$$
$$B_1 = b_0 + b_1 + b_2 = 0.04$$
$$B_2 = b_0 + 2b_1 + 4b_2 = 0.02$$

Thus, the lag pattern indicates that the heaviest weighting is in the current period.

A potential problem with the polynomial lag approach is that the constructed variables may exhibit multicollinearity. Note the extremely high simple correlations in Demo 6.6. Consequently, we must be cautious in interpreting the regression results. However, the problem of multicollinearity is usually less with the Almon method than by directly applying OLS to a model of the form represented by Equation (6.1).

summary

Economic relationships are usually more complex than the static models presented in introductory economics textbooks. A major factor accounting for this complexity is time. The time factor may be incorporated into a regression model by way of a time lag. There is strong theoretical and practical justification for specifying models with lags. A theoretical justification is provided by the economic notion of the *short run* and *long run*. One practical justification was mentioned in the preceding chapter with regard to the difficulty of estimating the forecast error variance if the independent variables are not lagged.

Two basic types of dynamic models have been discussed in this chapter. The first is the *distributed lag model* in which the independent variables represent current and lagged values of an explanatory variable. The second is an *autoregressive model* in which a lagged value of the dependent variable is actually an independent variable and therefore appears on the right side of the regression equation.

Examples of dynamic models are the Koyck, adaptive expectation, and stock adjustment models and the Almon polynomial lag. The Koyck model is useful if it is theorized that the βs decline geometrically over time, while the Almon polynomial lag is preferred if a more-complicated pattern for the βs is theorized. The adaptive and stock adjustment models are of interest in cases in which one of the variables (independent and dependent, respectively) takes on expected or optimum values.

A major problem in estimating distributed lag models is that of multicollinearity. Because the simple correlations of the independent variables may be extremely high, examination of the correlation matrix can be a quick way to detect this problem.

Two major problems exist in estimating autoregressive models. First, the inclusion of a lagged dependent variable as one of the independent variables violates the assumption of the regression model that the Xs are nonstochastic. The violation of this assumption can lead to biased and inefficient parameter estimates. Second, autocorrelation cannot be detected by the conventional Durbin-Watson statistic because it is biased toward two.

Nonetheless, the dynamic models discussed in this chapter are reasonable approaches to the problem of how to account for the time-lag factor. Because economic theory often strongly supports the specification of models with time lags, it is useful to study these models.

examples

example 1

Derive Equation (6.3), the Koyck autoregressive model, by substituting Equation (6.2) into (6.1).

Substituting Equation (6.2) into (6.1):

$$Y = \alpha + \beta_0 X_t + \beta_0 L X_{t-1} + \beta_0 L^2 X_{t-2} + \cdots + \cdots + \epsilon_t \tag{1}$$

And this equation is equivalent to

$$Y_{t-1} = \alpha + \beta_0 X_{t-1} + \beta_0 L X_{t-2} + \beta_0 L^2 X_{t-3} + \cdots + \cdots + \epsilon_{t-1} \tag{2}$$

Multiply (2) by L:

$$LY_{t-1} = L\alpha + \beta_0 L X_{t-1} + \beta_0 L^2 X_{t-2} + \beta_0 L^3 X_{t-3} + \cdots + \cdots + L\epsilon_{t-1} \tag{3}$$

Subtract (3) from (1) and cancel and collect terms:

$$Y_t = \alpha(1 - L) + \beta_0 X_t + LY_{t-1} + u_t \tag{6.3}$$

where $u_t = \epsilon_t - L\epsilon_{t-1}$.

example 2

Derive Equation (6.7), the adaptive expectation autoregressive model, by substituting Equation (6.6) into (6.5).

Substituting Equation (6.6) into (6.5):

$$Y_t = \beta_0 + g\beta_1 X_t + (1 - g)\beta_1 X^*_{t-1} + \epsilon_t \tag{1}$$

Lag (6.5) by one period:

$$Y_{t-1} = \beta_0 + \beta_1 X^*_{t-1} + \epsilon_{t-1} \tag{2}$$

Multiply Equation (2) by $(1 - g)$, subtract the result from Equation (1), and collect terms:

$$Y_t = g\beta_0 + g\beta_1 X_t + (1 - g)X_{t-1} + u_t \tag{6.7}$$

where

$$u_t = \epsilon_t - (1 - g)\epsilon_{t-1}$$

example 3

Derive Equation (6.10), the stock adjustment autoregressive model.

This can be accomplished by simply substituting Equation (6.8) into (6.9):

$$Y_t = p\beta_0 + p\beta_1 X_t + (1 - p)Y_{t-1} + u_t \tag{6.10}$$

where

$$u = p\epsilon.$$

exercises

1. In the Koyck model, why is L termed the "rate of decline" and $(1 - L)$ the "speed of adjustment"?

2. In the adaptive expectation model, what is the importance of the size of g?

3. In the stock adjustment model, what is the importance of the size of p?

4. Suppose that you have the following data (hypothetical) on capital stock and output. Using the stock adjustment model, estimate β_0, β_1, and p. Interpret your results.

Time	Capital Stock	Output
1	33	15
2	35	17
3	40	19
4	43	20
5	45	22
6	44	22
7	46	25
8	50	25
9	52	24
10	48	24
11	50	25
12	52	26

5. What would Equation (6.17) look like if the length of the lag were four and the degree of the polynomial were three?

computer exercises

1. Referring to the Koyck model, the impact of changes in β_0 and L can be examined with the following program, which was used to generate Demo 6.4. Run the program a few times. Do your results coincide with Equation (6.4)? Answer Exercise 1.

```
10PRINT "SHORT-RUN MPC"
15INPUT M
20PRINT "RATE OF DECLINE"
25INPUT L
30FOR K=1 TO 26
35LET B=M*L**(K-1)
40PRINT B;"TIME=";K-1
43LET S=S+B
45NEXT K
50PRINT
55PRINT "SUM OF B'S=";S
60END
```

2. Work Exercise 4 with the computer program in Demo 4.19.

3. Suppose that you theorize that stock prices (Standard and Poor's Index) are affected by the change in the consumer price index (ΔCPI) with a lag of three:

$$Y_t = \alpha + \beta_0 X_t + \beta_1 X_{t-1} + \beta_2 X_{t-2} + \beta_3 X_{t-3} + \epsilon_t$$

where Y is stock prices and X is ΔCPI. Furthermore, you hypothesize an Almon lag in which $p = 2$. Estimate this model with the following 16 quarters of data and interpret your results. You will have to make use of the computer program in Demo 4.19.

Quarter-Year	Stock Prices	ΔCPI
2–72	$108.16	.008
3–72	109.20	.010
4–72	114.04	.009
1–73	115.00	.020
2–73	107.41	.020
3–73	105.08	.023
4–73	102.22	.022
1–74	95.67	.033
2–74	90.64	.027
3–74	75.66	.033
4–74	69.42	.024
1–75	78.81	.015
2–75	89.07	.017
3–75	87.62	.019
4–75	89.11	.014
1–76	99.53	–.003

7

simultaneous equations models

The preceding chapters have discussed the theory underlying single equation econometric models. This chapter and the next consider models containing more than one equation—*simultaneous equations models.* In a single equation model, the line of causation is from the independent variables (Xs) to the dependent variable (Y). In a simultaneous equations model, the line of causation is from Y to X and from X to Y, thereby rendering the distinction between *dependent* and *independent* meaningless. For example, supply and demand simultaneously determine the equilibrium price and quantity in a market, and therefore both a supply and a demand equation must be specified in order to describe a market. Price and quantity are interdependent, or jointly determined, and are termed *endogenous* variables. In effect, the endogenous variables are stochastic, while variables that are predetermined outside of the simultaneous model are termed *exogenous* and considered nonstochastic. For purposes of notation, we will assign $Y\,(Y_1 \ldots Y_M)$ to the endogenous variables in a model and $X\,(X_1 \ldots X_I)$ to the exogenous variables, where M is the number of endogenous variables or equations and I the number of exogenous variables.

As will be demonstrated, ordinary least squares (OLS) cannot be utilized to estimate the parameters of a simultaneous equations model. Consequently, other estimation techniques have been developed which can be applied to simultaneous equations models. The two methods discussed in this chapter are *indirect least squares* (ILS) and *two-stage least squares* (2SLS). These techniques are known as *single equation*, or *limited information*, methods because each equation is estimated separately. In contrast, *full information*, or *systems*, methods involve obtaining a solution simultaneously; thus, all the equations are solved at the same time. Discussion of full information methods is beyond the scope of this book, and therefore the interested reader should refer to a more-advanced book (see the Bibliography).

a brief review of the concept of simultaneity

The reader may recall from an earlier mathematics course (such as linear algebra) the meaning of the concept of simultaneity and some of the rules for solving a simple system of simultaneous equations. Because the econometric methods developed in this chapter build upon this earlier mathematics, we present a brief review in this section.

Consider the following equation:

$$x_1 + x_2 = 5 \tag{7.1}$$

Is it possible to obtain a unique solution to this equation? Since there are an infinite number of values for x_1 and x_2 that satisfy this equation, the answer is no. For example, $x_1 = 2$ and $x_2 = 3$ satisfy this equation, as do $x_1 = 1$ and $x_2 = 4$. Thus, we need additional information in order to obtain unique values for x_1 and x_2.

Suppose we add an equation to the system:

$$2x_1 + 2x_2 = 10 \tag{7.2}$$

Does Equation (7.2) provide enough additional information so that we can now arrive at a unique solution? Since Equation (7.2) is merely a multiple (by two) of Equation (7.1), no additional information is contained in Equation (7.2), and therefore a unique solution cannot be obtained. The Equations (7.1) and (7.2) are not "linearly independent," as one is a linear function of the other.

But now consider the following two equations:

$$x_1 + x_2 = 5 \tag{7.1}$$

$$x_1 - x_2 = 3 \tag{7.3}$$

Equation (7.3) adds the information needed to arrive at a unique solution, as it is linearly independent of Equation (7.1); it adds the "restriction" that $x_1 - x_2$ must equal 3. The reader can easily verify that the unique solution is $x_1 = 4$ and $x_2 = 1$. The Equations (7.1) and (7.3) represent a "simultaneous" system because one equation cannot be solved without considering the additional information or the restriction imposed by the other equation.

A simultaneous system such as that in Equations (7.1) and (7.2) or Equations (7.1) and (7.3) can be written in matrix notation:

$$AX = C \tag{7.4}$$

where A is a matrix of coefficients on X $(X_1, X_2, \ldots, X_I)$, and C is a matrix of constants. Thus, the A, X, and C matrices for the system (7.1) and (7.2) are

$$A = \begin{matrix} 1 & 1 \\ 2 & 2 \end{matrix} \qquad X = \begin{matrix} X_1 \\ X_2 \end{matrix} \qquad C = \begin{matrix} 5 \\ 10 \end{matrix}$$

The matrices for the system (7.1) and (7.3) are

$$A = \begin{matrix} 1 & 1 \\ 1 & -1 \end{matrix} \qquad X = \begin{matrix} X_1 \\ X_2 \end{matrix} \qquad C = \begin{matrix} 5 \\ 3 \end{matrix}$$

A unique solution to (7.4) is given by

$$X = A^{-1}C \tag{7.5}$$

where A^{-1} is the "inverse matrix of A," as defined in Chapter 4.

Suppose (7.5) is used to obtain a solution to the two systems (7.1) and (7.2), and (7.1) and (7.3). The results of attempting to solve these systems are presented in Demo 7.1. Note that the computer prints out that the inverse matrix cannot be calculated for the former system, while the inverse matrix for the latter system is

$$A^{-1} = \begin{matrix} .5 & .5 \\ .5 & -.5 \end{matrix}$$

As already mentioned, a unique solution exists only if the equations are linearly independent. Another way of stating this principle is that the matrix A^{-1} must exist. We will see the importance of this principle later in the chapter when the problem of *identification* is discussed.

```
SYSTEM 1
      CAN'T INVERT MATRIX AT LINE 40
SYSTEM 2
      INVERSE MATRIX
               .5         .5
               .5        -.5
      X MATRIX
               4       1
```

demo 7.1. Computer Solutions for Systems 1 and 2

simultaneous versus recursive equation systems

Consider the following system of three equations:

$$Y_1 = \alpha_0 + \alpha_1 Y_2 + \alpha_2 Y_3 + \beta_1 X_1 + \beta_2 X_2 + \epsilon_1 \quad (7.6)$$

$$Y_2 = \alpha_3 + \alpha_4 Y_1 + \alpha_5 Y_3 + \beta_3 X_3 + \epsilon_2 \quad (7.7)$$

$$Y_3 = \alpha_6 + \alpha_7 Y_1 + \alpha_8 Y_2 + \beta_4 X_1 + \beta_5 X_3 + \epsilon_3 \quad (7.8)$$

where the Ys represent the endogenous variables, the Xs represent the exogenous variables, the αs are the population parameters on the endogenous variables, and the βs are the population parameters on the exogenous variables. In Equation (7.6), Y_1 is a function of both Y_2 and Y_3; while in Equation (7.7), Y_2 is a function of both Y_1 and Y_3. Similarly, in Equation (7.8), Y_3 is a function of the other two endogenous variables, Y_1 and Y_2. This is a simultaneous system because the parameters of one equation cannot be estimated without considering the information provided by the other two equations.

But now look at the following system:

$$Y_1 = \alpha_0 + \beta_1 X_1 + \beta_2 X_2 + \epsilon_1 \quad (7.9)$$

$$Y_2 = \alpha_1 + \alpha_2 Y_1 + \beta_3 X_3 + \epsilon_2 \quad (7.10)$$

$$Y_3 = \alpha_3 + \alpha_4 Y_1 + \alpha_5 Y_2 + \beta_4 X_1 + \beta_5 X_2 + \epsilon_3 \quad (7.11)$$

Although this system would appear to be a simultaneous system, it is actually a "recursive" system. In Equation (7.9), Y_1 is solely a function of the exogenous variables; no endogenous variables appear on the right-hand side, and therefore this equation can be treated separately from the others. In Equation (7.10), Y_2 is a function of Y_1, and in no other equation is Y_1 a function of Y_2. Thus, Equation (7.10) can be estimated separately. Similarly, in Equation (7.11), Y_3 is a function of Y_1 and Y_2, but Y_1 and Y_2 are not functions of Y_3 in any other equation: Equation (7.11) can therefore be treated separately. The system is "recursive" because each equation can be estimated in sequential order. The distinction between simultaneous and recursive systems can be brought out by diagramming the two systems, as in Figure 7.1. Note the relative simplicity of the recursive system. In contrast to a simultaneous equation system, ordinary least squares can be applied to a recursive system.

examples of simultaneous equations models

As already mentioned, a supply and demand model is a good example of a simultaneous equations system. If it is assumed that the supply and demand curves are linear (Figure 7.2), such a model may be represented by the following

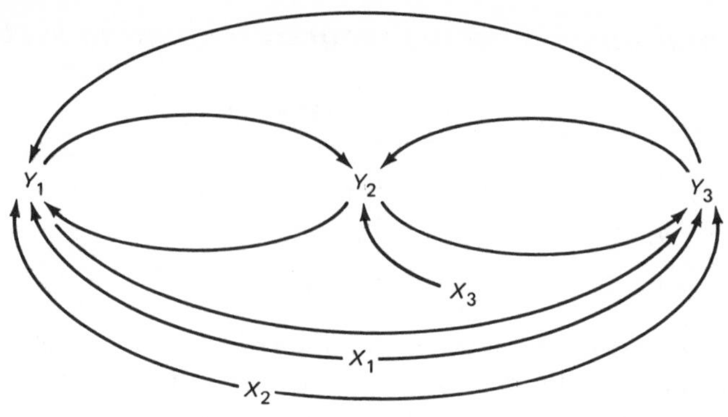

Simultaneous System

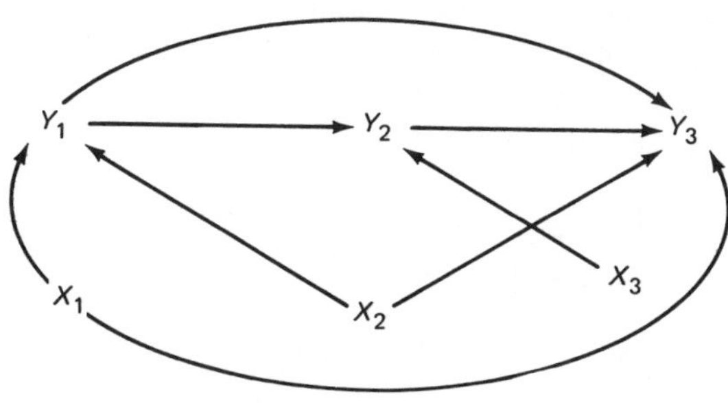

Recursive System

figure 7.1. Simultaneous vs. Recursive System

two equations:

$$Y_1 = \alpha_0 + \alpha_1 Y_2 + \epsilon_1 \quad (7.12)$$

$$Y_3 = \alpha_2 + \alpha_3 Y_2 + \epsilon_2 \quad (7.13)$$

where Y_1 = quantity supplied
Y_2 = price
Y_3 = quantity demanded
$Y_1 = Y_3$ at equilibrium

An upward-sloping supply curve and downward-sloping demand curve, as in Figure 7.2, imply that α_1 is greater than zero and α_3 is less than zero. Note that all variables in this model are endogenous.

The error term ϵ_1 in Equation (7.12) includes all other variables that might affect supply, such as technological change. Similarly, the error term ϵ_2 in

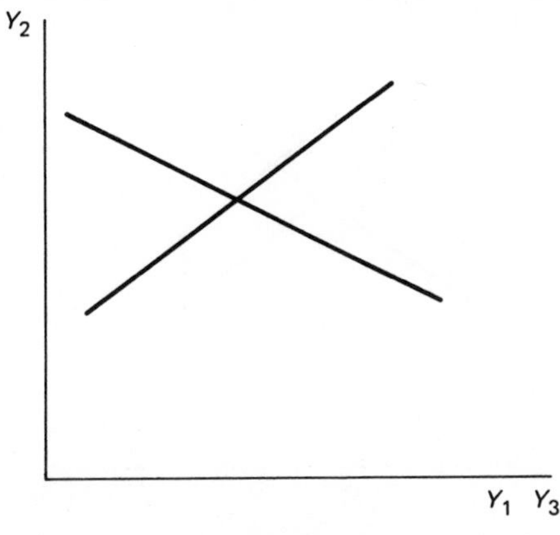

figure 7.2

Equation (7.13) includes all other variables that might affect demand, such as income. If, for example, there is a change in technology, ϵ_1 reflects this change and the supply curve shifts to the right (Figure 7.3). The price (Y_2) decreases and the equilibrium quantity ($Y_1 = Y_3$) increases. Thus, ϵ_1 and Y_2 are correlated with each other in Equation (7.12), thereby violating an important assumption of the classical regression model developed in earlier chapters. Consequently, ordinary least squares cannot be applied to Equation (7.12). Similarly, it can be shown that ϵ_2 and Y_2 are correlated with each other in Equation (7.13). This is illustrated in Figure 7.4 for the case of a shift in the demand curve to the right.

Another example of a simultaneous equations system is a macroeconomic

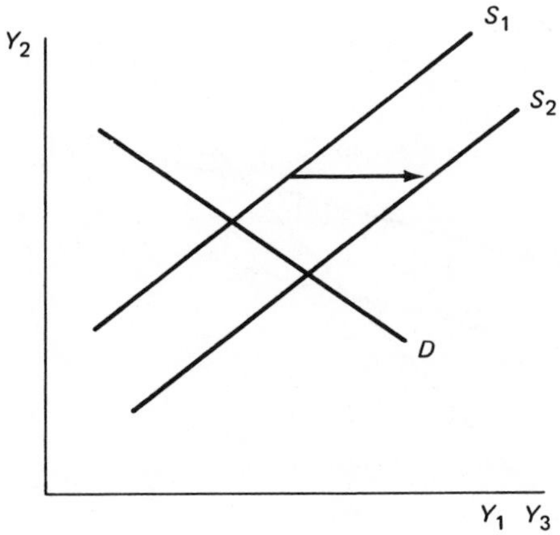

figure 7.3

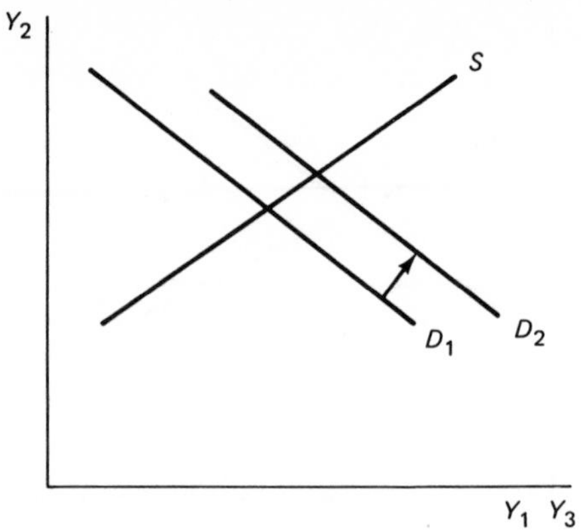

figure 7.4

model of income determination:

$$Y_1 = \alpha_0 + \alpha_1 Y_2 + \epsilon_1 \tag{7.14}$$

$$Y_2 = Y_1 + X_1 + X_2 \tag{7.15}$$

where Y_1 = consumption
Y_2 = income
X_1 = investment
X_2 = government spending

Note that Equation (7.15) is an identity and that there are two endogenous and two exogenous variables. This system is graphed in Figure 7.5. The slope of

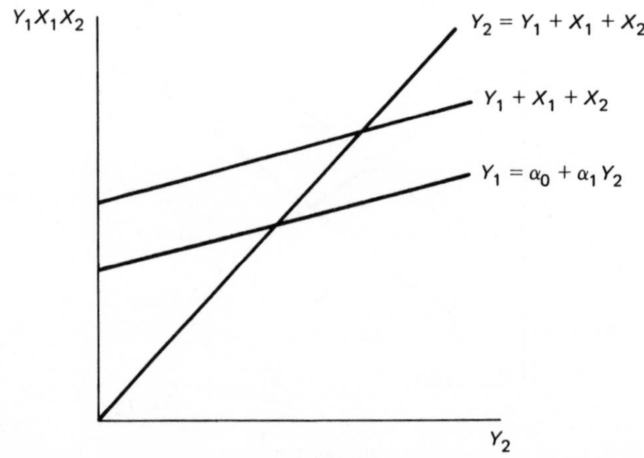

figure 7.5. Macroeconomic Model of Income Determination

Equation (7.14), α_1, is the marginal propensity to consume. The equilibrium level of income is indicated in this figure and is determined by simultaneously solving this system of two equations.

Simultaneous macroeconomic models are in common use today. In theory, there is virtually no limit to the number of equations and variables that could exist in these models. In practice, though, the cost of estimation places a restriction on their size. As an example of a larger macroeconomic model than the preceding one, consider the following system of six equations:[1]

$$Y_1 = \alpha_0 + \alpha_1 Y_2 + \alpha_2 Y_3 + \epsilon_1 \tag{7.16}$$

$$Y_4 = \alpha_3 + \alpha_4 Y_3 + \beta_1 X_1 + \beta_2 X_2 + \epsilon_2 \tag{7.17}$$

$$Y_2 = \alpha_5 + \alpha_6 Y_5 + \beta_3 X_3 + \beta_4 X_4 + \epsilon_3 \tag{7.18}$$

$$Y_1 + Y_4 + X_5 = Y_5 \tag{7.19}$$

$$Y_3 + Y_2 = Y_5 \tag{7.20}$$

$$\Delta Y_6 = Y_4 \tag{7.21}$$

where Y_1 = consumption
Y_2 = wages
Y_3 = profits
Y_4 = investment
Y_5 = output or income
Y_6 = capital stock
X_1 = profits in the previous period; that is, X_1 is equal to Y_3 lagged one period: $Y_3(-1)$. A lagged endogenous variable is considered exogenous because its value is known in the present period.
X_2 = capital stock in the previous period: $Y_6(-1)$
X_3 = output in the previous period: $Y_5(-1)$
X_4 = time
X_5 = government spending

Equation (7.16) describes consumer behavior and is a departure from the traditional consumption function in that income is divided into two components—wages and profits. Thus, the hypothesis that the marginal propensity to consume is different for these two types of income can be tested by this equation. Equation (7.17) describes business behavior and expresses investment as a function of profits (current and lagged) and the capital stock (lagged). Equation (7.18) represents the labor market and hypothesizes that wages are a function of output (current and lagged) and a time trend. The remaining three equations are identities. The sum of consumption, investment, and government

[1]This model is one of several developed by Lawrence R. Klein, *Economic Fluctuations in the United States, 1921–1941* (New York: John Wiley, 1950).

spending is equal to output or income (Equation (7.19)). The sum of profits and wages is equal to output or income (Equation (7.20)). The change in the capital stock from the beginning to the end of the time period is equal to investment for that time period (Equation (7.21)).

Although simple, this model is a good example of the simultaneous macroeconomic models that have been constructed by econometricians. Obviously, the economy is considerably more complex than the one represented by this model. For example, taxes and the foreign trade sector are excluded. Even though no model can do justice to the complexity of a modern-day economy, many econometricians feel that large multiequation models serve a useful purpose. Still others believe that the benefits do not outweight the costs. It is not our purpose to enter this debate, but rather to make the reader aware that such models are now widely used and accepted.

identification

Suppose that we are interested in estimating the parameters of the supply and demand model specified by Equations (7.12) and (7.13):

$$\text{Supply:} \quad Q = \alpha_0 + \alpha_1 P + \epsilon_1 \tag{7.22}$$

$$\text{Demand:} \quad Q = \alpha_2 + \alpha_3 P + \epsilon_2 \tag{7.23}$$

where Q = quantity
P = price

Furthermore, data on the price and quantity of bananas (50-lb. bunch) are available for ten time periods, as in Table 7.1. Is it possible to estimate the parameters of our supply and demand model with these data?

table 7.1. Hypothetical Price and Quantity Data for Bunches of Bananas

Time Period	Price ($)	Quantity (000)
1	10	50
2	12	54
3	9	65
4	15	84
5	14	75
6	15	85
7	16	90
8	14	60
9	17	40
10	19	70

Assuming that the quantity supplied is equal to the quantity demanded at any point in time, the data in Table 7.1 merely represent the points of intersection of particular supply and demand curves, as illustrated in Figure 7.6. Consequently, it would be impossible to obtain parameter estimates of our supply and demand model with these data. Each equation of the model, as well as the overall model, is said to be "unidentified."

Alternatively, consider the following model, which includes two additional variables (both exogenous):

$$\text{Supply:} \quad Q = \alpha_0 + \alpha_1 P + \beta_1 S + \epsilon_1 \tag{7.24}$$

$$\text{Demand:} \quad Q = \alpha_2 + \alpha_3 P + \beta_2 I + \epsilon_2 \tag{7.25}$$

where S = state of technology
I = income

Note that technology is included in the supply equation but not the demand equation, and that income is included in the demand equation but not the supply equation. We will see later when discussing the "order condition" for identification that there is considerable significance to the fact that each equation excludes one variable appearing in the other equation.

In a moment we will demonstrate mathematically that the addition of the two exogenous variables makes it possible to estimate the parameters of the supply and demand model represented by Equations (7.24) and (7.25). This point is graphically brought out in Figure 7.7. In Figure 7.7A the additional

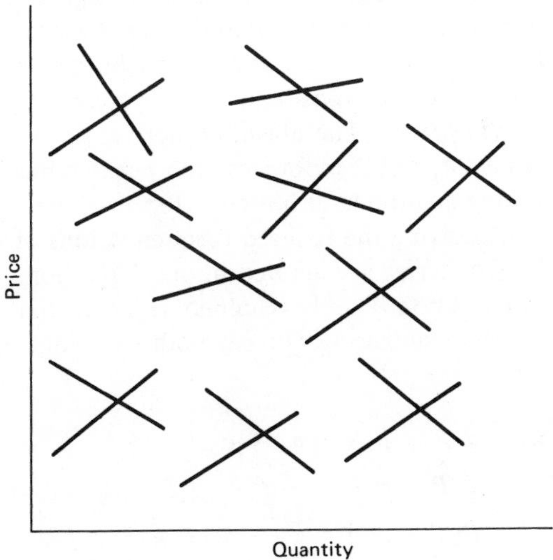

figure 7.6. Supply and Demand Curves at Different Points in Time

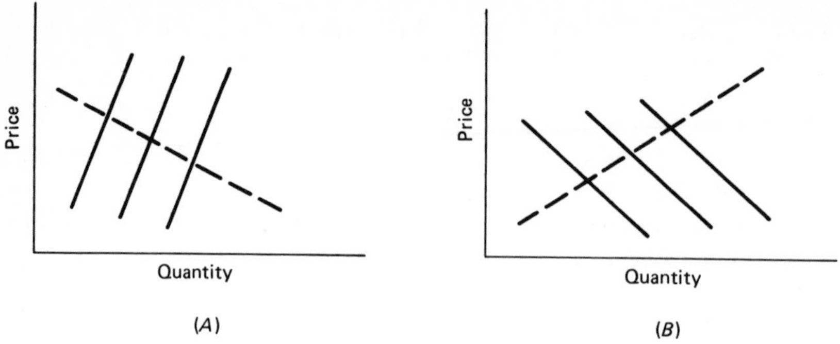

figure 7.7. Identification of Demand and Supply Curves

information provided by the technology variable allows us to identify the demand equation by assuming that changes in technology cause the supply curve to shift in a predictable manner, thereby tracing out the fixed demand curve. Similarly, in Figure 7.7B changes in income shift the demand curve, and the desired supply curve is traced out. Without this additional information, it would be impossible to identify the parameters of the model.

The identification problem can be analyzed by expressing the endogenous variables as functions of the exogenous variables only. Thus, an equation can be derived expressing Q as a function of S and I, and P as a function of S and I. Such equations are termed *reduced form*. If unique estimates of the parameters of an underlying or "structural" equation such as (7.24) or (7.25) can be derived from the reduced form equations, the equation is *identified* or *exactly identified* or *just* or *fully identified*. If no estimate can be derived, the equation is *unidentified* or *underidentified*. If more than one estimate can be derived, the equation is *overidentified*. For purposes of exposition, we will use the terms *just identified*, *unidentified*, and *overidentified*. The algebraic derivation of the reduced form equations is often difficult, and therefore less-complicated means of determining the identification of an equation have been developed. However, we will demonstrate the concept by deriving the reduced form equations of (7.24) and (7.25). For simplicity, the error terms are ignored in our derivation.

The equilibrium condition (supply = demand) means that (7.24) and (7.25) can be equated, thereby eliminating Q from both equations, and solving for P in terms of S and I:

$$\alpha_0 + \alpha_1 P + \beta_1 S = \alpha_2 + \alpha_3 P + \beta_2 I$$

$$\alpha_1 P - \alpha_3 P = -\alpha_0 - \beta_1 S + \alpha_2 + \beta_2 I$$

$$P(\alpha_1 - \alpha_3) = \alpha_2 - \alpha_0 - \beta_1 S + \beta_2 I$$

$$P = \frac{\alpha_2 - \alpha_0}{\alpha_1 - \alpha_3} - \frac{\beta_1}{\alpha_1 - \alpha_3} S + \frac{\beta_2}{\alpha_1 - \alpha_3} I \tag{7.26}$$

Equation (7.26) is one of the desired reduced form equations. Note that P is expressed solely as a function of the two exogenous variables, S and I.

The other reduced form equation can be derived by substituting the value of P from Equation (7.26) into Equation (7.24) or (7.25). We will show the derivation by substituting into (7.24). The reader is encouraged to check this result by substituting into (7.25).

$$Q = \alpha_0 + \alpha_1\left[\frac{\alpha_2 - \alpha_0}{\alpha_1 - \alpha_3} = \frac{\beta_1}{\alpha_1 - \alpha_3}S + \frac{\beta_2}{\alpha_1 - \alpha_3}I\right] + \beta_1 S$$

$$= \alpha_0 + \frac{\alpha_1(\alpha_2 - \alpha_0)}{\alpha_1 - \alpha_3} - \frac{\alpha_1\beta_1}{\alpha_1 - \alpha_3}S + \frac{\alpha_1\beta_2}{\alpha_1 - \alpha_3}I + \beta_1 S$$

$$= \frac{\alpha_0\alpha_1 - \alpha_0\alpha_3 + \alpha_1\alpha_2 - \alpha_0\alpha_1}{\alpha_1 - \alpha_3} + \frac{\alpha_1\beta_1 - \alpha_3\beta_1 - \alpha_1\beta_1}{\alpha_1 - \alpha_3}S + \frac{\alpha_1\beta_2}{\alpha_1 - \alpha_3}I$$

$$Q = \frac{\alpha_1\alpha_2 - \alpha_0\alpha_3}{\alpha_1 - \alpha_3} - \frac{\alpha_3\beta_1}{\alpha_1 - \alpha_3}S + \frac{\alpha_1\beta_2}{\alpha_1 - \alpha_3}I \tag{7.27}$$

In a form similar to that in Equation (7.26), Equation (7.27) expresses Q solely as a function of S and I.

The reduced form equations are of the form:

$$P = c_1 + c_2 S + c_3 I \tag{7.28}$$

$$Q = c_4 + c_5 S + c_6 I \tag{7.29}$$

where

$$c_1 = \frac{\alpha_2 - \alpha_0}{\alpha_1 - \alpha_3}, \quad c_2 = \frac{-\beta_1}{\alpha_1 - \alpha_3}, \quad c_3 = \frac{\beta_2}{\alpha_1 - \alpha_3},$$

$$c_4 = \frac{\alpha_1\alpha_2 - \alpha_0\alpha_3}{\alpha_1 - \alpha_3}, \quad c_5 = \frac{-\alpha_3\beta_1}{\alpha_1 - \alpha_3}, \quad c_6 \frac{\alpha_1\beta_2}{\alpha_1 - \alpha_3}$$

Can unique estimates be derived from the reduced form equations for the structural parameters of Equations (7.24) and (7.25)? The answer is yes and is provided by the following equations:

$$\alpha_1 = \frac{c_6}{c_3} \tag{7.30}$$

$$\alpha_3 = \frac{c_5}{c_2} \tag{7.31}$$

$$\beta_1 = -c_2(\alpha_1 - \alpha_3) \tag{7.32}$$

$$\beta_2 = c_3(\alpha_1 - \alpha_3) \tag{7.33}$$

$$\alpha_0 = c_4 - \alpha_1 c_1 \tag{7.34}$$

$$\alpha_2 = c_4 - \alpha_3 c_1 \tag{7.35}$$

The reader should check the algebra of the above equations to see if any other equations for the parameters can be derived.

Alternatively, if the model is specified with no exogenous variable in the demand equation, the supply equation is unidentified, while the demand equation is still identified:

$$\text{Supply:} \quad Q = \alpha_0 + \alpha_1 P + \beta_1 S + \epsilon_1 \tag{7.36}$$

$$\text{Demand:} \quad Q = \alpha_2 + \alpha_3 P \qquad\qquad + \epsilon_2 \tag{7.37}$$

The reduced form equations are

$$P = \frac{\alpha_2 - \alpha_0}{\alpha_1 - \alpha_3} - \frac{\beta_1}{\alpha_1 - \alpha_3} S \tag{7.38}$$

$$Q = \frac{\alpha_1 \alpha_2 - \alpha_0 \alpha_3}{\alpha_1 - \alpha_3} - \frac{\alpha_3 \beta_1}{\alpha_1 - \alpha_3} S \tag{7.39}$$

Equations (7.38) and (7.39) can simply be expressed as

$$P = c_1 + c_2 S \tag{7.40}$$

$$Q = c_3 + c_4 S \tag{7.41}$$

The parameters in the demand equation (7.37), α_2 and α_3, can be estimated by the following equations:

$$\alpha_3 = \frac{c_4}{c_2} \tag{7.42}$$

$$\alpha_2 = c_3 - \alpha_3 c_1 \tag{7.43}$$

However, the parameters of the supply equation (7.36) cannot be retrieved from the coefficients of the reduced form equations.

In contrast to the model represented by Equations (7.36) and (7.37), the following supply equation is identified, but not the demand equation:

$$\text{Supply:} \quad Q = \alpha_0 + \alpha_1 P \qquad\qquad + \epsilon_1 \tag{7.44}$$

$$\text{Demand:} \quad Q = \alpha_2 + \alpha_3 P + \alpha_4 I + \epsilon_2 \tag{7.45}$$

As an exercise, the reader may wish to derive the reduced form equations of this model and show that α_0 and α_1 may be estimated from the coefficients of the reduced form equations.

Now consider the following model, which provides an example of an over-identified equation:

$$\text{Supply:} \quad Q = \alpha_0 + \alpha_1 P \qquad\qquad\qquad + \epsilon_1 \tag{7.46}$$

$$\text{Demand:} \quad Q = \alpha_2 + \alpha_3 P + \beta_1 I + \beta_2 T + \epsilon_2 \tag{7.47}$$

where T (tastes) is an additional exogenous variable in the demand equation. The reduced form equations are

$$P = \frac{\alpha_2 - \alpha_0}{\alpha_1 - \alpha_3} + \frac{\beta_1}{\alpha_1 - \alpha_3} I + \frac{\beta_2}{\alpha_1 - \alpha_3} T \tag{7.48}$$

$$Q = \frac{\alpha_1\alpha_2 - \alpha_0\alpha_3}{\alpha_1 - \alpha_3} + \frac{\alpha_1\beta_1}{\alpha_1 - \alpha_3} I + \frac{\alpha_1\beta_2}{\alpha_1 - \alpha_3} T \tag{7.49}$$

or

$$P = c_1 + c_2 I + c_3 T \tag{7.50}$$

$$Q = c_4 + c_5 I + c_6 T \tag{7.51}$$

Note that there are two estimates of α_1:

$$\alpha_1 = \frac{c_5}{c_2} \tag{7.52}$$

$$\alpha_1 = \frac{c_6}{c_3} \tag{7.53}$$

And Equations (7.52) and (7.53) need not be equal. For each estimate of α_1, two estimates can be obtained for α_0:

$$\alpha_0 = c_4 - \alpha_1 c_1 \tag{7.54}$$

Since estimates of the parameters of the demand equation (7.47) cannot be derived from the coefficients of the reduced form equations, the demand equation is unidentified, although the supply equation (7.46), as just noted, is overidentified.

Determining the identification of an equation by way of the reduced form equations is usually quite difficult if there are many equations in the simultaneous system. The analysis just presented is for a system of only two equations; the reader should now be easily able to imagine the difficulty of deriving the reduced form equations for simultaneous systems containing more than two equations. Consequently, it is fortunate that there is another method for determining the identification of an equation. This method involves applying the "order" and "rank" conditions of identification.

The order condition is very simple to apply. A simultaneous system contains M endogenous variables and M equations. An equation is just identified if the number of excluded variables (endogenous plus exogenous) in that equation is equal to $M - 1$. It is unidentified if the number of excluded variables is less than $M - 1$, and overidentified if the number of excluded variables is more than $M - 1$. Table 7.2 summarizes the order condition for identification.

Let us apply the order condition to the supply and demand model represented by Equations (7.22) and (7.23). The number of endogenous variables (M) is equal to two, and there are no exogenous variables in the system. There are no

table 7.2. Order Condition for Identification

	Number of Excluded Variables
Unidentified equation	$< (M - 1)$
Just identified equation	$= (M - 1)$
Overidentified equation	$> (M - 1)$

missing variables in either equation, and therefore both equations are unidentified:

$$0 < (M - 1)$$
$$\text{i.e., } 0 < 1$$

Applying the order condition to the model represented by Equations (7.24) and (7.25), we find that both equations are just identified, since each excludes one exogenous variable:

$$1 = (M - 1)$$
$$\text{i.e., } 1 = 1$$

Applying the order condition to Equations (7.46) and (7.47), we see that the supply equation is overidentified because it excludes two variables (I and T):

$$2 > (M - 1)$$
$$\text{i.e., } 2 > 1$$

The demand equation is unidentified because no variables are excluded from that equation.

Unfortunately, the easy-to-apply order condition is a necessary, but not sufficient, condition for identification. A necessary and sufficient condition for identification is the rank condition. For example, it is possible for an equation to be identified on the basis of the order condition, but fail to be identified by the rank condition. The rank condition is difficult to apply because it involves determining whether or not a matrix can be inverted. Fortunately, computer programs (see the computer exercises) can do this work for us.

To illustrate the rank condition, let us consider the following three-equation simultaneous model:

$$Y_1 = \alpha_0 + \alpha_1 Y_2 + \alpha_2 Y_3 + \beta_1 X_1 + \beta_2 X_2 + \epsilon_1 \qquad (7.55)$$
$$Y_2 = \alpha_3 + \alpha_4 Y_1 + \alpha_5 Y_3 + \beta_3 X_3 \qquad + \epsilon_2 \qquad (7.56)$$
$$Y_3 = \alpha_6 + \alpha_7 Y_1 + \alpha_8 Y_2 \qquad + \epsilon_3 \qquad (7.57)$$

This model can be represented by an M-row-by-K-column matrix, where M is the number of equations and K is the number of variables (endogenous plus exogenous) in the system. The error term is excluded to simplify the analysis:

	Y_1	Y_2	Y_3	X_1	X_2	X_3
Equation (7.55)	1	1	1	1	1	0
Equation (7.56)	1	1	1	0	0	1
Equation (7.57)	1	1	1	0	0	0

Note that if a variable is present in an equation, a one is assigned in the appropriate column; if a variable is excluded, a zero is assigned.

It is interesting to first apply the order condition to this system. Since $M - 1$ is equal to two, an equation is just identified only if the number of excluded variables is equal to two. Thus, by the order condition, the only equation that is just identified is Equation (7.56), as there are two zeros in the second row corresponding to the excluded variables X_1 and X_2. Equation (7.55) is unidentified because there are less than two zeros in that row, and Equation (7.57) is overidentified because there are more than two zeros in that row.

The application of the "rank" condition involves deleting the particular equation under consideration and then including the columns of the remaining equations in which zeros appear in the deleted equation. From these columns, if a matrix of order $(M - 1)$ by $(M - 1)$ can be formed that possesses an inverse, then that particular equation is just identified or overidentified.[2] Because methods exist for estimating overidentified equations, it is not important that the rank condition cannot distinguish between just identified and overidentified equations. Rather, it is important to know whether or not an equation is unidentified. In any event, the application of the order condition can tell us whether an equation is just identified or overidentified.

For the system represented by Equations (7.55), (7.56), and (7.57), a matrix of order two by two must exist, and this matrix must have an inverse. Let us apply the rank condition to each equation. Deleting the first equation, there is only one column in which a zero appears:

$$\begin{matrix} 1 \\ 0 \end{matrix}$$

Since the order of this matrix is two rows by one column, a two-by-two matrix cannot be formed. Thus, Equation (7.55) is unidentified, as was discovered by applying the order condition.

Deleting the second equation, a two-by-two matrix can be formed with the columns in which zero appears in the deleted equation:

$$\begin{matrix} 1 & 1 \\ 0 & 0 \end{matrix}$$

[2]For those familiar with matrix algebra, the "determinant" of the $(M - 1)$ matrix must be nonzero.

However, if we asked a computer to calculate the inverse of this matrix, it would tell us that this matrix does not possess an inverse. Therefore, Equation (7.56) is unidentified, even though the order condition suggested that it was identified. This is a good example of how the application of the order condition alone can lead to error.

Deleting the third equation, a two-by-three matrix can be formed with the columns in which zero appears in the deleted equation:

$$\begin{matrix} 1 & 1 & 0 \\ 0 & 0 & 1 \end{matrix}$$

From this matrix, three unique two-by-two matrices ($M1$, $M2$, $M3$) can be formed. The rank condition is satisfied if only one of these has an inverse:

$$M1 = \begin{matrix} 1 & 1 \\ 0 & 0 \end{matrix}$$

$$M2 = \begin{matrix} 1 & 0 \\ 0 & 1 \end{matrix}$$

$$M3 = \begin{matrix} 0 & 1 \\ 1 & 0 \end{matrix}$$

Although $M1$ does not have an inverse, both $M2$ and $M3$ do have inverses, and therefore Equation (7.57) is just identified or overidentified. From the order condition, we know that it is overidentified.

This completes our discussion of identification. If the reader does not have access to a computer, he or she may be content with applying the order condition. The computer exercises contain a simple program for applying the rank condition. For large simultaneous systems of equations, there is really no alternative to the computer.

estimation by indirect least squares (ILS)

In this section we discuss a commonly used method for estimating the parameters of an equation that is just identified—*indirect least squares* (ILS). The ILS method consists of applying ordinary least squares (OLS) to the reduced form equations and then obtaining estimates of the parameters from the coefficients of the reduced form equations. Because the reduced form equations express the endogenous variables as a function of the exogenous variables only, it is permissible to apply OLS to the reduced form equations and then "indirectly" obtain estimates of the parameters from the reduced form coefficients.

To illustrate the ILS method, reconsider the supply and demand model presented in the preceding section:

$$\text{Supply:} \quad Q = \alpha_0 + \alpha_1 P + \beta_1 S + \epsilon_1 \tag{7.24}$$

$$\text{Demand:} \quad Q = \alpha_2 + \alpha_3 P + \beta_2 I + \epsilon_2 \tag{7.25}$$

The reduced form equations are

$$P = c_1 + c_2 S + c_3 I + u_1 \tag{7.58}$$

$$Q = c_4 + c_5 S + c_6 I + u_2 \tag{7.59}$$

where

$$c_1 = \frac{\alpha_2 - \alpha_0}{\alpha_1 - \alpha_3}$$

$$c_2 = \frac{-\beta_1}{\alpha_1 - \alpha_3}$$

$$c_3 = \frac{\beta_2}{\alpha_1 - \alpha_3}$$

$$c_4 = \frac{\alpha_1 \alpha_2 - \alpha_0 \alpha_3}{\alpha_1 - \alpha_3}$$

$$c_5 = \frac{-\alpha_3 \beta_1}{\alpha_1 - \alpha_3}$$

$$c_6 = \frac{\alpha_1 \beta_2}{\alpha_1 - \alpha_3}$$

$$u_1, u_2 = \text{error terms}$$

Suppose we estimate the parameters of this model with the hypothetical data in Table 7.3.

table 7.3. Hypothetical Supply and Demand Data

Time Period	P	Q	S	I
1	10	50	100	15
2	12	54	102	12
3	9	65	105	11
4	15	84	107	17
5	14	75	110	19
6	15	85	111	30
7	16	90	111	28
8	14	60	113	25
9	17	40	117	23
10	19	70	120	35

The estimating equations (T values in parentheses) are

$$\hat{P} = -19.65 + .28S + .14I \qquad (7.60)$$
$$(1.4) \quad (1.9) \quad (1.2)$$

$$\hat{Q} = 215.03 - 1.71S + 1.87I \qquad (7.61)$$
$$(1.5) \quad (1.1) \quad (1.6)$$

Substituting into Equations (7.30)–(7.35), estimates of the underlying structural parameters can be derived:[3]

$$\alpha_1 = \frac{c_6}{c_3} = 13.36$$

$$\alpha_3 = \frac{c_5}{c_2} = -6.11$$

$$\beta_1 = -c_2(\alpha_1 - \alpha_3) = -5.45$$

$$\beta_2 = c_3(\alpha_1 - \alpha_3) = 2.73$$

$$\alpha_0 = c_4 - \alpha_1 c_1 = 477.55$$

$$\alpha_2 = c_4 - \alpha_3 c_1 = 94.97$$

It is interesting to compare the ILS estimates above with those obtained by mistakenly applying OLS to the structural equations, (7.24) and (7.25):

$$\alpha_1 = 3.95$$

$$\alpha_3 = -.86$$

$$\beta_1 = -1.42$$

$$\beta_2 = 1.03$$

$$\alpha_0 = 167.53$$

$$\alpha_2 = 57.33$$

Thus, the equations estimated by ILS are

$$\text{Supply:} \quad \hat{Q} = 477.55 + 13.36P - 5.45S \qquad (7.62)$$

$$\text{Demand:} \quad \hat{Q} = 94.97 - 6.11P + 2.73I \qquad (7.63)$$

And the equations estimated by OLS are

$$\text{Supply:} \quad \hat{Q} = 167.53 + 3.95P - 1.42S \qquad (7.64)$$

$$\text{Demand:} \quad \hat{Q} = 57.33 - .86P + 1.03I \qquad (7.65)$$

[3]The calculation of the standard errors is very difficult and beyond the scope of this book. It should also be pointed out that ILS estimates may be biased for small samples.

This example demonstrates the danger of inappropriately applying OLS to a system of simultaneous equations. It can be proven that the OLS estimates are biased (note the large difference between Equations (7.62) and (7.64) or between Equations (7.63) and (7.65)) and do not converge to their population values even for large N. Thus, the OLS estimates are inconsistent.

estimation by two-stage least squares (2SLS)

There are two major problems with the ILS technique. First, it can be applied to just identified, but not to overidentified, equations. Second, the derivation of the reduced form equations can be difficult, since considerable algebraic manipulation of the underlying structural equations may be required. A solution to both of these problems is to apply two-stage least squares (2SLS), instead of ILS, to a system of simultaneous equations.

To demonstrate the 2SLS method, let us again consider the supply and demand model that was estimated by ILS in the preceding section:

$$\text{Supply:} \quad Q = \alpha_0 + \alpha_1 P + \beta_1 S + \epsilon_1 \tag{7.24}$$

$$\text{Demand:} \quad Q = \alpha_2 + \alpha_3 P + \beta_2 I + \epsilon_2 \tag{7.25}$$

We have seen that the problem with applying OLS to these equations concerns the likely correlation of ϵ_1 with P in Equation (7.24), and ϵ_2 with P in Equation (7.25). But suppose we could construct a variable that is highly correlated with P, but not with ϵ_1 or ϵ_2. Such a variable is termed a *proxy* or *instrumental* variable. This is the essence of the 2SLS technique, which consists of the following two stages:

stage 1

Each endogenous variable appearing on the right side of the equations is regressed on all the exogenous variables in the model. For example, there is only one endogenous variable (P) on the right side of Equations (7.24) and (7.25). P is regressed on the two exogenous variables, S and I:

$$P = \beta_3 + \beta_4 S + \beta_5 I + u \tag{7.66}$$

The estimated regression coefficients from Equation (7.66) are used to construct the "instrumental variable," $\hat{P}$:

$$\hat{P} = B_3 + B_4 S + B_5 I \tag{7.67}$$

Since only exogenous variables appear on the right side of Equation (7.66), the presumption is that $\hat{P}$ is uncorrelated with ϵ_1 and ϵ_2. Note that if the R^2 of

Equation (7.66) is one, P is equal to $\hat{P}$, and there would be no difference between the OLS and 2SLS estimates.

stage 2

The instrumental variables are substituted for the respective endogenous variables on the right side of the model, and each equation is estimated by OLS:

$$Q = \alpha_0 + \alpha_1\hat{P} + B_1S + \epsilon_1 \tag{7.68}$$

$$Q = \alpha_2 + \alpha_3\hat{P} + \beta_2I + \epsilon_2 \tag{7.69}$$

Estimates for β_3, β_4, and β_5 have already been obtained from the reduced form equation (7.60): -19.65, .28, and .14, respectively. The resulting values for $\hat{P}$ are presented in Table 7.4.

table 7.4. Instrumental Variable Constructed from Equation (7.67)

Time Period	$\hat{P}$
1	10.50
2	10.65
3	11.35
4	12.75
5	13.87
6	15.67
7	15.39
8	15.54
9	16.39
10	18.89

The parameter estimates obtained by applying 2SLS are

$$\alpha_1 = 13.53$$

$$\alpha_3 = -6.09$$

$$\beta_1 = -5.52$$

$$\beta_2 = 2.71$$

$$\alpha_0 = 481.92$$

$$\alpha_2 = 94.91$$

It is interesting to compare the 2SLS with the ILS parameter estimates. The reader should immediately see how close the estimates are. In fact, the difference between the ILS and 2SLS estimates results solely from the rounding of $\hat{P}$ in Table 7.4. Thus, if an equation is just identified, ILS and 2SLS are equivalent. But since equations of the form of (7.30) to (7.35) need not be derived, 2SLS is superior to ILS.

Although ILS cannot be applied to an overidentified equation, 2SLS is often used to obtain estimates of the parameters of an overidentified equation. Earlier in the chapter we presented a supply and demand model containing an overidentified equation:

$$\text{Supply:} \quad Q = \alpha_0 + \alpha_1 P \qquad\qquad\qquad\qquad + \epsilon_1 \tag{7.46}$$

$$\text{Demand:} \quad Q = \alpha_2 + \alpha_3 P + \beta_1 I + \beta_2 T + \epsilon_2 \tag{7.47}$$

The reader can easily verify by way of the order condition that the supply equation is overidentified, while the demand equation is unidentified. Suppose we attempt to estimate the parameters of the supply equation by way of ILS. The reduced form equations have previously been presented (without the error terms):

$$P = c_1 + c_2 I + c_3 T + u_1 \tag{7.50}$$

$$Q = c_4 + c_5 I + c_6 T + u_2 \tag{7.51}$$

Furthermore, T (tastes) takes on the hypothetical values in Table 7.5, while the values for P, Q, and I are the same as before (Table 7.3).

table 7.5. Hypothetical Data on Tastes (T)

Time Period	T
1	125
2	140
3	155
4	170
5	160
6	175
7	150
8	135
9	140
10	145

Estimation of Equations (7.50) and (7.51) leads to the following regression coefficients:

$$c_1 = 5.10$$
$$c_2 = 0.32$$
$$c_3 = 0.015$$
$$c_4 = -57.65$$
$$c_5 = 0.53$$
$$c_6 = 0.76$$

Two estimates of α_0 and α_1 can be derived from these coefficients. The reader should refer to Equations (7.52), (7.53), and (7.54):

$$\alpha_1 = \frac{c_5}{c_2} = 1.66$$

or

$$\alpha_1 = \frac{c_6}{c_3} = 50.67$$

$$\alpha_0 = c_4 - \alpha_1 c_1 = -66.12$$

or

$$\alpha_0 = -316.07$$

Thus, ILS does not lead to unique estimates of the parameters of an overidentified equation. In contrast, it can be proven that 2SLS does provide us with unique estimates of the parameters of an overidentified equation. The instrumental variable, $\hat{P}$, is constructed from Equation (7.50):

$$\hat{P} = 5.1 + .32I + .015T$$

The values of $\hat{P}$ are given in Table 7.6. Q is then regressed on $\hat{P}$, resulting in the following parameter estimates:

$$Q = 28.94 + 2.72\hat{P}$$

table 7.6. Values of $\hat{P}$ from Equation (7.50)

Time Period	$\hat{P}$
1	11.68
2	10.95
3	10.85
4	12.97
5	13.46
6	17.17
7	16.17
8	15.00
9	14.44
10	18.31

summary

In this chapter we briefly introduced the reader to simultaneous equations models. If at least two variables in an economic model are interdependent or jointly determined, such as price and quantity in a supply and demand model, a simultaneous model must be specified. A simultaneous model contains M endogenous variables (and M equations in order to estimate the parameters of the model), and any number of exogenous variables.

A simultaneous system of equations can be written in "reduced form" by expressing each endogenous variable as solely a function of the exogenous variables in the model. If the parameters of an underlying structural equation can be retrieved from the coefficients of the reduced form equations, the structural equation is said to be *just identified.* If no estimate of the parameters can be made, the equation is *unidentified*; if more than one estimate can be obtained, the equation is *overidentified.* A necessary and sufficient condition for identification is the "rank" condition. Unfortunately, the rank condition is difficult to apply because it involves determining whether an inverse matrix exists. A simple alternative is the "order" condition, which is a necessary, but not sufficient, condition.

The parameters of a just identified equation may be estimated by either *indirect least squares* (ILS) or *two-stage least squares* (2SLS). Indirect least squares, as its name implies, involves obtaining estimates of the parameters indirectly from the reduced form equations. Ordinary least squares cannot be directly applied to the underlying structural equations because of the likely correlation of the endogenous variables with the error term. By constructing instrumental variables that are correlated with the endogenous variables, but uncorrelated with the error terms, two-stage least squares permits the direct application of ordinary least squares to the structural equations. Two-stage least squares can also be used to obtain unique estimates of the parameters of an overidentified equation. Several other methods exist for estimating the parameters of a simultaneous equations system, but a discussion of these is beyond the scope of this book. The interested reader should refer to the Bibliography.

examples

example 1

Derive the reduced form equations for the simple Keynesian model represented by Equations (7.14) and (7.15).

Substituting Equation (7.15) into (7.14) and solving for Y_1:

$$Y_1 = \alpha_0 + \alpha_1 Y_1 + \alpha_1 X_1 + \alpha_1 X_2$$

$$Y_1 - \alpha_1 Y_1 = \alpha_0 + \alpha_1 X_1 + \alpha_1 X_2$$

$$Y_1 = \frac{\alpha_0}{1 - \alpha_1} + \frac{\alpha_1}{1 - \alpha_1} X_1 + \frac{\alpha_1}{1 - \alpha_1} X_2 \tag{7.70}$$

Substituting Equation (7.70) into (7.15):

$$Y_2 = \frac{\alpha_0}{1 - \alpha_1} + \frac{\alpha_1}{1 - \alpha_1} X_1 + \frac{\alpha_1}{1 - \alpha_1} X_2 + X_1 + X_2$$

$$Y_2 = \frac{\alpha_0}{1 - \alpha_1} + \frac{1}{1 - \alpha_1} X_1 + \frac{1}{1 - \alpha_1} X_2 \tag{7.71}$$

example 2

The reduced form equations derived in Example 1 show what impact changes in the exogenous variables have on the endogenous variables. Suppose that the marginal propensity to consume is .75. How will a change in government spending of 100 affect consumption? Income?

From Equation (7.70) it can be seen that if government spending (X_2) increases by 100, consumption (Y_1) will increase by

$$\frac{\alpha_1}{1 - \alpha_1} X_2 = \frac{.75}{.25}(100) = 300$$

From Equation (7.71), income (Y_2) will increase by

$$\frac{1}{1 - \alpha_1} X_2 = \frac{1}{.25}(100) = 400$$

Thus, the total increase in income of 400 can be broken down into a government spending increase of 100 and a consumption increase of 300. This mathematics should be familiar to any introductory economics student.

example 3

Can unique estimates of the parameters (α_0, α_1) of the Keynesian model be derived from the reduced form equations (7.70) and (7.71)?

Rewriting Equations (7.70) and (7.71):

$$Y_1 = c_1 + c_2 X_1 + c_2 X_2$$

$$Y_2 = c_1 + c_3 X_1 + c_3 X_2$$

where $\quad c_1 = \dfrac{\alpha_0}{1 - \alpha_1}, \quad c_2 = \dfrac{\alpha_1}{1 - \alpha_1}, \quad c_3 = \dfrac{1}{1 - \alpha_1}$

$$\alpha_1 = \frac{c_2}{c_3}$$

$$\alpha_0 = (1 - \alpha_1)c_1$$

These estimates are unique.

example 4

Are the equations of the Keynesian model just identified?

Yes, since unique estimates of the parameters can be obtained from the reduced form equations.

Which estimation technique—ILS or 2SLS—could be used to estimate the parameters of the Keynesian model?

Because the equations are just identified, either technique can be used.

example 5

Klein's "Model I"[4] is

$$Y_1 = \alpha_0 + \alpha_1 Y_2 + \alpha_2(Y_3 + X_6) + \beta_1 X_1 + \epsilon_1$$

$$Y_4 = \alpha_3 + \alpha_4 Y_2 + \beta_2 X_1 + \beta_3 X_2 \qquad + \epsilon_2$$

$$Y_3 = \alpha_5 + \alpha_6(Y_5 + X_3 - X_6) + \beta_4(Y_5 + X_3 - X_6)_{-1} + \beta_5 X_4 + \epsilon_3$$

$$Y_5 + X_3 = Y_1 + Y_4 + X_5$$

$$Y_5 = Y_3 + X_6 + Y_2$$

$$Y_6 = X_2 + Y_4$$

where Y_1 = consumption spending
Y_2 = profits
Y_3 = private wages
Y_4 = investment spending
Y_5 = income less taxes
Y_6 = capital stock
$X_1 = Y_2(-1)$
$X_2 = Y_6(-1)$
X_3 = taxes
X_4 = time
X_5 = government spending
X_6 = government wages

Note that the sum of an endogenous and exogenous variable—e.g., $(Y_3 + X_6)$—is treated as endogenous except when it is lagged: $(Y_5 + X_3 - X_6)_{-1}$. Assuming the equations are just identified (or overidentified), how would you apply 2SLS to this system?

Since the last three equations are identities, we are concerned with constructing instrumental variables for the endogenous variables on the right side of the first three equations: Y_2, $(Y_3 + X_6)$, and $(Y_5 + X_3 - X_6)$. These can be

[4]Klein, *Economic Fluctuations.*

regressed on the exogenous variables: X_1, X_2, $(Y_5 + X_3 - X_6)_{-1}$, X_4, and X_5.

The instrumental variables can be substituted for the original variables in the first three equations, and OLS can be applied to obtain consistent parameter estimates.

exercises

1. Consider the following Keynesian model:

$$Y_1 = \alpha_0 + \alpha_1 Y_2 + \epsilon_1 \tag{7.72}$$

$$Y_2 = Y_1 + X_1 \tag{7.73}$$

where Y_1 = consumption
Y_2 = income
X_1 = investment

Are the equations just identified? Using data for the years 1964–78, estimate the parameters of the model by OLS and 2SLS and compare your results.

Billions of Dollars

	Consumption	*Income*	*Investment*	*Government Spending*
1964	400.4	635.7	96.6	129.8
1965	430.2	688.1	112.0	138.4
1966	464.8	753.0	124.5	158.7
1967	490.4	796.3	120.8	180.2
1968	535.9	868.5	131.5	198.7
1969	579.7	935.5	146.2	207.9
1970	618.8	982.4	140.8	218.9
1971	668.2	1063.4	160.0	233.7
1972	733.0	1171.1	188.3	253.1
1973	809.9	1306.6	220.0	269.5
1974	889.6	1412.9	214.6	302.7
1975	979.1	1528.8	190.9	338.4
1976	1089.9	1702.2	243.0	361.3
1977	1210.0	1899.5	303.3	396.2
1978	1350.8	2127.6	351.5	435.6

2. Suppose the Keynesian model in the preceding exercise is revised by adding a government sector and making investment endogenous.

$$Y_1 = \alpha_0 + \alpha_1 Y_2 + \epsilon_1 \tag{7.72}$$

$$Y_3 = \alpha_2 + \alpha_3 Y_2 + \epsilon_2 \tag{7.74}$$

$$Y_2 = Y_1 + Y_3 + X_1 \tag{7.75}$$

where Y_1 = consumption
Y_2 = income
Y_3 = investment
X_1 = government spending

Derive the reduced form equations for this model and determine whether or not the equations are just identified by seeing if unique parameter estimates can be obtained from the coefficients of the reduced form equations. Check your results by applying the order condition for identification. What estimation technique would you use to estimate the parameters of this model?

3. Estimate by 2SLS the parameters of the model in the preceding exercise. Use the data given in Exercise 1. Reestimate the model by OLS and compare your results.

4. Equations (7.16)–(7.21) were given as an example of a larger macroeconomic model. Check on the identification of each equation by way of the order condition. How would you estimate the parameters of this model?

5. Equation (7.27) was derived by substituting Equation (7.26) into (7.24). Show that the result is the same if Equation (7.26) is substituted into (7.25).

6. Consider the following model:

$$Y_1 = \alpha_0 + \alpha_1 Y_2 + \beta_1 X_1 + \epsilon_1$$
$$Y_2 = \alpha_2 + \alpha_3 Y_1 + \alpha_4 Y_3 + \epsilon_2$$
$$Y_3 = \alpha_5 + \alpha_6 Y_1 + \beta_2 X_2 + \epsilon_3$$

Determine whether or not the equations are just identified by way of the order condition. How would you estimate the parameters of this model?

7. Consider the following model:

$$Y_1 = \alpha_0 + \beta_1 X_1 + \beta_2 X_2 + \beta_3 X_3 + \epsilon_1$$
$$Y_2 = \alpha_1 + \alpha_2 Y_1 + \beta_4 X_1 + \beta_5 X_3 + \epsilon_2$$
$$Y_3 = \alpha_3 + \alpha_4 Y_1 + \alpha_5 Y_2 + \beta_6 X_3 + \epsilon_3$$

How would you estimate the parameters of this model?

computer exercises

The rank condition can be checked with the simple program shown in Demo 7.2, which determines whether or not a matrix possesses an inverse.

```
10DIM  A(2,2),B(2,2)
20MAT  READ  A
30MAT  B=INV(A)
40MAT  PRINT  B;
50DATA  1,1,0,0
60END
RUN

?Can't invert matrix at line 30

50DATA  1,1,1,-1
RUN

   .5      .5
   .5     -.5
```

demo 7.2. Program That Tests Rank Condition by Printing Inverse Matrix If It Exists

This program is run on the following two matrices:

$$\begin{matrix} 1 & 1 \\ 0 & 0 \end{matrix} \qquad \begin{matrix} 1 & 1 \\ 1 & -1 \end{matrix}$$

The DATA statement (50) must be changed each time the program is run (data are input row by row). The DIM statement (10) must be changed for larger matrices. For example, for a three-by-three matrix:

```
10DIM  A(3,3),B(3,3)
```

1. Use this program to determine the identification of the equations in Exercise 6.

2. The following two statements can be added to the multiple regression program presented in Chapter 4 in order to print out the values of the instrumental variable used in the second stage of 2SLS. Use this program to work Exercise 3.

```
493 PRINT "INSTRUMENTAL VARIABLE"
495 MAT PRINT Z;
```

8

introduction to simulation

Often in econometric work, we wish to study the "dynamic behavior" of a model, a form of which can be defined in terms of the time path of the endogenous variables, given changes in the exogenous variables.[1] A time path is termed *stable* if the variable converges to an equilibrium value over time, and *unstable* if there is no equilibrium. Figure 8.1 shows two stable time paths; one of these paths is cyclical, and the other is noncyclical. Similarly, Figure 8.2 shows two examples of unstable time paths.

Simulation can be defined as the derivation of the time path of a mathematical model. There are two basic techniques by which a time path can be derived. The first is by mathematical or algebraic solution, and the second is by computer simulation. For most practical problems, the method of mathematical solution is too complex. Consequently, computer simulation is the preferred technique. The Appendix to this chapter demonstrates how to write a BASIC computer program to solve a typical simulation problem.

[1]A simulation model is normally a multiequation simultaneous model, although a simple model may be a single equation. In the latter case, we would be concerned with the time path of the dependent variable, given changes in the independent variables.

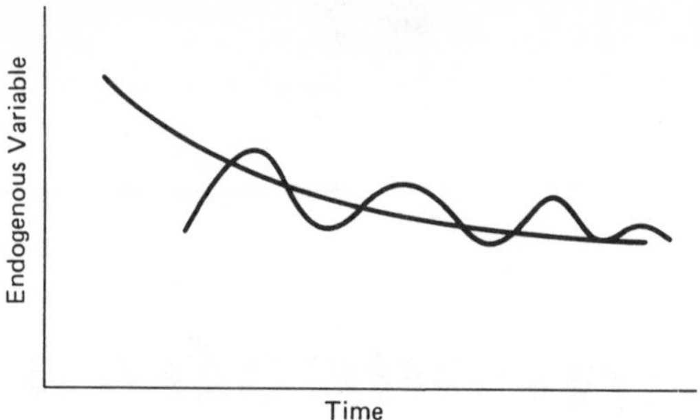

figure 8.1. Stable Time Paths

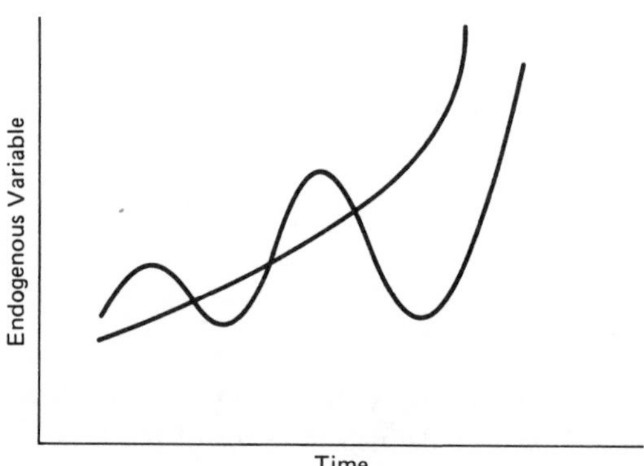

figure 8.2. Unstable Time Paths

a growth model example

A simple growth model that relates output (Y) to time (T) can be represented by the following equation:

$$Y = Ae^{rT} \tag{8.1}$$

where A and r are parameters to be estimated, and e is the natural exponential (2.71828). For simplicity, the error term is excluded. Because Equation (8.1) is nonlinear in the parameters, it is necessary to linearize this equation in order to apply the classical regression model discussed earlier in the book. This may be accomplished by taking the log of both sides:

$$\log Y = \log A + rT \tag{8.2}$$

Suppose that Equation (8.2) is estimated with the available data and that the parameter estimates are

$$\log A = 10$$
$$r = .05$$

Substituting these values into Equation (8.2), the initial value ($T = 0$) of Y is 22,026. What is the time path of Y over the next twenty-five years? Obviously, the mathematical solution to this simulation problem is simple, as we merely substitute various values of T ranging from 1 to 25 directly into Equation (8.2). For example, for $T = 1$:

$$\log Y = 10 + .05(1) = 10.05$$

or

$$Y = 23{,}156$$

For $T = 25$:

$$\log Y = 10 + .05(25) = 11.25$$

or

$$Y = 76{,}880$$

The time path of Y for all twenty-five years is presented in Table 8.1. Note that the log of Y grows at the constant rate of $r = .05$.

table 8.1. Simulation of Growth Model

Time	Y (r = .05)	Log Y (r = .05)	Y (r = .10)
0	22,026	10.00	22,026
1	23,156	10.05	24,343
2	24,343	10.10	26,903
3	25,591	10.15	29,733
4	26,903	10.20	32,860
5	28,282	10.25	36,316
6	29,733	10.30	40,135
7	31,257	10.35	44,356
8	32,860	10.40	49,021
9	34,544	10.45	54,176
10	36,316	10.50	59,874
11	38,177	10.55	66,171
12	40,135	10.60	73,130
13	42,193	10.65	80,822
14	44,356	10.70	89,322
15	46,630	10.75	98,716
16	49,021	10.80	109,098
17	51,534	10.85	120,572
18	54,176	10.90	133,252
19	56,954	10.95	147,267
20	59,874	11.00	162,755
21	62,944	11.05	179,872
22	66,171	11.10	198,789
23	69,564	11.15	219,696
24	73,130	11.20	242,802
25	76,880	11.25	268,337

Suppose there is reason to believe that r may not be fixed. For example, we may be interested in obtaining the time path of Y given an r equal to .10. The latter time path is given in the last column of Table 8.1. It is interesting to compare the time in which output doubles given the two values for r (14 years and 7 years, respectively).

a multiplier-accelerator model example

An example of a simultaneous simulation model (Model I) is given by the following equations (the error terms are excluded):

$$C_t = \beta_1 + \beta_2 Y_t \tag{8.3}$$

$$I_t = \beta_3 + \beta_4(Y_{t-1} - Y_{t-2}) \tag{8.4}$$

$$Y_t = C_t + I_t + G_t \tag{8.5}$$

where C = consumption
I = investment
Y = output or income
G = government spending

The reader may recognize this as a form of the multiplier-accelerator model often presented in macroeconomics courses.

It is interesting to examine the time path of the endogenous variables (C, I, Y) given a change in the exogenous variable (G). Suppose that the parameter estimates of the multiplier-accelerator model are

$$B_1 = 100$$
$$B_2 = .75$$
$$B_3 = 50$$
$$B_4 = .25$$

Furthermore, the values for the variables in the first period ($t = 1$) are

$$C_1 = 1{,}150$$
$$I_1 = 50$$
$$G_1 = 200$$
$$Y_1 = Y_0 = Y_{-1} = 1{,}400$$

If government spending should increase by 40 in the second period, how does this affect the endogenous variables over the next twenty-five years ($t = 25$)? This question can be explored by substituting Equations (8.3) and (8.4) into Equation (8.5), and then solving for Y_t:

$$Y_t = \frac{B_1 + B_3 + B_4(Y_{t-1} - Y_{t-2}) + G_t}{1 - B_2} \tag{8.6}$$

For example, in the second period ($t = 2$):

$$Y_2 = \frac{100 + 50 + .25(1{,}400 - 1{,}400) + 240}{1 - .75} = 1{,}560$$

$$C_2 = 100 + .75(1{,}560) = 1{,}270$$

$$I_2 = 50 + .25(1{,}400 - 1{,}400) = 50$$

In the third period ($t = 3$):

$$Y_3 = \frac{100 + 50 + .25(1{,}560 - 1{,}400) + 240}{.25} = 1{,}720$$

$$C_3 = 100 + .75(1{,}720) = 1{,}390$$

$$I_3 = 50 + .25(1{,}560 - 1{,}400) = 90$$

Similarly, the other values can be calculated. The simulation results for all twenty-five years are presented in Table 8.2.

A graph (Figure 8.3) of these results reveals that this model is unstable and cyclical. However, the cycles are regular and predictable. Often, a slight model modification can lead to drastically different results. For example, consider the

table 8.2. Simulation Results for Multiplier-Accelerator Model I

Time	C	I	Y
1	1150	50	1400
2	1270	50	1560
3	1390	90	1720
4	1390	90	1720
5	1270	50	1560
6	1150	10	1400
7	1150	10	1400
8	1270	50	1560
9	1390	90	1720
10	1390	90	1720
11	1270	50	1560
12	1150	10	1400
13	1150	10	1400
14	1270	50	1560
15	1390	90	1720
16	1390	90	1720
17	1270	50	1560
18	1150	10	1400
19	1150	10	1400
20	1270	50	1560
21	1390	90	1720
22	1390	90	1720
23	1270	50	1560
24	1150	10	1400
25	1150	10	1400

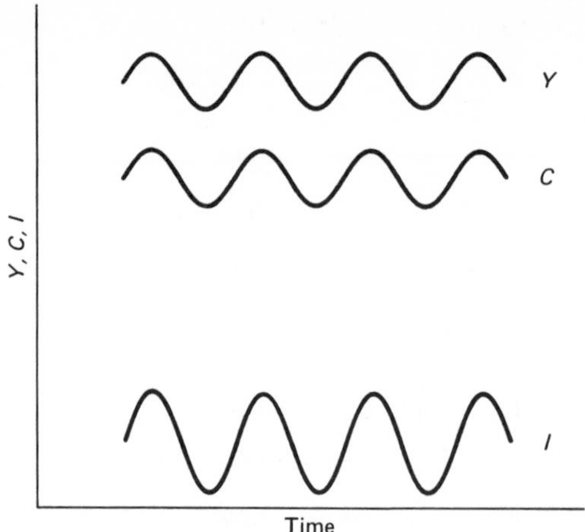

figure 8.3. Graph (Continuous) of Model I

following model (Model II) in which Equation (8.3) is altered so that consumption is a function of income lagged one time period.

$$C_t = \beta_1 + \beta_2 Y_{t-1} \quad (8.7)$$

$$I_t = \beta_3 + \beta_4(Y_{t-1} - Y_{t-2}) \quad (8.4)$$

$$Y_t = C_t + I_t + G_t \quad (8.5)$$

Substituting Equations (8.7) and (8.4) into Equation (8.5), Y_t can be expressed as a function of the exogenous variables in the model:

$$Y_t = B_1 + B_3 + (B_2 + B_4)Y_{t-1} - B_4 Y_{t-2} + G_t \quad (8.8)$$

Given the same parameter and initial variable values as before, the results of simulating this model for twenty-five time periods are presented in Table 8.3. Note that this model is stable because the endogenous variables converge to an equilibrium and then remain constant. Both income and consumption behave in a noncyclical manner as they steadily increase to their equilibrium values (1,560 and 1,270, respectively) while investment moves cyclically until reaching a stable equilibrium at 50 (see Figure 8.4).

dynamic multipliers

Referring to Table 8.3, we see that the initial increase in government spending of 40 in the first time period leads to an increase in income of 40 in the second time period, 40 in the third period, 30 in the fourth period, 20 in the fifth period, 12.5 in the sixth period, and so forth. In the seventeenth period, the increase in income is zero and a stable equilibrium has been reached. For each time period, the *dynamic multiplier* is defined as the ratio of the increase in income to the

table 8.3. Simulation of Multiplier-Accelerator Model II

Time	C	I	Y
1	1150.0	50.0	1400.0
2	1150.0	50.0	1440.0
3	1180.0	60.0	1480.0
4	1210.0	60.0	1510.0
5	1232.5	57.5	1530.0
6	1247.5	55.0	1542.5
7	1256.9	53.1	1550.0
8	1262.5	51.9	1554.4
9	1265.8	51.1	1556.9
10	1267.7	50.6	1558.3
11	1268.7	50.4	1559.1
12	1269.3	50.2	1559.5
13	1269.6	50.1	1559.7
14	1269.8	50.1	1559.9
15	1269.9	50.0	1559.9
16	1269.9	50.0	1560.0
17	1270.0	50.0	1560.0
18	1270.0	50.0	1560.0
19	1270.0	50.0	1560.0
20	1270.0	50.0	1560.0
21	1270.0	50.0	1560.0
22	1270.0	50.0	1560.0
23	1270.0	50.0	1560.0
24	1270.0	50.0	1560.0
25	1270.0	50.0	1560.0

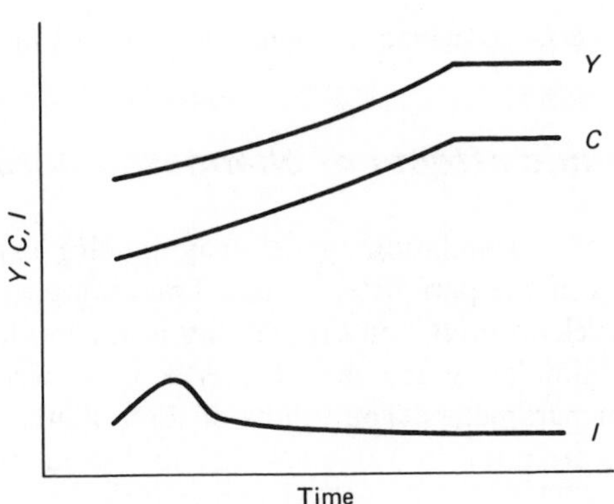

figure 8.4. Graph of Model II

initial change in government spending. Thus, the dynamic multiplier is 1 in the second and third periods, .75 in the fourth, .50 in the fifth, .31 in the sixth, and so forth. The sum of all the dynamic multipliers is equal to the *long-run multiplier*, which is four in this example. The dynamic multipliers and their sum are presented in Demo 8.1.

TIME PERIOD	DYNAMIC MULTIPLIER
2	1
3	1
4	.75
5	.5
6	.3125
7	.1875
8	.109375
9	.0625
10	.351563E−1
11	.195313E−1
12	.107422E−1
13	.585938E−2
14	.317383E−2
15	.170898E−2
16	.915527E−3
17	.488281E−3
18	.259399E−3
19	.137329E−3
20	.724792E−4
21	.38147E−4
22	.200272E−4
23	.104904E−4
24	.548363E−5
25	.286102E−5
	SUM = 4

demo 8.1. Dynamic Multipliers and Long-Run Multiplier

dynamic effects of changes in parameters

The analysis of a simulation model may involve exploring the dynamic effects of changes in the parameter values. For example, what is the effect of changes in the accelerator (B_4) on the stability of the model? This question can be answered by simulating the model over a long period of time, holding constant all other parameters. The results of three simulations of Model II for fifty time periods are given in Table 8.4. The first simulation (SIM 1) assumes that B_4 is equal to .75, the second (SIM 2) that B_4 is 1.25, and the third (SIM 3) that B_4 is 3.5. SIM 1 is cyclical but stable, with income approaching an equilibrium value of 1,560 after fifty years. SIM 2 is cyclical and unstable, while

SIM 3 is noncyclical and unstable. In all three simulations, B_2 (marginal propensity to consume) is held constant at .75.

table 8.4. Model II Simulations Given Three Different Values for the Accelerator

Time	Y (SIM 1)	Y (SIM 2)	Y (SIM 3)
1	1400	1400	1400
2	1440	1440	1440
3	1500	1520	1610
4	1560	1630	2193
5	1605	1750	4073
6	1628	1852	10027
7	1628	1908	28749
8	1611	1889	87478
9	1585	1784	271552
10	1560	1597	848311
11	1541	1354	.3E7
12	1532	1101	.8E7
13	1532	900	.3E8
14	1539	813	.8E8
15	1549	892	.3E9
16	1560	1158	.8E9
17	1568	1590	.3E10
18	1572	2123	.8E10
19	1572	2648	.2E11
20	1569	3033	.8E11
21	1565	3146	.2E12
22	1560	2890	.8E12
23	1557	2238	.2E13
24	1555	1254	.7E13
25	1555	100	.2E14
50	1560	17252	.6E26

forecasting with a simulation model

Often a simulation model is constructed for the purpose of forecasting. As an example, the multiplier-accelerator model (Model II) represented by Equations (8.7), (8.4), and (8.5) was estimated by OLS with data for the years 1964–78. The estimating equations are (T values in parentheses):

$$C_t = -64.213 + .745Y_{t-1} \tag{8.7}$$
$$\quad (6.4) \qquad (90.5) \qquad R^2 = .99 \quad DW = 1.81$$

$$I_t = 58.495 + 1.404(Y_{t-1} - Y_{t-2}) \tag{8.4}$$
$$\quad (4.2) \qquad (10.9) \qquad R^2 = .91 \quad DW = 1.91$$

$$Y_t = C_t + I_t + G_t \tag{8.5}$$

Given values for the exogenous variables Y_{t-1}, Y_{t-2}, and G_t, Equations (8.8), (8.7), and (8.4) can be solved in sequential order to yield forecasted values for the endogenous variables Y_t, C_t, and I_t. For example, given Y_{1964}, Y_{1965}, and $G_{1966-78}$, the endogenous variables can be simulated over the 1966–78 period. The simulation model can then be evaluated by comparing the forecasted with the actual values of Y, C, and I. This is done in Table 8.5 where the superscript S refers to the simulated value, and the superscript A refers to the actual value.

table 8.5. Simulated (S) and Actual (A) Values for Model II (Billions of Current Dollars)

Time	Y^A	Y^S	C^A	C^S	I^A	I^S	G
1966	753.0	739.2	464.8	448.4	124.5	132.1	158.7
1967	796.3	796.9	490.4	486.5	120.8	130.2	180.2
1968	868.5	867.7	535.9	529.5	131.5	139.5	198.7
1969	935.5	948.0	579.7	582.2	146.2	157.9	207.9
1970	982.4	1032.2	618.8	642.1	140.8	171.3	218.9
1971	1063.4	1115.2	668.2	704.8	160.0	176.7	233.7
1972	1171.1	1194.8	733.0	766.6	188.3	175.0	253.1
1973	1306.6	1265.5	809.9	825.9	220.0	170.1	269.5
1974	1412.9	1339.2	889.6	878.6	214.6	157.9	302.7
1975	1528.8	1433.7	979.1	933.5	190.9	161.9	338.4
1976	1702.2	1556.5	1089.9	1003.9	243.0	191.3	361.3
1977	1899.5	1722.4	1210.0	1095.4	303.3	230.9	396.2
1978	2127.6	1946.1	1350.8	1219.0	351.5	291.5	435.6

$Y^A(1964) = 635.7$

$Y^A(1965) = 688.1$

To aid in the evaluation of the performance of the simulation model, the data in Table 8.5 are graphed in Figure 8.5, and the RMS error and RMS percent error are presented for each of the three simulations.[2]

In Figure 8.5 the actual and simulated values for income and consumption are extremely close over the 1966–69 time period, and the RMS percent errors for both of these variables over the entire 1966–78 time period are low (5.31 percent and 5.22 percent, respectively). In contrast, the model does not perform as well for the investment variable (RMS percent error of 16.61 percent). Because the accelerator in the model can translate small changes in income into large swings in investment, it is not surprising that the investment variable is more difficult to predict than consumption and income. The volatility of investment over time is one of the factors that makes its forecasting so difficult.

Suppose we wish to forecast the values of the endogenous variables to 1990.

[2]The reader should refer to Equations (5.12) and (5.13) for definitions of these error concepts.

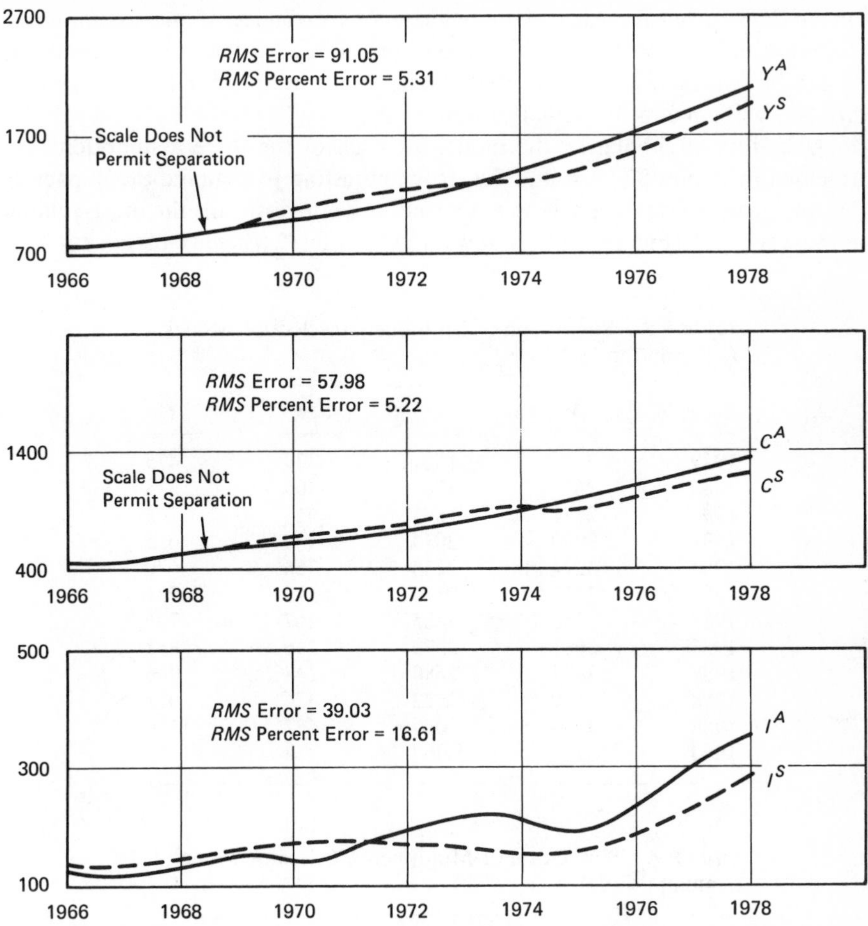

figure 8.5. Graphs of Simulated and Actual Values for Model II

In order to do so, some assumption must be made regarding the movement of government spending (G) during these years. For example, one possibility is that G will continue to grow at the same rate as in the recent past (Assumption I). For the period over which the model was estimated (1964–78), Assumption I translates into a 9 percent annual growth rate for G. Assumption I might be considered a midpoint of the possible range for the growth rate of G and could be compared with two other assumptions:

Assumption II—5 percent annual growth rate of G to 1990

Assumption III—13 percent annual growth rate of G to 1990

Assumption II represents a lower bound, and Assumption III an upper bound. By simulating the model for each of the three assumptions, an interval forecast can be constructed for each of the endogenous variables. If our assumptions encompass a large portion of the range of possibility for the growth rate of G, we can be reasonably confident that the interval forecasts for the endogenous variables will contain the actual values.[3]

The results of simulating the model for each of the three assumptions are presented in Tables 8.6, 8.7, and 8.8. It is interesting to examine the impact of differing growth rates of government spending on investment, the most volatile of the variables (Figure 8.6). A low growth rate (5 percent) of government

table 8.6. Simulation of Multiplier-Accelerator Model (Assumption I)

Time	Y	C	I	G
1979	2374	1521	379	475
1980	2627	1705	405	518
1981	2871	1893	414	564
1982	3090	2074	400	615
1983	3274	2238	366	670
1984	3422	2375	317	731
1985	3548	2485	267	796
1986	3683	2579	236	868
1987	3874	2680	248	946
1988	4179	2822	326	1031
1989	4660	3049	487	1124
1990	5366	3407	734	1225

table 8.7. Simulation of Multiplier-Accelerator Model (Assumption II)

Time	Y	C	I	G
1979	2357	1521	379	457
1980	2553	1692	381	480
1981	2675	1837	333	504
1982	2688	1928	230	529
1983	2571	1938	77	556
1984	2330	1851	−105	584
1985	2004	1672	−280	613
1986	1674	1429	−399	644
1987	1453	1183	−406	676
1988	1476	1018	−252	710
1989	1871	1035	91	745
1990	2726	1330	614	782

[3]By way of "stochastic simulation," a probability can be assigned to an interval forecast. The interested reader is referred to R. S. Pindyck and D. L. Rubinfeld, *Econometric Models and Econometric Forecasts* (New York: McGraw-Hill, 1976), pp. 360–67.

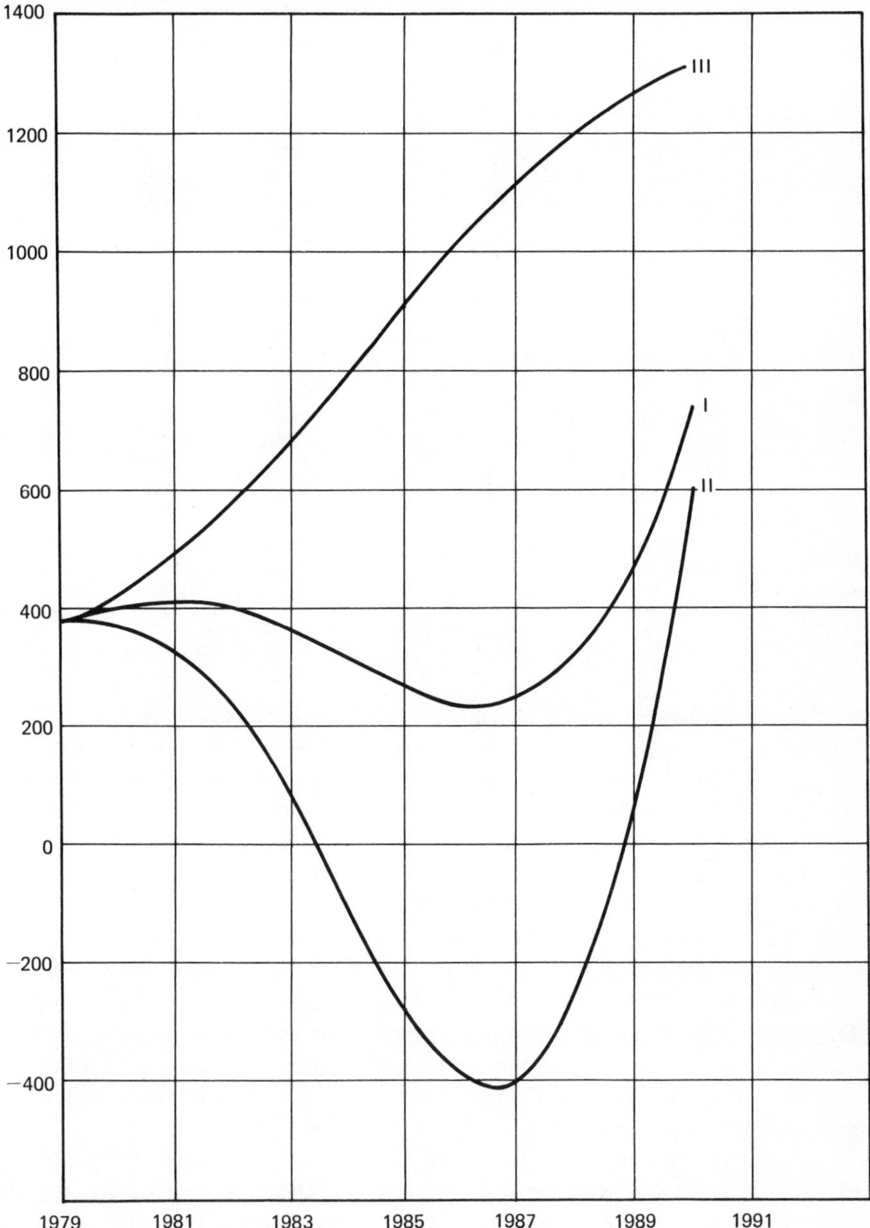

figure 8.6. Simulations of Investment Under Three Different Assumptions

spending actually leads to negative investment from 1984 to 1988. A forecast interval for investment, or any of the other endogenous variables, can be constructed from the low and high values for any particular year. For example, the range for investment in 1990 is from $614 to $1,314 billion.

table 8.8. Simulation of Multiplier-Accelerator Model (Assumption III)

Time	Y	C	I	G
1979	2392	1521	379	492
1980	2703	1718	429	556
1981	3074	1950	496	629
1982	3516	2226	579	710
1983	4035	2555	678	803
1984	4638	2942	789	907
1985	5320	3391	904	1025
1986	6073	3899	1016	1158
1987	6884	4460	1116	1309
1988	7742	5065	1198	1479
1989	8636	5703	1262	1671
1990	9572	6370	1314	1888

summary

The dynamic behavior of a mathematical model is often of considerable interest to an econometrician. One aspect of dynamic behavior is defined by the time paths of the endogenous variables and is termed *simulation.* Given changes in the exogenous variables, simulation involves the derivation of the time paths of the endogenous variables. Ordinarily, simulation is accomplished by a computer. The interested reader should refer to the Appendix to this chapter, "How to Write a Computer Simulation."

A change in an exogenous variable will probably not have the same impact on the endogenous variables within each time period. Consequently, we may wish to examine the *dynamic multipliers,* which measure the difference in impact. The sum of the dynamic multipliers for all time periods in the simulation is termed the *long-run multiplier.* Since a simulation may not be carried out over an infinite number of time periods, the long-run multiplier is not necessarily equal to its maximum possible value.

Analysis of the time path of a model allows a determination of whether the model is stable, and whether it is cyclical. Because the parameters are not necessarily fixed over time, it is often important to examine the dynamic effects of changes in the parameters on the stability and cyclical nature of a model. This can easily be accomplished by way of computer simulation.

An econometric model may be evaluated on the basis of how close its simulated or forecasted values of the endogenous variables are to the actual values. A common means of comparing and evaluating more than one simulation is the RMS percent error.

Given various assumptions on the movement of the exogenous variables over time, a simulation that forecasts the endogenous variables into the future can be performed. If the assumptions represent a broad range of possibility, then a forecast interval can be constructed with a high probability that it will contain the actual value of the endogenous variable.

exercises

1. Model II (Equations (8.7), (8.4), and (8.5)) was estimated by OLS. Is OLS the appropriate estimation technique?

2. Model I (Equations (8.3), (8.4), and (8.5)) could be estimated by OLS or 2SLS. Which is the better technique?

3. Estimate the parameters of Model I using OLS. The data are in Table 8.5.

4. Estimate the parameters of Model I using 2SLS and compare your results with those obtained in the preceding exercise.

5. Use the OLS parameter estimates of Model I to obtain simulated values of Y, C, and I for the 1966–78 time period (see Table 8.5, which presents actual and simulated values of Model II).

6. Repeat Exercise 5 using the 2SLS parameter estimates.

computer exercises

1. Work Exercise 3 with the regression program presented in Demo 4.19.

2. Work Exercise 4 with the regression program presented in Demo 4.19. (You should refer to Computer Exercise 2 in Chapter 7.)

3. Work Exercise 5 by way of the following computer program, which simulates Model I given the OLS parameter estimates entered into the program at Statements 10, 20, 30, and 40. Thus, you must type in the actual parameter estimates after the equal sign. The parameter estimates of Model II are input for illustrative purposes.

4. Repeat Computer Exercise 3 using the 2SLS parameter estimates.

5. Select a particular value for the annual growth rate (input .01 for 1 percent, .02 for 2 percent, etc.) of G and forecast the endogenous variables in Model II using the program in Demo 8.3. What would happen if G grew at an annual rate of -1 percent?

```
10LET B1=-64.213
20LET B2=.745
30LET B3=58.495
40LET B4=1.404
50DIM Y(15),C(15),I(15),G(15)
60LET Y(1)=635.7
70LET Y(2)=688.1
80FOR T=3 TO 15
90READ G(T)
100NEXT T
110DATA 158.7,180.2,198.7,207.9
120DATA 218.9,233.7,253.1,269.5,302.7
130DATA 338.4,361.3,396.2,435.6
140PRINT "Y","C","I","T"
150FOR T=3 TO 15
160LET Y(T)=(B1+B3+B4*(Y(T-1)-Y(T-2))+G(T))/(1-B2)
170LET C(T)=B1+B2*Y(T)
180LET I(T)=B3+B4*(Y(T-1)-Y(T-2))
190PRINT Y(T),C(T),I(T),T+1963
200PRINT
210NEXT T
220END
```

demo 8.2. Program That Simulates Model I

```
10LET B1=-64.213
20LET B2=.745
30LET B3=58.495
40LET B4=1.404
50DIM Y(15),C(15),I(15),G(15)
60LET Y(1)=1899.5
70LET Y(2)=2127.6
80LET G(2)=435.6
90PRINT "RATE OF GROWTH OF G"
100INPUT R
140PRINT "Y","C","I","G","T"
150FOR T=3 TO 15
155LET G(T)=G(T-1)+R*G(T-1)
160LET Y(T)=B1+B3+(B2+B4)*Y(T-1)-B4*Y(T-2)+G(T)
170LET C(T)=B1+B2*Y(T-1)
180LET I(T)=B3+B4*(Y(T-1)-Y(T-2))
190PRINT Y(T),C(T),I(T),G(T),T+1976
200PRINT
210NEXT T
220END
```

demo 8.3. Model II Forecasting Program

appendix 8.1

how to write a computer simulation

A computer simulation is not difficult to write. To generate the desired simulated values for the endogenous variables in a model, the computer must be given the following information:

1. Parameter values
2. Length of simulation (time)
3. Initial starting values of endogenous variables
4. Values of exogenous variables
5. Equations in model

We will illustrate by writing a computer program to simulate Model II. First, the parameter values are assigned:

```
10LET B1=-64.213
20LET B2=.745
30LET B3=58.495
40LET B4=1.404
```

Second, the length of the simulation is specified by way of a DIM statement. Since income is lagged two periods and values are simulated for thirteen periods

(1966–78), the DIM statement tells the computer to store space for 15 values (2 + 13):

```
50DIM Y(15),C(15),I(15),G(15)
```

Third, the initial starting values for income (1964 and 1965) must be assigned:

```
60LET Y(1)=635.7
70LET Y(2)=688.1
```

Note that $Y(1)$ is the income value for 1964, and $Y(2)$ is the value for 1965. Thus, time periods 3–15 correspond to the simulation period, 1966–78.

Fourth, the values of the exogenous variables must be input into the program. There is only one exogenous variable in Model II:

```
80FOR T=3 TO 15
90READ G(T)
100NEXT T
110DATA 158.7,180.2,198.7,207.9
120DATA 218.9,233.7,253.1,269.5,302.7
130DATA 338.4,361.3,396.2,435.6
```

If there is more than one exogenous variable, this series of statements will have to be repeated. Any number of DATA statements may be used.

Fifth, the equations must be given, along with print statements to output the results:

```
140PRINT "Y","C","I","T"
150FOR T=3 TO 15
160LET Y(T)=B1+B3+(B2+B4)*Y(T-1)-B4*Y(T-2)+G(T)
170LET C(T)=B1+B2*Y(T-1)
180LET I(T)=B3+B4*(Y(T-1)-Y(T-2))
190PRINT Y(T),C(T),I(T),T+1963
200PRINT
210NEXT T
220END
```

Only twenty-two statements are required to write this computer simulation. When this program is run, the results are as in Table 8.5.

The forecasts in Tables 8.6, 8.7, and 8.8 were constructed by assuming that

G grows at a specified rate. The above program can be simply modified by eliminating Statements 80–130 and initializing *G* at its starting value (1978):

```
80LET G(2)=435.6
```

Note that as long as the forecast period in the simulation (1979–90) is not longer than fifteen periods, the DIM statement need not be altered. Thus, we assume that $G(2) = G(1978)$ and that the first period of the forecast (1979) corresponds to $G(3)$. Assuming a 9 percent growth rate of G ($R = .09$), the following statement is placed in the loop:

```
155LET G(T)=G(T-1)+R*G(T-1)
```

Furthermore, $Y(1)$ and $Y(2)$ are initialized at their values in 1977 and 1978:

```
60LET Y(1)=1899.5
70LET Y(2)=2127.6
```

The PRINT statements at 140 and 190 are altered to print *G* and *T*:

```
140PRINT "Y","C","I","G","T"
190PRINT Y(T),C(T),I(T),G(T),T+1976
```

A listing of this program is in Computer Exercise 5 (Demo 8.3).

appendix A

introduction to the computer and to BASIC programming

When doing the exercises on a computer, you may need to know how to store or save a computer program for future use. In some instances your instructor may have already done this work for you, but you will still need to know how to access and run computer programs that have previously been saved. This section explains what you need to know to do the computer exercises in this book. Should you or your instructor desire to modify programs or add programs not given in the textbook, this Appendix provides an introduction to the computer and BASIC programming. Careful study of this material should enable you to write computer programs intermediate in difficulty; but without considerable practice, do not expect to become an expert.

You should first familiarize yourself with the computer environment at your school. Just as a reference librarian can demonstrate how to use the microfilm reader, a computer consultant employed in the computer center can show you where the terminals are and how to use them. The computer center will assign you or your class a number which must be typed in when "logging in" to the computer. Although the logging-in process varies from school to school, an example is given in Demo A.1. The carriage return is always hit after typing in your response. Lines not followed by "hit carriage return" are the computer responses.

```
HELLO        (Hit carriage return)

05-OCT-81        09:39
#
200,6        (Hit carriage return)

** LOGGED IN AT 09:39,        05-OCT-81 **
READY
```

demo A.1. Logging In

In the example in Demo A.1, you first type in HELLO and the computer responds with the DATE, the TIME, and the symbol "#," which tells you to type in your number: 200,6. Then the computer prints "**LOGGED IN AT 09:39,05-OCT-81**" and "READY," which indicates that the computer is ready to take your commands. With a few minutes of practice, you will be an expert at logging in.

You do not need to know anything about programming in order to use a computer program. Suppose you wish to run the program in Demo A.2, which

```
5PRINT "NUMBER OF COIN TOSSES"
10INPUT N
20RANDOM
30LET H=0
40FOR I=1 TO N
50LET X=RND
60IF X>.5 THEN 80
70LET H=H+1
80NEXT I
90PRINT "NUMBER OF HEADS=";H
100PRINT "NUMBER OF TAILS=";N-H
110PRINT "PERCENTAGE HEADS=";H/N*100
120PRINT
130END
```

demo A.2.

simulates the tossing of a coin. In the READY mode you would first type a name for the program in the following way:

```
NEW COIN        (Hit carriage return)
```

You are defining a new program not already stored on your computer number, and which you have chosen to name "COIN." The name of a program must always begin with an alphabetic character (*A*, *B*, *C*, etc.) and can contain anywhere from one to six alphabetic or numerical characters (on some computers the limit is eight characters). The following names would therefore have been acceptable: C1, C12, CN, COINTS, H12345, HD12TL. After naming your program, the computer will respond READY and you can then type in the program, hitting the carriage return after each line has been typed. If you make an error in any one line, the line is simply retyped. Note that in BASIC, the number in front of each line tells the computer the order of execution. Therefore, the lines can be typed in any order. If the wrong line number is accidentally typed, that line can be deleted by simply typing the wrong number and hitting the carriage return; then the correct line number along with the line can be typed in. For example, suppose you had typed 45LET X = RND when the line should read 50LET X = RND. You would type the following:

```
45        (Hit carriage return)
50LET X=RND        (Hit carriage return)
```

Once a program has been typed, it should be run to see if it is performing properly. All the programs in this book have sample runs that demonstrate what the output should look like. If an error occurs, each line of the program should be checked. A listing of the program can be output by typing LIST. To run a program, simply type RUN, as in Demo A.3. You will note that in this program,

```
RUN

NUMBER OF COIN TOSSES
? 100
NUMBER OF HEADS= 49
NUMBER OF TAILS= 51
PERCENTAGE HEADS= 49
```

demo A.3

the computer prints "NUMBER OF COIN TOSSES" with a question mark (?). You then type in the number of desired coin tosses after the question mark, hit the carriage return, and the computer will print out the "NUMBER OF HEADS," the "NUMBER OF TAILS," and the "PERCENTAGE HEADS." If a program is functioning as it should, type SAVE to store the program for future use. If you are good at copying, you should have little trouble getting the programs in this book to run.[1] However, do not be discouraged if you initially have problems. As with the learning of any skill, practice is required.

[1]A problem may exist in the use of the RANDOM statement. The following four statements may be used in place of the random statement and should be numbered with the line numbers 1, 2, 3, 4:

```
1 INPUT R
2 FOR I= 1 TO R
3 LET X= RND
4 NEXT R
```

When finished on the computer, it is time to "log off." You must ask a computer consultant about the logging off, since this command varies from place to place. (One of the most common log-off commands is "BYE.") Should you later decide to run a previously saved program such as the COIN program, you would log in and type OLD COIN, which tells the computer to find COIN so that it can be either run or revised. Some of the exercises require that a statement be revised or added. This can be accomplished by simply typing the revised or added line and then running the program. If you wish to save a revised program for future use, a computer consultant can explain how to do this. Usually this is done by typing SAVE again, but occasionally the command is different. If the revised program is not saved for future use, then the original program is saved by the computer.

introduction to the computer

The physical computing devices are termed *hardware*. Such terms as *bits*, *bytes*, *core*, *input-output*, *central processing unit*, *control unit*, *arithmetic-logic unit*, *magnetic drums* and *discs*, *magnetic* and *paper tape*, *card punches* and *readers*, *terminals*, and *line printers* are the jargon used to describe computer hardware. Computer hardware comprises three main components: (1) central processing unit (CPU), (2) memory (core), and (3) input-ouput (I/O). The central processing unit is composed of the control and arithmetic logic units, and it controls the order in which operations of the computer are performed and also does the actual arithmetical and logical operations.

The core of a computer is capable of storing various amounts of information depending on its size (memory). Core size is typically measured in bytes equal to groups of four, six, or eight bits. A digital computer is so named because of its use of the binary number system, which represents a piece of information in terms of zeros and ones. The reason for the use of the binary system is that electricity is capable of magnetizing a wire core either positively or negatively. Thus, a negative polarity can mean a zero; and a positive polarity, a one.

For example, the eight-bit (one byte) representation 10111001 means the following number: $1\times2^7 + 0\times2^6 + 1\times2^5 + 1\times2^4 + 1\times2^3 + 0\times2^2 + 0\times2^1 + 1\times2^0 = 128+0+32+16+8+0+0+1 = 185$. One byte is capable of storing the numbers 0 through 255, or a total of 256 numbers ($2^8 = 256$). Of course, larger numbers can be represented by using more than one byte. The alphabet and other characters are also represented by a certain byte configuration.

Input-output can be divided into separate devices for input and output, although some devices can be used for both. The typical computer user is most

---

where *R* is any positive integer input in the program after the first question mark. Line 20 would then be eliminated. *R* should be different each time the program is run. Note also that LET can be omitted on some machines, although its inclusion would not cause an error.

familiar with using cards and a card reader for input and seeing the output printed on paper by a line printer. However, magnetic drums, discs, and tapes are often used to store large files for input and output. The advantages of such devices are that they increase the memory of a computer at much lower cost than adding additional core, and they are more easily handled than cards.

A terminal or teletype, which functions in the same manner as a typewriter, is another device for I/O that enables the user to interact with the computer. This is done by typing in a program or running a previously saved program. Interaction is of great advantage over batch (cards), since results can be obtained immediately and any errors can be detected and corrected without waiting a long time—sometimes several hours—for batch.

The interactive use of a computer via terminal is termed *time sharing*, since the user actually shares computer time with other users. Although it appears to the user that no one else is using the computer, the computer is actually sharing its CPU time with many users. The tremendous speed of response of the computer might deceive a person into thinking that he or she is the only one using computer time. In addition, paper tape with specific programs and/or data can be input via a terminal, also allowing for interaction.

Primarily because of the more-expensive I/O devices required, the interactive use of a computer is more costly than batch in many applications. However, there has been a rapid reduction in the cost of interactive computing over the past few years, especially with the advent of minicomputers. As the calculator has replaced the slide rule, so might the minicomputers of the next decade lead to the replacement of batch processing with interactive time sharing. The following *Wall Street Journal* article is of interest:

> International Data Corp., a Waltham, Mass., computer-industry research firm, is optimistic about the sales of so-called personal computers. About the size of a typewriter, the personal computer is used to play electronic games, balance checkbooks, keep track of recipes and perform a variety of other tasks around the home. International Data estimates that sales of personal computers, which retail for an average of about $3,000, should reach $300 million annually by 1980—and twice that if there is a breakthrough in developing programs that are cheaper and easier to use. (March 27, 1978, p. 1).

The informational component of the computer is known as *software*. Software is the sum total of all the computer programs available to the hardware. The computer programs contained in this book are written in BASIC (Beginners All-Purpose Symbolic Instruction Code), which is available at almost every computer installation in the country. Another common computer language is FORTRAN (Formula Translation). BASIC is actually a simpler version of FORTRAN without the complicated input-output of FORTRAN. BASIC is an excellent interactive language.

A line number must precede each BASIC statement. The value for the line number is arbitrary. There is only one rule in assigning line numbers: A line that must be executed before another line must have a smaller line number. It is common practice to begin numbering a program at 5 or 10, and then number each successive line in steps of 5 or 10: 5, 10, 15 or 10, 20, 30. This procedure allows lines to be added between existing line numbers should it be necessary to revise or correct an error in a program. Some computer systems have an automatic line number function which types the line number for you. You should check with a computer consultant to see if such an option is available. If so, it will save you a considerable amount of time, as you will not need to type in the line numbers yourself.

In BASIC, a syntax rule is used to define a variable: a single letter of the alphabet, or a single letter followed by a single digit. For example, *A*, *X*, *Y*2, *B*1, *J*9, and *K* are valid, while *X*15 (more than two characters) and 1*Y* (starts with a digit) are invalid. To assign a value to a variable, the variable name is specified along with an equal sign:

```
10N=12     or     10LET N=12
```

Line 10 defines the variable, *N*, and assigns a 12 to it. *N* might be the number of observations in a sample. Statement 10 is termed an *assignment* and may have to begin with "LET" in some systems (check with a computer consultant). The "=" sign is not the "=" of an equation. It is a device to show assignment. This subtlety must be appreciated. For example, the next statement could be:

```
20N=N-1     (i.e., N = Value previously stored in N minus one).
```

N would now contain the number 11. Note that if $N = N - 1$ were an equation instead of an assignment, rules of algebra would be violated.

As an example of the use of statements of assignment, consider the following program:

```
10A=4
20B=10
30C=5
40D=-B+A**2+A*B-C/B
50E=(-B+A)**2+A*(B-C)/B
60F=((-B+A)**2+A*(B-C)/B)*2
70G1=A/4*2
80G1=G1+1
```

In Table A.1 the arithmetic operations allowed on the right-hand side of the equal sign of an assignment statement are listed in order of computer execution. All of these symbols are used in the above program. Exponentiation (rais-

table A.1. Arithmetic Operators

Operator	Name	Example	Example
↑	Exponentiation	A↑2	10↑2
**	Exponentiation	10.5**2	B**.5
−	Prefix minus	−0.5	$-A$
* or /	Multiplication or division	11.3*x	A/B
+ or −	Addition or subtraction	$A + 5.5$	$B - C$

ing a number to a power) is performed before prefix minus (a negative of a single number), multiplication or division, and addition or subtraction. Similarly, prefix minus takes priority over multiplication or division, which in turn is performed before addition or subtraction. Note that exponentiation is indicated by either "**" or "↑", and therefore you must check with a computer consultant as to which one to use. For example, the computer will scan Statement 40 and first calculate A**2 (A^2). Then it will calculate $-B$ (prefix minus after exponentiation). Since multiplication and division are at the same level of priority, it will make the calculations on a left-to-right basis. Thus, A*B will first be calculated and then C/B. Finally, the computer will perform the specified addition and subtraction:

```
D=-10+16+40-.5=45.5
```

It is frequently necessary to use the parentheses pair "( )" to avoid ambiguity. In any statement, the number of left parentheses must equal the number of right parentheses. Thus, in Statement 50, we desire to add A to minus B before squaring the result, and subtract C from B before dividing by B:

$$E=(-10+4)^2+4(10-5)/10=36+2=38.0$$

If we wish to multiply the result in Statement 50 by two, an additional parentheses pair could be added, as in Statement 60. Alternatively, Statement 60 could be written as $F = 2$*E or $F = E$*2. In Statement 70, $G1$ is equal to 2, not

.5, since the operations (equal priority for multiplication and division) are performed from left to right. If Statement 70 read $G1 = A/(4*2)$, then the result would be .5. If a variable has not been defined in an assignment statement, any use of the variable name will cause the computer to initially assign it a value of zero. Thus, if $G1$ had not been defined in Statement 70, Statement 80 would assign a one to $G1$ ($G1 = 0+1 = 1$).

There are four BASIC techniques for assigning numbers to variables. The first has already been presented—the assignment statement (e.g., $A = 4$). The second method is done with a pair of statements: READ and DATA. The syntax of these statements is as follows:

READ: The word READ followed by variable names separated by commas. If only one variable name is referenced, no commas are needed.

DATA: The word DATA followed by numbers separated by commas. If only one number is on a line, no commas are needed.

Statements 10, 20, and 30 could be replaced by the following READ–DATA statements:

```
10READ A,B,C
20DATA 4,10,5
```

The computer will assign 4 to A, 10 to B, and 5 to C. Any number of DATA statements may be used, as the computer will read the numbers on the DATA statements until the total numbers that are read equal the number of variables on the READ statement:

```
10READ A,B,C
20DATA 4
30DATA 10,5
```

Similarly, more than one READ statement may be used:

```
10READ A
20READ B
30READ C
40DATA 4,10,5,6
```

The computer will ignore the 6 in Statement 40 because only three variables are being read.

The third method of assignment is done with the INPUT statement and is exactly like the READ statement except that data are input by the user while executing a program. The terminal will type a "?" each time an INPUT statement is executed, and the user will type the appropriate number and hit the carriage return. The syntax of the INPUT statement is:

INPUT: The word INPUT followed by variable names separated by commas. If only one variable name is referenced, no commas are needed.

For example, the following statement would assign values for *A*, *B*, and *C*, replacing Statements 10, 20, and 30:

```
10INPUT A,B,C
```

The terminal will print question marks until all the variables referenced in the INPUT statement have been assigned values:

```
? 4 (Hit carriage return)
? 10 (Hit carriage return)
? 5 (Hit carriage return)
```

The fourth method of assignment is more complicated and is done when a particular variable takes on more than one value. As an example, suppose we have data on the IQ of ten individuals: 80, 95, 100, 101, 103, 115, 105, 116, 120, and 110. The following program defines a variable, *Q*, which will contain the ten observations on IQ:

```
10N=10
20DIM Q(10)
30FOR I=1 TO N
40READ Q(I)
50NEXT I
60DATA 80,95,100,101,103,115,105,116,120,110
```

Statement 10 assigns 10 to the number of observations in *Q*, and Statement 20 dimensions and defines the variable *Q*. In effect, Statement 20 stores room for ten numbers in *Q*. Unfortunately, the statement DIM Q(N) is illegal in BASIC, and therefore the dimension of *Q* must be changed each time the program is run with a different number of observations. Similarly, Statement 10 must be changed if the number of observations on IQ is altered.[2] More than one variable may be referenced on a DIM statement:

```
10DIM Q(10), E(10)
```

Statements 30 through 50 compose a "loop" which reads in the data one step at a time. All statements between FOR and NEXT are executed N times. Thus, the first time through the loop, $I = 1$; the second time, $I = 2$; the third time, $I = 3$, and so forth, until $I = 10$. Statement 40 is therefore executed ten times: READ $Q(1)$, READ $Q(2)$, READ $Q(3)$, . . . , READ $Q(10)$. The first value of Q that is read is 80, the second value is 95, and the tenth value is 110. Q now contains all ten values of IQ. This computer program can be used on any size data set by simply changing Statements 10, 20, and 60. If one desires to type in the values for the variable at the terminal, Statement 60 would be deleted and Statement 40 would read:

```
40INPUT Q(I)
```

Statement 40 is executed N times and causes a "?" to be printed for each value. For large amounts of data, however, it is better to use DATA statements, since they can be saved by the computer. The data can therefore be used again without having to retype all the numbers.

Instead of saving DATA statements, another method for data storage consists of creating a data file. Although the procedure for creating a file is relatively easy, you should actually have a computer consultant do this for you because the procedure varies from place to place. Once a data file is created, it can be used in any program because it is permanently stored under a particular name, just like any program that is saved for future use. The following program creates a file containing the ten values of IQ:

```
5OPEN "IQ" AS FILE 1
10DIM #1,Q(10)
15N=10
20FOR I=1 TO N
30READ Q(I)
40NEXT I
50DATA 80,95,100,101,103,115,105,116,120,110
60CLOSE 1
70END
```

[2]Alternatively, if you knew that the largest data set on which the program would ever be used was, for example, equal to 100, Statement 20 could read: 20DIM Q(100). However, many programs in this book make use of the MAT (matrix) statement. If MAT statements exist in a program, the dimensions specified must be exact.

Statement 5 defines the name, IQ, of the first data file to be stored on your number. Statement 10 dimensions the size of File 1. After running this program (type RUN), a file named IQ will be stored on your number.

All files must be closed (Statement 60) before the end (Statement 70) of program execution. Now suppose you wish to use the IQ data in another program or in a newly created program. The first two statements of the program would be:

```
5OPEN "IQ" AS FILE 1
10DIM #1, Q(10)
```

CLOSE statement is placed just before END of program. The data are available to the program without having to read it again.

Output of answers and desired labels (literals) is accomplished by the PRINT statement. A *literal* is any group of characters—numeric, alphabetic, =, #, etc.—that is enclosed in quotes. These characters are printed out just as they appear within quotes. A literal can be as long as the typewriter carriage permits on the terminal. The syntax of the PRINT statement is:

PRINT: The word PRINT followed by variables and/or literals separated by commas or semicolons. The use of a semicolon reduces the spacing between the variables and/or literals being printed.

The programs in Demos A.4 and A.5 demonstrate the use of the PRINT statement.

```
10A=4
20B=10
30C=5
40D=-B+A**2+A*B-C/B
50E=(-B+A)**2+A*(B-C)/B
60F=((-B+A)**2+A*(B-C)/B)*2
70G1=A/4*2
75PRINT "G1=";G1
80G1=G1+1
90PRINT "G1=";G1
100PRINT "D=",D
110PRINT "E=",E
120PRINT "F=",F
130END

RUN

G1= 2
G1= 3
D=              45.5
E=              38
F=              76
```

demo A.4.

```
10N=10
20DIM Q(10)
30FOR I=1 TO N
40READ Q(I)
45PRINT Q(I)
50NEXT I
60DATA 80,95,100,101,103,115,105,116,120,110
70END

RUN

80
95
100
101
103
115
105
116
120
110

45PRINT Q(I);
RUN

80 95 100 101 103 115 105 116 120 110
```

demo A.5.

Statements 75 and 90 in DEMO A.4 print out the two values for *G*1 defined in Statements 70 and 80. Because of the use of the semicolon in these PRINT statements, there is only one space between the literal (*G*1=) and the value of *G*1. Statements 100, 110, and 120 print out the values for *D*, *E*, and *F* defined in Statements 40, 50, and 60; the comma in the PRINT statements increases the spacing between the literals and the variable values. Alternatively, an assignment statement and a PRINT statement could be combined into one PRINT statement:

```
100PRINT "D=", -B+A**2+A*B-C/B
```

Thus, a PRINT statement may also include a formula evaluation provided that any variables used in the formula have previously been defined in assignment statements (10, 20, and 30). With Statement 100 above, Statement 40 could obviously be deleted.

The PRINT statement within the loop (FOR–NEXT) in Demo A.5 is performed ten times: each time a value of *Q* is read by Statement 40, Statement 45 is then executed, causing that value to be printed. Without a semicolon at the end of the PRINT statement, the numbers are printed in a column. If a semicolon is added to the PRINT statement, the numbers are printed in a row.

One of the most important statistical operators is the summation, $\sum$. Many formulas require that a series of numbers be summed. For example, the formula for the mean is

$$\bar{X} = \frac{\sum_{I=1}^{N} X_I}{N} \qquad (1)$$

This formula indicates that the N values of the variable, X, are to be summed: $X_1+X_2+X_3+X_4+\cdots+X_N$: This sum is then divided by N to get the mean. The reader may already have guessed that the FOR–NEXT loop is the appropriate programming technique to use in calculating a sum. The following program calculates the mean of the ten observations on IQ in Demo A.5:

```
10N=10
20DIM Q(10)
30FOR I=1 TO N
40READ A(I)
45S=S+Q(I)
50NEXT I
60DATA 80,95,100,101,103,115,105,116,120,110
70PRINT "MEAN ="; S/N
```

To demonstrate how the loop calculates the desired sum, let us run through the loop for each I (Statement 45):

```
I=1  S=S+Q(1)=0+80=80
I=2  S=S+Q(2)=80+95=175
I=3  S=S+Q(3)=175+100=275
I=4  S=S+Q(4)=275+101=376
I=5  S=S+Q(5)=376+103=479
I=6  S=S+Q(6)=479+115=594
I=7  S=S+Q(7)=594+105=699
I=8  S=S+Q(8)=699+116=815
I=9  S=S+Q(9)=815+120=935
I=10 S=S+Q(10)=935+110=1045
```

When $I = 10$, Statement 45 is executed for the last time and S now contains the sum of the ten observations on IQ. Statement 70 prints out the mean, $1045/10 = 104.5$.

The formula for the standard deviation is

$$S = \sqrt{\frac{\sum_{I=1}^{N} (X - \bar{X})^2}{N - 1}} \qquad (2)$$

The following statements could be added to the previous program to calculate the standard deviation of the IQ data:

```
80S=S/N
90FOR I=1 TO N
100S1=S1+(Q(I)-S)**2
110NEXT I
120PRINT "STANDARD DEVIATION="; SQR(S1/(N-1))
130END
```

$(Q(I)-S)**2$ is equivalent to $(X-\bar{X})**2$. In general, the form of the summation statement (Statements 45 and 100) is $S = S + F$, where S is the variable name of the variable storing the sum, and F is the formula following the summation sign.

The *SQR* in Statement 120 directs the computer to calculate the square root of whatever is contained in parentheses: $S1/(N - 1)$. It is only one of many BASIC functions that permit quick calculations of complicated mathematical functions. The BASIC mathematical functions for which you may have use are listed in Table A.2. You should check with a computer consultant to make certain that these are the same at your installation.

table A.2. Mathematical Functions

ABS(X)	Calculates the absolute value of X
SQR(X)	Calculates the square root of X
EXP(X)	Calculates $e**X$, where $e = 2.71828\ldots$
LOG(X)	Calculates the natural logarithm of X, $\log_e X$
LOG10(X)	Calculates the logarithm of X to the base 10, $\log_{10} X$
INT(X)	Calculates the greatest integer of X that is less than or equal to X

In addition to the mathematical functions given in Table A.2, it is frequently necessary to use "relational symbols" in order to compare two values. Table A.3 presents these symbols.

Relational symbols are often used with the logical espression IF THEN:

```
40FOR I=1 TO N
50X=RND
60IF X>.5 THEN 80
70H=H+1
80NEXT I
```

table A.3. Relational Symbols

Equal	=
Not Equal	# or < >[a]
Less Than	<
Greater Than	>
Less Than or Equal	< =
Greater Than or Equal	> =

[a]Check with a computer consultant as to which one to use.

Statement 50 generates a random number between zero and one and assigns that value to X (N random numbers are generated). If X is greater than .5, then control switches to Statement 80, skipping Statement 70. Only if X is less than .5 is Statement 70 executed, which is termed a *counter*. Statement 70 counts the number of heads generated by the random number function, RND. Thus, Statement 60 tests each of the N random numbers and counts a head only if the random number is less than .5. Each time Statement 80 is executed, I is incremented by one and a new random number is generated. When $I = N$, no more random numbers are generated.

Suppose we wished to calculate the lowest and highest price of XYZ stock traded on a particular day on the New York Stock Exchange (this information is regularly reported in the financial news). The prices of XYZ in the order that shares were traded on this day are given in Table A.4.

table A.4. Prices of *XYZ*

27.25
28.50
30.00
29.25
30.50
28.00
28.50
29.50
30.25
29.75
30.25
28.75

The following statements would calculate and print out the maximum value of the stock price data:

```
220Z=X(1)
230FOR I=2 TO N
240IF (Z-X(I))>=0 THEN 270
260Z=X(I)
270NEXT I
280PRINT "MAXIMUM VALUE IS";Z
```

Statement 220 assigns the first value of X (27.25) to Z. Let us run through the loop a few times to see what it is doing:

```
230I=2
240IF (27.25-28.50) >=0 THEN 270
260Z=28.50
270NEXT I

230I=3
240IF (28.50-30) >=0 THEN 270
260Z=30
270NEXT I

230I=4
240IF (30-29.25) >=0 THEN 270
270NEXT I

230I=5
240IF (30-30.50) >=0 THEN 270
260Z=30.50
270NEXT I
```

The first time through the loop, $I = 2$, $Z = X(1) = 27.25$ (Statement 220), and $X(2) = 28.50$. If $Z - X(2)$ is greater than or equal to zero, then Z is larger than $X(2)$ and Statement 260 is skipped. In this case however, Z is not larger than $X(2)$, and therefore Statement 260 is executed which assigns the larger value to Z. In this manner, each value of X is compared with all other values of X until the largest value of X is found. The fourth time through the loop ($I = 5$), Statement 260 is executed for the last time, since 30.50 is the largest value of X. Z now contains 30.50, and this value is printed out by Statement 280. The program in Demo A.6 prints out the minimum, maximum, and range of the stock price data. Statements 100 and 110 indicate the size of the data set. Statements 120 through 140 and Statement 310 read in the data. Statements 150 through 210 calculate and print out the minimum value. Statements 220 through 280 do the same for the maximum value, and Statement 290 prints out the range ($Z - Y$). By changing Statements 100, 110, and 310, this program can be used on any data set.

```
100DIM X(12)
110N=12
120FOR I=1 TO N
130READ X(I)
140NEXT I
150Y=X(1)
160FOR I=2 TO N
170IF (Y-X(I)) <=0 THEN 200
190Y=X(I)
200NEXT I
210PRINT "MINIMUM VALUE IS";Y
220Z=X(1)
230FOR I=2 TO N
240IF (Z-X(I)) >=0 THEN 270
260Z=X(I)
270NEXT I
280PRINT "MAXIMUM VALUE IS";Z
290PRINT "RANGE IS"; Z-Y
310DATA 27.25,28.5,30,29.25,30.5,28,28.5,29.5,30.25,29.75,30.25,28.75
320END

RUN

MINIMUM VALUE IS 27.25
MAXIMUM VALUE IS 30.5
RANGE IS 3.25
```

demo A.6.

Although you may not have noticed, the concept of a "matrix" has already been introduced in the section dealing with dimensioned variables. A *matrix* is a rectangular array of numbers. The IQ data can be presented as a column matrix of dimension 10 rows by 1 column (10, 1):

80
95
100
101
103
115
105
116
120
110

or as a row matrix of dimension 1 row by 10 columns (1, 10):

80 95 100 101 103 115 105 116 120 110

Letting N stand for the number of observations and K for the number of variables, an N-row-by-K-column matrix can be dimensioned to store a data set. For example, suppose we had data on the income, IQ, and education ($K = 3$) of ten individuals ($N = 10$). These data could be stored in a 10-row-by-3-column matrix:

$$A = \begin{matrix} 5000 & 80 & 9 \\ 6000 & 95 & 8 \\ 7000 & 100 & 10 \\ 8000 & 101 & 10 \\ 9000 & 103 & 11 \\ 10000 & 115 & 14 \\ 11000 & 105 & 15 \\ 12000 & 116 & 13 \\ 13000 & 120 & 16 \\ 14000 & 110 & 17 \end{matrix}$$

The BASIC statement DIM A(10,3) would define a matrix, A, to store these data. A is a doubly dimensioned variable, which is constructed using the same syntax rule for defining any variable—a single letter or a single letter followed by a single digit.[3]

It is customary to allow I to stand for the row number and J for the column number of the matrix. Thus, $A(I,J)$ represents the I row, J column element of the matrix, A. For example, $A(1,1)$, $A(1,2)$, and $A(1,3)$ are the respective variable values for the first observation (first row): 5000, 80, and 9. $A(10,1)$, $A(10,2)$, and $A(10,3)$ are the values for the tenth observation: 14000, 110, and 17. Similarly, $A(5,2)$ is the IQ of the fifth observation (103), and $A(6,1)$ is the income of the sixth observation (10000). $A(7,3)$ is the years of education for the seventh observation (15). There are two general methods for reading the data into a matrix. The first makes use of a "nested loop," which is also an extremely important programming concept in other applications. The second method uses the MAT READ statement.

A nested loop is a loop within a loop. As an example, consider the following program:

```
10FOR I=1 TO 3
20FOR J=1 TO 2
30PRINT I*J
40NEXT J
50NEXT I
60END
```

[3]Some machines will only allow dimensioned variables to be defined by a single letter.

The outer loop (FOR I, NEXT I) comprises Statements 10 and 50. The inner or nested loop (Statements 20 through 40) is executed two times (FOR $J = 1$ TO 2) for each I. Thus, the total number of times Statement 30 is executed is six (3*2). Let us run through the program:

```
I=1,J=1    30PRINT 1*1
I=1,J=2    30PRINT 1*2
I=2,J=1    30PRINT 2*1
I=2,J=2    30PRINT 2*2
I=3,J=1    30PRINT 3*1
I=3,J=2    30PRINT 3*2
```

When this program is run, the following numbers are therefore printed: 1, 2, 2, 4, 3, 6. More than one nested loop can be in a program, as in Demo A.7. Note the use of the command "LIST," which lists a program.

```
LIST

10FOR K=1 TO 4
20FOR I=1 TO 3
30FOR J=1 TO 2
40PRINT K*I*J
50NEXT J
60NEXT I
70NEXT K
80END

RUN

1
2
2
4      K=1
3
6

2
4
4
8      K=2
6
12

3
6
6
12     K=3
9
18
```

demo A.7.

```
4
8
8
16     K=4
12
24
```

demo A.7. Continued

The placement of Statements 10 and 70 (FOR $K = 1$ TO 4, NEXT K) around the original program containing the I and J loops only, and the change in the PRINT statement (PRINT $I*J$) to PRINT $K*I*J$, cause a total of twenty-four numbers to be printed (4*3*2). The first six numbers are the same as before because $K = 1$, but the next three sets of six numbers are respectively two, three, and four times the original numbers ($K = 2$, $K = 3$, $K = 4$).

The following program, which contains only one nested loop, reads the income, IQ, and education data into a matrix named A, as above.

```
10DIM A(10,3)
20FOR I=1 TO 10
30FOR J=1 TO 3
40READ A(I,J)
50NEXT J
60NEXT I
70DATA 5000,80,9,6000,95,8,7000,100,10,8000,101,10
75DATA 9000,103,11,10000,115,14,11000,105,15
80DATA 12000,116,13,13000,120,16,14000,110,17
```

To use the above program, the data must be organized in row order. Alternatively, the data could be organized in column order if the following program were used:

```
10DIM A(10,3)
20FOR J=1 TO 3
30FOR I=1 TO 10
40READ A(I,J)
50NEXT I
60NEXT J
70DATA 5000,6000,7000,8000,9000,10000,11000,12000,13000,14000
75DATA 80,95,100,101,103,115,105,116,120,110
80DATA 9,8,10,10,11,14,15,13,16,17
```

Thus, in the first program, the J loop is the nested loop; in the second program, it is the I loop. The selection of a specific method is a matter of personal preference, although the second method of data organization seems easier. However, if the data are organized in row order, a MAT READ statement can be used instead of a nested loop:

```
10DIM A(10,3)
20MAT READ A
70DATA 5000,80,9,6000,95,8,7000,100,10,8000,101,10
75DATA 9000,103,11,10000,115,14,11000,105,15
80DATA 12000,116,13,13000,120,16,14000,110,17
```

Regardless of which method is chosen to read in the data, the most convenient way of printing a matrix is with the MAT PRINT statement (Demo A.8).

```
10DIM A(10,3)
20MAT READ A
30MAT PRINT A;
70DATA 5000,80,9,6000,95,8,7000,100,10,8000,101,10
75DATA 9000,103,11,10000,115,14,11000,105,15
80DATA 12000,116,13,13000,120,16,14000,110,17
90END

RUN
  5000    80    9
  6000    95    8
  7000   100   10
  8000   101   10
  9000   103   11
 10000   115   14
 11000   105   15
 12000   116   13
 13000   120   16
 14000   110   17
```

demo A.8.

In addition to reading data and printing matrices, MAT statements can be used to add, subtract, and multiply matrices, and to calculate inverses and transposes. Two matrices can be added or subtracted only if their dimensions are the same. As an example, consider the following matrices of order four by three:

$$A = \begin{matrix} 1 & 5 & 7 \\ 2 & 3 & 1 \\ 1 & 4 & 3 \\ 9 & 8 & 6 \end{matrix} \qquad B = \begin{matrix} 3 & 2 & 2 \\ 5 & 5 & 7 \\ 3 & 4 & 9 \\ 1 & 1 & 8 \end{matrix}$$

The sum and difference of these matrices are:

$$A + B = \begin{matrix} 4 & 7 & 9 \\ 7 & 8 & 8 \\ 4 & 8 & 12 \\ 10 & 9 & 14 \end{matrix} \qquad A - B = \begin{matrix} -2 & 3 & 5 \\ -3 & -2 & -6 \\ -2 & 0 & -6 \\ 8 & 7 & -2 \end{matrix}$$

Two matrices can be multiplied only if the number of columns of the first matrix equals the number of rows of the second matrix. Since the number of columns in A is three, and the number of rows in B is four, $A*B$ cannot be calculated. The *transpose* of a matrix is defined as that matrix in which the first row becomes the first column, the second row the second column, and so forth. The transposes of A and B (a prime indicates a transpose) are:

$$A' = \begin{matrix} 1 & 2 & 1 & 9 \\ 5 & 3 & 4 & 8 \\ 7 & 1 & 3 & 6 \end{matrix} \qquad B' = \begin{matrix} 3 & 5 & 3 & 1 \\ 2 & 5 & 4 & 1 \\ 2 & 7 & 9 & 8 \end{matrix}$$

Because the dimension of A' is (3,4) and that of A is (4,3), $A'*A$ or $A*A'$ can be calculated. An easy way to check whether or not two matrices can be multiplied is to write down their dimensions in the order in which multiplication is to take place. Thus, $A*A'$ is (4,3)*(3,4). Since the two inner numbers are equal (3), they are conformable to multiplication. The two outer numbers indicate the dimensions of the resulting matrix; the first number (4) is the number of rows, and the last number (also 4) is the number of columns. The resulting matrix is therefore (4,4). Similarly, $A'*A$ is (3,4)*(4,3) = (3,3).

Letting (I,J) stand for the ijth element of the resulting matrix, $A*A'$, (I,J) is obtained by multiplying the respective elements in the ith row by the jth column and then summing these numbers. For example, (1,1) = 1*1 + 5*5 + 7*7 = 75; (2,3) = 2*1 + 3*4 + 1*3 = 17.

$$\begin{matrix} 1 & 5 & 7 \\ 2 & 3 & 1 \\ 1 & 4 & 3 \\ 9 & 8 & 6 \end{matrix} * \begin{matrix} 1 & 2 & 1 & 9 \\ 5 & 3 & 4 & 8 \\ 7 & 1 & 3 & 6 \end{matrix} = \begin{matrix} 75 & 24 & 42 & 91 \\ 24 & 14 & 17 & 48 \\ 42 & 17 & 26 & 59 \\ 91 & 48 & 59 & 181 \end{matrix}$$

Calculating $A'*A$ in a similar manner:

$$\begin{matrix} 1 & 2 & 1 & 9 \\ 5 & 3 & 4 & 8 \\ 7 & 1 & 3 & 6 \end{matrix} * \begin{matrix} 1 & 5 & 7 \\ 2 & 3 & 1 \\ 1 & 4 & 3 \\ 9 & 8 & 6 \end{matrix} = \begin{matrix} 87 & 87 & 66 \\ 87 & 114 & 98 \\ 66 & 98 & 95 \end{matrix}$$

The extremely simple program in Demo A.9 does all this work for us. Matrix C (MAT C) is the transpose (TRN) of A, MAT D is $A*A'$, and MAT E is $A'*A$.

```
10DIM A(4,3),C(3,4),D(4,4),E(3,3)
20MAT READ A
30DATA 1,5,7,2,3,1,1,4,3,9,8,6
40MAT C=TRN(A)
50MAT D=A*C
60MAT E=C*A
70MAT PRINT A;
80MAT PRINT C;
90MAT PRINT D;
100MAT PRINT E;
110END

RUN

 1   5   7
 2   3   1
 1   4   3
 9   8   6

 1   2   1   9
 5   3   4   8
 7   1   3   6

 75   24    42   91
 24   14    17   48
 42   17    26   59
 91   48    59   181

 87   87    66
 87   114   98
 66   98    95
```

demo A.9.

An *inverse* of a matrix is defined as that matrix which, when multiplied by the original matrix, results in an identity matrix. Only square matrices (same number of rows as columns) possess inverses. An identity matrix has ones down the main diagonal (left to right) and zeros elsewhere. As an example of an inverse matrix, consider the last matrix printed in Demo A.9 (MAT E). For small matrices, the work of calculating an inverse matrix is tedious, but not impossible. But since most econometric applications require the calculation of fairly large inverse matrices, we will examine only the computer solution. The inverse of E is:

$$E^{-1} = \begin{matrix} .075 & -.109 & .061 \\ -.109 & .238 & -.169 \\ .061 & -.169 & .143 \end{matrix}$$

$E*E^{-1}$ or $E^{-1}*E$ is equal to the identity matrix:

$$\begin{matrix} 1 & 0 & 0 \\ 0 & 1 & 0 \\ 0 & 0 & 1 \end{matrix}$$

In Demo A.10, E, E^{-1}, and $E*E^{-1}$ (the identity matrix) are printed. Due to rounding error, the computer prints out the extremely small numbers .476837E-6 and —.953674E-6 instead of zeros.

```
10DIM  E(3,3),F(3,3),G(3,3)
20MAT  READ  E
30DATA  87,87,66,87,114,98,66,98,95
40MAT  F=INV(E)
50MAT  G=E*F
60MAT  PRINT  E;
70MAT  PRINT  F;
80MAT  PRINT  G;
90END

RUN
  87    87    66
  87    114   98
  66    98    95
     .745062E-1     -.109207     .608933E-1
    -.109207     .237557     -.169189
     .608934E-1     -.169189     .142753
     1   0   0
     .476837E-6     1     -.953674E-6
     0   0   1
```

demo A.10.

appendix B

statistical tables

statistical table 1 Areas Under the Standardized Normal Distribution

Z	.00	.01	.02	.03	.04	.05	.06	.07	.08	.09
0.0	.0000	.0040	.0080	.0120	.0160	.0199	.0239	.0279	.0319	.0359
0.1	.0398	.0438	.0478	.0517	.0557	.0596	.0636	.0675	.0714	.0753
0.2	.0793	.0832	.0871	.0910	.0948	.0987	.1026	.1064	.1103	.1141
0.3	.1179	.1217	.1255	.1293	.1331	.1368	.1406	.1443	.1480	.1517
0.4	.1554	.1591	.1628	.1664	.1700	.1736	.1772	.1808	.1844	.1879
0.5	.1915	.1950	.1985	.2019	.2054	.2088	.2123	.2157	.2190	.2224
0.6	.2257	.2291	.2324	.2357	.2389	.2422	.2454	.2486	.2517	.2549
0.7	.2580	.2611	.2642	.2673	.2704	.2734	.2764	.2794	.2823	.2852
0.8	.2881	.2910	.2939	.2967	.2995	.3023	.3051	.3078	.3106	.3133
0.9	.3159	.3186	.3212	.3238	.3264	.3289	.3315	.3340	.3365	.3389
1.0	.3413	.3438	.3461	.3485	.3508	.3531	.3554	.3577	.3599	.3621
1.1	.3643	.3665	.3686	.3708	.3729	.3749	.3770	.3790	.3810	.3830
1.2	.3849	.3869	.3888	.3907	.3925	.3944	.3962	.3980	.3997	.4015
1.3	.4032	.4049	.4066	.4082	.4099	.4115	.4131	.4147	.4162	.4177
1.4	.4192	.4207	.4222	.4236	.4251	.4265	.4279	.4292	.4306	.4319
1.5	.4332	.4345	.4357	.4370	.4382	.4394	.4406	.4418	.4429	.4441
1.6	.4452	.4463	.4474	.4484	.4495	.4505	.4515	.4525	.4535	.4545
1.7	.4554	.4564	.4573	.4582	.4591	.4599	.4608	.4616	.4625	.4633
1.8	.4641	.4649	.4656	.4664	.4671	.4678	.4686	.4693	.4699	.4706
1.9	.4713	.4719	.4726	.4732	.4738	.4744	.4750	.4756	.4761	.4767
2.0	.4772	.4778	.4783	.4788	.4793	.4798	.4803	.4808	.4812	.4817
2.1	.4821	.4826	.4830	.4834	.4838	.4842	.4846	.4850	.4854	.4857
2.2	.4861	.4864	.4868	.4871	.4875	.4878	.4881	.4884	.4887	.4890
2.3	.4893	.4896	.4898	.4901	.4904	.4906	.4909	.4911	.4913	.4916
2.4	.4918	.4920	.4922	.4925	.4927	.4929	.4931	.4932	.4934	.4936
2.5	.4938	.4940	.4941	.4943	.4945	.4946	.4948	.4949	.4951	.4952
2.6	.4953	.4955	.4956	.4957	.4959	.4960	.4961	.4962	.4963	.4964
2.7	.4965	.4966	.4967	.4968	.4969	.4970	.4971	.4972	.4973	.4974
2.8	.4974	.4975	.4976	.4977	.4977	.4978	.4979	.4979	.4980	.4981
2.9	.4981	.4982	.4982	.4983	.4984	.4984	.4985	.4985	.4986	.4986
3.0	.4987	.4987	.4987	.4988	.4988	.4989	.4989	.4989	.4990	.4990

statistical table 2 Critical Values of the t Distribution (Two-Tailed)

Pr / df	0.50	0.20	0.10	0.05	0.02	0.010	0.002
1	1.000	3.078	6.314	12.706	31.821	63.657	318.31
2	0.816	1.886	2.920	4.303	6.965	9.925	22.327
3	0.765	1.638	2.353	3.182	4.541	5.841	10.214
4	0.741	1.533	2.132	2.776	3.747	4.604	7.173
5	0.727	1.476	2.015	2.571	3.365	4.032	5.893
6	0.718	1.440	1.943	2.447	3.143	3.707	5.208
7	0.711	1.415	1.895	2.365	2.998	3.499	4.785
8	0.706	1.397	1.860	2.306	2.896	3.355	4.501
9	0.703	1.383	1.833	2.262	2.821	3.250	4.297
10	0.700	1.372	1.812	2.228	2.764	3.169	4.144
11	0.697	1.363	1.796	2.201	2.718	3.106	4.025
12	0.695	1.356	1.782	2.179	2.681	3.055	3.930
13	0.694	1.350	1.771	2.160	2.650	3.012	3.852
14	0.692	1.345	1.761	2.145	2.624	2.977	3.787
15	0.691	1.341	1.753	2.131	2.602	2.947	3.733
16	0.690	1.337	1.746	2.120	2.583	2.921	3.686
17	0.689	1.333	1.740	2.110	2.567	2.898	3.646
18	0.688	1.330	1.734	2.101	2.552	2.878	3.610
19	0.688	1.328	1.729	2.093	2.539	2.861	3.579
20	0.687	1.325	1.725	2.086	2.528	2.845	3.552
21	.0686	1.323	1.721	2.080	2.518	2.831	3.527
22	0.686	1.321	1.717	2.074	2.508	2.819	3.505
23	0.685	1.319	1.714	2.069	2.500	2.807	3.485
24	0.685	1.318	1.711	2.064	2.492	2.797	3.467
25	0.684	1.316	1.708	2.060	2.485	2.787	3.450
26	0.684	1.315	1.706	2.056	2.479	2.779	3.435
27	0.684	1.314	1.703	2.052	2.473	2.771	3.421
28	0.683	1.313	1.701	2.048	2.467	2.763	3.408
29	0.683	1.311	1.699	2.045	2.462	2.756	3.396
30	0.683	1.310	1.697	2.042	2.457	2.750	3.385
40	0.681	1.303	1.684	2.021	2.423	2.704	3.307
60	0.679	1.296	1.671	2.000	2.390	2.660	3.232
120	0.677	1.289	1.658	1.980	2.358	2.617	3.160
∞	0.674	1.282	1.645	1.960	2.326	2.576	3.090

Source: From E. S. Pearson and H. O. Hartley, eds., *Biometrika Tables for Statisticians* (New York: Cambridge University Press, 1966), 3rd ed., Vol. 1, Table 12. Reproduced by permission of the Biometrika trustees.

statistical table 3A The F Distribution (Values of $F_{0.01}$)

Degrees of Freedom for Denominator	Degrees of Freedom for Numerator																		
	1	2	3	4	5	6	7	8	9	10	12	15	20	24	30	40	60	120	∞
1	4,052	5,000	5,403	5,625	5,764	5,859	5,928	5,982	6,023	6,056	6,106	6,157	6,209	6,235	6,261	6,287	6,313	6,339	6,366
2	98.5	99.0	99.2	99.2	99.3	99.3	99.4	99.4	99.4	99.4	99.4	99.4	99.4	99.5	99.5	99.5	99.5	99.5	99.5
3	34.1	30.8	29.5	28.7	28.2	27.9	27.7	27.5	27.3	27.2	27.1	26.9	26.7	26.6	26.5	26.4	26.3	26.2	26.1
4	21.2	18.0	16.7	16.0	15.5	15.2	15.0	14.8	14.7	14.5	14.4	14.2	14.0	13.9	13.8	13.7	13.7	13.6	13.5
5	16.3	13.3	12.1	11.4	11.0	10.7	10.5	10.3	10.2	10.1	9.89	9.72	9.55	9.47	9.38	9.29	9.20	9.11	9.02
6	13.7	10.9	9.78	9.15	8.75	8.47	8.26	8.10	7.98	7.87	7.72	7.56	7.40	7.31	7.23	7.14	7.06	6.97	6.88
7	12.2	9.55	8.45	7.85	7.46	7.19	6.99	6.84	6.72	6.62	6.47	6.31	6.16	6.07	5.99	5.91	5.82	5.74	5.65
8	11.3	8.65	7.59	7.01	6.63	6.37	6.18	6.03	5.91	5.81	5.67	5.52	5.36	5.28	5.20	5.12	5.03	4.95	4.86
9	10.6	8.02	6.99	6.42	6.06	5.80	5.61	5.47	5.35	5.26	5.11	4.96	4.81	4.73	4.65	4.57	4.48	4.40	4.31
10	10.0	7.56	6.55	5.99	5.64	5.39	5.20	5.06	4.94	4.85	4.71	4.56	4.41	4.33	4.25	4.17	4.08	4.00	3.91
11	9.65	7.21	6.22	5.67	5.32	5.07	4.89	4.74	4.63	4.54	4.40	4.25	4.10	4.02	3.94	3.86	3.78	3.69	3.60
12	9.33	6.93	5.95	5.41	5.06	4.82	4.64	4.50	4.39	4.30	4.16	4.01	3.86	3.78	3.70	3.62	3.54	3.45	3.36
13	9.07	6.70	5.74	5.21	4.86	4.62	4.44	4.30	4.19	4.10	3.96	3.82	3.66	3.59	3.51	3.43	3.34	3.25	3.17
14	8.86	6.51	5.56	5.04	4.70	4.46	4.28	4.14	4.03	3.94	3.80	3.66	3.51	3.43	3.35	3.27	3.18	3.09	3.00
15	8.68	6.36	5.42	4.89	4.56	4.32	4.14	4.00	3.89	3.80	3.67	3.52	3.37	3.29	3.21	3.13	3.05	2.96	2.87
16	8.53	6.23	5.29	4.77	4.44	4.20	4.03	3.89	3.78	3.69	3.55	3.41	3.26	3.18	3.10	3.02	2.93	2.84	2.75
17	8.40	6.11	5.19	4.67	4.34	4.10	3.93	3.79	3.68	3.59	3.46	3.31	3.16	3.08	3.00	2.92	2.83	2.75	2.65
18	8.29	6.01	5.09	4.58	4.25	4.01	3.84	3.71	3.60	3.51	3.37	3.23	3.08	3.00	2.92	2.84	2.75	2.66	2.57
19	8.19	5.93	5.01	4.50	4.17	3.94	3.77	3.63	3.52	3.43	3.30	3.15	3.00	2.92	2.84	2.76	2.67	2.58	2.49
20	8.10	5.85	4.94	4.43	4.10	3.87	3.70	3.56	3.46	3.37	3.23	3.09	2.94	2.86	2.78	2.69	2.61	2.52	2.42
21	8.02	5.78	4.87	4.37	4.04	3.81	3.64	3.51	3.40	3.31	3.17	3.03	2.88	2.80	2.72	2.64	2.55	2.46	2.36
22	7.95	5.72	4.82	4.31	3.99	3.76	3.59	3.45	3.35	3.26	3.12	2.98	2.83	2.75	2.67	2.58	2.50	2.40	2.31
23	7.88	5.66	4.76	4.26	3.94	3.71	3.54	3.41	3.30	3.21	3.07	2.93	2.78	2.70	2.62	2.54	2.45	2.35	2.26
24	7.82	5.61	4.72	4.22	3.90	3.67	3.50	3.36	3.26	3.17	3.03	2.89	2.74	2.66	2.58	2.49	2.40	2.31	2.21
25	7.77	5.57	4.68	4.18	3.86	3.63	3.46	3.32	3.22	3.13	2.99	2.85	2.70	2.62	2.53	2.45	2.36	2.27	2.17
30	7.56	5.39	4.51	4.02	3.70	3.47	3.30	3.17	3.07	2.98	2.84	2.70	2.55	2.47	2.39	2.30	2.21	2.11	2.01
40	7.31	5.18	4.31	3.83	3.51	3.29	3.12	2.99	2.89	2.80	2.66	2.52	2.37	2.29	2.20	2.11	2.02	1.92	1.80
60	7.08	4.98	4.13	3.65	3.34	3.12	2.95	2.82	2.72	2.63	2.50	2.35	2.20	2.12	2.03	1.94	1.84	1.73	1.60
120	6.85	4.79	3.95	3.48	3.17	2.96	2.79	2.66	2.56	2.47	2.34	2.19	2.03	1.95	1.86	1.76	1.66	1.53	1.38
∞	6.63	4.61	3.78	3.32	3.02	2.80	2.64	2.51	2.41	2.32	2.18	2.04	1.88	1.79	1.70	1.59	1.47	1.32	1.00

Source: M. Merrington and C. M. Thompson, "Tables of Percentage Points of the Inverted Beta (F) Distribution," *Biometrika*, 1943, Vol. 33. Reproduced by permission of the Biometrika trustees.

statistical table 3B The F Distribution (Values of $F_{0.05}$)

Degrees of Freedom for Denominator	Degrees of Freedom for Numerator 1	2	3	4	5	6	7	8	9	10	12	15	20	24	30	40	60	120	∞
1	161	200	216	225	230	234	237	239	241	242	244	246	248	249	250	251	252	253	254
2	18.5	19.0	19.2	19.2	19.3	19.3	19.4	19.4	19.4	19.4	19.4	19.4	19.4	19.5	19.5	19.5	19.5	19.5	19.5
3	10.1	9.55	9.28	9.12	9.01	8.94	8.89	8.85	8.81	8.79	8.74	8.70	8.66	8.64	8.62	8.59	8.57	8.55	8.53
4	7.71	6.94	6.59	6.39	6.26	6.16	6.09	6.04	6.00	5.96	5.91	5.86	5.80	5.77	5.75	5.72	5.69	5.66	5.63
5	6.61	5.79	5.41	5.19	5.05	4.95	4.88	4.82	4.77	4.74	4.68	4.62	4.56	4.53	4.50	4.46	4.43	4.40	4.37
6	5.99	5.14	4.76	4.53	4.39	4.28	4.21	4.15	4.10	4.06	4.00	3.94	3.87	3.84	3.81	3.77	3.74	3.70	3.67
7	5.59	4.74	4.35	4.12	3.97	3.87	3.79	3.73	3.68	3.64	3.57	3.51	3.44	3.41	3.38	3.34	3.30	3.27	3.23
8	5.32	4.46	4.07	3.84	3.69	3.58	3.50	3.44	3.39	3.35	3.28	3.22	3.15	3.12	3.08	3.04	3.01	2.97	2.93
9	5.12	4.26	3.86	3.63	3.48	3.37	3.29	3.23	3.18	3.14	3.07	3.01	2.94	2.90	2.86	2.83	2.79	2.75	2.71
10	4.96	4.10	3.71	3.48	3.33	3.22	3.14	3.07	3.02	2.98	2.91	2.85	2.77	2.74	2.70	2.66	2.62	2.58	2.54
11	4.84	3.98	3.59	3.36	3.20	3.09	3.01	2.95	2.90	2.85	2.79	2.72	2.65	2.61	2.57	2.53	2.49	2.45	2.40
12	4.75	3.89	3.49	3.26	3.11	3.00	2.91	2.85	2.80	2.75	2.69	2.62	2.54	2.51	2.47	2.43	2.38	2.34	2.30
13	4.67	3.81	3.41	3.18	3.03	2.92	2.83	2.77	2.71	2.67	2.60	2.53	2.46	2.42	2.38	2.34	2.30	2.25	2.21
14	4.60	3.74	3.34	3.11	2.96	2.85	2.76	2.70	2.65	2.60	2.53	2.46	2.39	2.35	2.31	2.27	2.22	2.18	2.13
15	4.54	3.68	3.29	3.06	2.90	2.79	2.71	2.64	2.59	2.54	2.48	2.40	2.33	2.29	2.25	2.20	2.16	2.11	2.07
16	4.49	3.63	3.24	3.01	2.85	2.74	2.66	2.59	2.54	2.49	2.42	2.35	2.28	2.24	2.19	2.15	2.11	2.06	2.01
17	4.45	3.59	3.20	2.96	2.81	2.70	2.61	2.55	2.49	2.45	2.38	2.31	2.23	2.19	2.15	2.10	2.06	2.01	1.96
18	4.41	3.55	3.16	2.93	2.77	2.66	2.58	2.51	2.46	2.41	2.34	2.27	2.19	2.15	2.11	2.06	2.02	1.97	1.92
19	4.38	3.52	3.13	2.90	2.74	2.63	2.54	2.48	2.42	2.38	2.31	2.23	2.16	2.11	2.07	2.03	1.98	1.93	1.88
20	4.35	3.49	3.10	2.87	2.71	2.60	2.51	2.45	2.39	2.35	2.28	2.20	2.12	2.08	2.04	1.99	1.95	1.90	1.84
21	4.32	3.47	3.07	2.84	2.68	2.57	2.49	2.42	2.37	2.32	2.25	2.18	2.10	2.05	2.01	1.96	1.92	1.87	1.81
22	4.30	3.44	3.05	2.82	2.66	2.55	2.46	2.40	2.34	2.30	2.23	2.15	2.07	2.03	1.98	1.94	1.89	1.84	1.78
23	4.28	3.42	3.03	2.80	2.64	2.53	2.44	2.37	2.32	2.27	2.20	2.13	2.05	2.01	1.96	1.91	1.86	1.81	1.76
24	4.26	3.40	3.01	2.78	2.62	2.51	2.42	2.36	2.30	2.25	2.18	2.11	2.03	1.98	1.94	1.89	1.84	1.79	1.73
25	4.24	3.39	2.99	2.76	2.60	2.49	2.40	2.34	2.28	2.24	2.16	2.09	2.01	1.96	1.92	1.87	1.82	1.77	1.71
30	4.17	3.32	2.92	2.69	2.53	2.42	2.33	2.27	2.21	2.16	2.09	2.01	1.93	1.89	1.84	1.79	1.74	1.68	1.62
40	4.08	3.23	2.84	2.61	2.45	2.34	2.25	2.18	2.12	2.08	2.00	1.92	1.84	1.79	1.74	1.69	1.64	1.58	1.51
60	4.00	3.15	2.76	2.53	2.37	2.25	2.17	2.10	2.04	1.99	1.92	1.84	1.75	1.70	1.65	1.59	1.53	1.47	1.39
120	3.92	3.07	2.68	2.45	2.29	2.18	2.09	2.02	1.96	1.91	1.83	1.75	1.66	1.61	1.55	1.50	1.43	1.35	1.25
∞	3.84	3.00	2.60	2.37	2.21	2.10	2.01	1.94	1.88	1.83	1.75	1.67	1.57	1.52	1.46	1.39	1.32	1.22	1.00

Source: M. Merrington and C. M. Thompson, "Tables of Percentage Points of the Inverted Beta (F) Distribution," *Biometrika*, 1943, Vol. 33. Reproduced by permission of the Biometrika trustees.

statistical table 4 Critical Values of the Swed and Eisenhart Test (.05 Level)

	N_2																		
N_1	**2**	**3**	**4**	**5**	**6**	**7**	**8**	**9**	**10**	**11**	**12**	**13**	**14**	**15**	**16**	**17**	**18**	**19**	**20**
2											2	2	2	2	2	2	2	2	2
3					2	2	2	2	2	2	2	2	2	3	3	3	3	3	3
4				2	2	2	3	3	3	3	3	3	3	3	4	4	4	4	4
5			2	2	3	3	3	3	3	4	4	4	4	4	4	4	5	5	5
6		2	2	3	3	3	3	4	4	4	4	5	5	5	5	5	5	6	6
7		2	2	3	3	3	4	4	5	5	5	5	5	6	6	6	6	6	6
8		2	3	3	3	4	4	5	5	5	6	6	6	6	6	7	7	7	7
9		2	3	3	4	4	5	5	5	6	6	6	7	7	7	7	8	8	8
10		2	3	3	4	5	5	5	6	6	7	7	7	7	8	8	8	8	9
11		2	3	4	4	5	5	6	6	7	7	7	8	8	8	9	9	9	9
12	2	2	3	4	4	5	6	6	7	7	7	8	8	8	9	9	9	10	10
13	2	2	3	4	5	5	6	6	7	7	8	8	9	9	9	10	10	10	10
14	2	2	3	4	5	5	6	7	7	8	8	9	9	9	10	10	10	11	11
15	2	3	3	4	5	6	6	7	7	8	8	9	9	10	10	11	11	11	12
16	2	3	4	4	5	6	6	7	8	8	9	9	10	10	11	11	11	12	12
17	2	3	4	4	5	6	7	7	8	9	9	10	10	11	11	11	12	12	13
18	2	3	4	5	5	6	7	8	8	9	9	10	10	11	11	12	12	13	13
19	2	3	4	5	6	6	7	8	8	9	10	10	11	11	12	12	13	13	13
20	2	3	4	5	6	6	7	8	9	9	10	10	11	12	12	13	13	13	14

	N_2																		
N_1	**2**	**3**	**4**	**5**	**6**	**7**	**8**	**9**	**10**	**11**	**12**	**13**	**14**	**15**	**16**	**17**	**18**	**19**	**20**
2																			
3																			
4				9	9														
5			9	10	10	11	11												
6			9	10	11	12	12	13	13	13	13								
7				11	12	13	13	14	14	14	14	15	15	15					
8				11	12	13	14	14	15	15	16	16	16	16	17	17	17	17	17
9					13	14	14	15	16	16	16	17	17	18	18	18	18	18	18
10					13	14	15	16	16	17	17	18	18	18	19	19	19	20	20
11					13	14	15	16	17	17	18	19	19	19	20	20	20	21	21
12					13	14	16	16	17	18	19	19	20	20	21	21	21	22	22
13						15	16	17	18	19	19	20	20	21	21	22	22	23	23
14						15	16	17	18	19	20	20	21	22	22	23	23	23	24
15						15	16	18	18	19	20	21	22	22	23	23	24	24	25
16							17	18	19	20	21	21	22	23	23	24	25	25	25
17							17	18	19	20	21	22	23	23	24	25	25	26	26
18							17	18	19	20	21	22	23	24	25	25	26	26	27
19							17	18	20	21	22	23	23	24	25	26	26	27	27
20							17	18	20	21	22	23	24	25	25	26	27	27	28

Source: Frieda S. Swed and C. Eisenhart, "Tables for Testing Randomness of Grouping in a Sequence of Alternatives," *Annals of Mathematical Statistics*, 1943, Vol. 14. Used by permission of *Annals of Mathematical Statistics.*

statistical table 5A Durbin-Watson Statistic (.01 Level)

	$k' = 1$		$k' = 2$		$k' = 3$		$k' = 4$		$k' = 5$	
n	d_L	d_U	d_L	d_U	d_L	d_U	d_L	d_U	d_L	d_U
15	0.81	1.07	0.70	1.25	0.59	1.46	0.49	1.70	0.39	1.96
16	0.84	1.09	0.74	1.25	0.63	1.44	0.53	1.66	0.44	1.90
17	0.87	1.10	0.77	1.25	0.67	1.43	0.57	1.63	0.48	1.85
18	0.90	1.12	0.80	1.26	0.71	1.42	0.61	1.60	0.52	1.80
19	0.93	1.13	0.83	1.26	0.74	1.41	0.65	1.58	0.56	1.77
20	0.95	1.15	0.86	1.27	0.77	1.41	0.68	1.57	0.60	1.74
21	0.97	1.16	0.89	1.27	0.80	1.41	0.72	1.55	0.63	1.71
22	1.00	1.17	0.91	1.28	0.83	1.40	0.75	1.54	0.66	1.69
23	1.02	1.19	0.94	1.29	0.86	1.40	0.77	1.53	0.70	1.67
24	1.04	1.20	0.96	1.30	0.88	1.41	0.80	1.53	0.72	1.66
25	1.05	1.21	0.98	1.30	0.90	1.41	0.83	1.52	0.75	1.65
26	1.07	1.22	1.00	1.31	0.93	1.41	0.85	1.52	0.78	1.64
27	1.09	1.23	1.02	1.32	0.95	1.41	0.88	1.51	0.81	1.63
28	1.10	1.24	1.04	1.32	0.97	1.41	0.90	1.51	0.83	1.62
29	1.12	1.25	1.05	1.33	0.99	1.42	0.92	1.51	0.85	1.61
30	1.13	1.26	1.07	1.34	1.01	1.42	0.94	1.51	0.88	1.61
31	1.15	1.27	1.08	1.34	1.02	1.42	0.96	1.51	0.90	1.60
32	1.16	1.28	1.10	1.35	1.04	1.43	0.98	1.51	0.92	1.60
33	1.17	1.29	1.11	1.36	1.05	1.43	1.00	1.51	0.94	1.59
34	1.18	1.30	1.13	1.36	1.07	1.43	1.01	1.51	0.95	1.59
35	1.19	1.31	1.14	1.37	1.08	1.44	1.03	1.51	0.97	1.59
36	1.21	1.32	1.15	1.38	1.10	1.44	1.04	1.51	0.99	1.59
37	1.22	1.32	1.16	1.38	1.11	1.45	1.06	1.51	1.00	1.59
38	1.23	1.33	1.18	1.39	1.12	1.45	1.07	1.52	1.02	1.58
39	1.24	1.34	1.19	1.39	1.14	1.45	1.09	1.52	1.03	1.58
40	1.25	1.34	1.20	1.40	1.15	1.46	1.10	1.52	1.05	1.58
45	1.29	1.38	1.24	1.42	1.20	1.48	1.16	1.53	1.11	1.58
50	1.32	1.40	1.28	1.45	1.24	1.49	1.20	1.54	1.16	1.59
55	1.36	1.43	1.32	1.47	1.28	1.51	1.25	1.55	1.21	1.59
60	1.38	1.45	1.35	1.48	1.32	1.52	1.28	1.56	1.25	1.60
65	1.41	1.47	1.38	1.50	1.35	1.53	1.31	1.57	1.28	1.61
70	1.43	1.49	1.40	1.52	1.37	1.55	1.34	1.58	1.31	1.61
75	1.45	1.50	1.42	1.53	1.39	1.56	1.37	1.59	1.34	1.62
80	1.47	1.52	1.44	1.54	1.42	1.57	1.39	1.60	1.36	1.62
85	1.48	1.53	1.46	1.55	1.43	1.58	1.41	1.60	1.39	1.63
90	1.50	1.54	1.47	1.56	1.45	1.59	1.43	1.61	1.41	1.64
95	1.51	1.55	1.49	1.57	1.47	1.60	1.45	1.62	1.42	1.64
100	1.52	1.56	1.50	1.58	1.48	1.60	1.46	1.63	1.44	1.65

Source: J. Durbin and G. S. Watson, "Testing for Serial Correlation in Least Squares Regression," *Biometrika*, 38 (1951), 159–77. Reproduced by permission of the Biometrika trustees.

statistical table 5B Durbin-Watson Statistic (.05 Level)

	$k'=1$		$k'=2$		$k'=3$		$k'=4$		$k'=5$	
n	d_L	d_U	d_L	d_U	d_L	d_U	d_L	d_U	d_L	d_U
15	1.08	1.36	0.95	1.54	0.82	1.75	0.69	1.97	0.56	2.21
16	1.10	1.37	0.98	1.54	0.86	1.73	0.74	1.93	0.62	2.15
17	1.13	1.38	1.02	1.54	0.90	1.71	0.78	1.90	0.67	2.10
18	1.16	1.39	1.05	1.53	0.93	1.69	0.82	1.87	0.71	2.06
19	1.18	1.40	1.08	1.53	0.97	1.68	0.86	1.85	0.75	2.02
20	1.20	1.41	1.10	1.54	1.00	1.68	0.90	1.83	0.79	1.99
21	1.22	1.42	1.13	1.54	1.03	1.67	0.93	1.81	0.83	1.96
22	1.24	1.43	1.15	1.54	1.05	1.66	0.96	1.80	0.86	1.94
23	1.26	1.44	1.17	1.54	1.08	1.66	0.99	1.79	0.90	1.92
24	1.27	1.45	1.19	1.55	1.10	1.66	1.01	1.78	0.93	1.90
25	1.29	1.45	1.21	1.55	1.12	1.66	1.04	1.77	0.95	1.89
26	1.30	1.46	1.22	1.55	1.14	1.65	1.06	1.76	0.98	1.88
27	1.32	1.47	1.24	1.56	1.16	1.65	1.08	1.76	1.01	1.86
28	1.33	1.48	1.26	1.56	1.18	1.65	1.10	1.75	1.03	1.85
29	1.34	1.48	1.27	1.56	1.20	1.65	1.12	1.74	1.05	1.84
30	1.35	1.49	1.28	1.57	1.21	1.65	1.14	1.74	1.07	1.83
31	1.36	1.50	1.30	1.57	1.23	1.65	1.16	1.74	1.09	1.83
32	1.37	1.50	1.31	1.57	1.24	1.65	1.18	1.73	1.11	1.82
33	1.38	1.51	1.32	1.58	1.26	1.65	1.19	1.73	1.13	1.81
34	1.39	1.51	1.33	1.58	1.27	1.65	1.21	1.73	1.15	1.81
35	1.40	1.52	1.34	1.58	1.28	1.65	1.22	1.73	1.16	1.80
36	1.41	1.52	1.35	1.59	1.29	1.65	1.24	1.73	1.18	1.80
37	1.42	1.53	1.36	1.59	1.31	1.66	1.25	1.72	1.19	1.80
38	1.43	1.54	1.37	1.59	1.32	1.66	1.26	1.72	1.21	1.79
39	1.43	1.54	1.38	1.60	1.33	1.66	1.27	1.72	1.22	1.79
40	1.44	1.54	1.39	1.60	1.34	1.66	1.29	1.72	1.23	1.79
45	1.48	1.57	1.43	1.62	1.38	1.67	1.34	1.72	1.29	1.78
50	1.50	1.59	1.46	1.63	1.42	1.67	1.38	1.72	1.34	1.77
55	1.53	1.60	1.49	1.64	1.45	1.68	1.41	1.72	1.38	1.77
60	1.55	1.62	1.51	1.65	1.48	1.69	1.44	1.73	1.41	1.77
65	1.57	1.63	1.54	1.66	1.50	1.70	1.47	1.73	1.44	1.77
70	1.58	1.64	1.55	1.67	1.52	1.70	1.49	1.74	1.46	1.77
75	1.60	1.65	1.57	1.68	1.54	1.71	1.51	1.74	1.49	1.77
80	1.61	1.66	1.59	1.69	1.56	1.72	1.53	1.74	1.51	1.77
85	1.62	1.67	1.60	1.70	1.57	1.72	1.55	1.75	1.52	1.77
90	1.63	1.68	1.61	1.70	1.59	1.73	1.57	1.75	1.54	1.78
95	1.64	1.69	1.62	1.71	1.60	1.73	1.58	1.75	1.56	1.78
100	1.65	1.69	1.63	1.72	1.61	1.74	1.59	1.76	1.57	1.78

Source: J. Durbin and G. S. Watson, "Testing for Serial Correlation in Least Squares Regression," *Biometrika*, 38 (1951), 159–77. Reproduced by permission of the Biometrika trustees.

selected bibliography

Aigner, D. J., *Basic Econometrics.* Englewood Cliffs, N.J.: Prentice-Hall, 1971.

Baumol, W. J., *Economic Dynamics.* New York: Macmillan, 1970.

Beals, Ralph E., *Statistics for Economists; An Introduction.* Chicago: Rand McNally, 1972.

Bridge, J. I., *Applied Econometrics.* Amsterdam: North-Holland, 1971.

Christ, C. F., *Econometric Models and Methods.* New York: John Wiley, 1966.

Cramer, J. S., *Empirical Econometrics.* Amsterdam: North-Holland, 1969.

Desai, Meghnad, *Applied Econometrics.* New York: McGraw-Hill, 1976.

Dhrymes, P. J., *Distributed Lags: Problems of Estimation and Formulation.* San Francisco: Holden-Day, 1971.

———, *Econometrics: Statistical Foundations and Applications.* New York: Harper & Row, Pub., 1970.

Elliott, J. W., *Econometric Analysis for Management Decisions.* Homewood, Ill.: Richard D. Irwin, 1973.

Fisher, F. M., *The Identification Problem in Econometrics.* New York: McGraw-Hill, 1966.

Frank, C. R., Jr., *Statistics and Econometrics.* New York: Holt, Rinehart & Winston, 1971.

Freund, John E., *Mathematical Statistics.* Englewood Cliffs, N.J.: Prentice-Hall, 1962.

———, *Statistics: A First Course* (2nd ed.). Englewood Cliffs, N.J.: Prentice-Hall, 1976.

Goldberger, A. S., *Econometric Theory.* New York: John Wiley, 1964.

———, *Topics in Regression Analysis.* New York: Macmillan, 1968.

Goldfeld, S. M., and R. E. Quandt, *Nonlinear Methods in Econometrics.* Amsterdam: North-Holland, 1972.

Graybill, F. A., *An Introduction to Linear Statistical Models,* Vol. 1. New York: McGraw-Hill, 1961.

Gujarati, Damodar, *Basic Econometrics.* New York: McGraw-Hill, 1978.

Hoel, P. G., *Introduction to Mathematical Statistics* (4th ed.). New York: John Wiley, 1971.

Hu, Teh-Wei, *Econometrics: An Introductory Analysis.* Baltimore: University Park Press, 1973.

Huang, D. S., *Regression and Econometric Methods.* New York: John Wiley, 1970.

Johnston, J., *Econometric Methods* (2nd ed.). New York: McGraw-Hill, 1972.

Kane, Edward J., *Economic Statistics and Econometrics.* New York: Harper & Row, Pub., 1968.

Kelejian, H. A., and W. E. Oates, *Introduction to Econometrics: Principles and Applications.* New York: Harper & Row, Pub., 1974.

Klein, Lawrence R., *An Introduction to Econometrics.* Englewood Cliffs, N.J.: Prentice-Hall, 1962.

———, *A Textbook of Econometrics* (2nd ed.). Englewood Cliffs, N.J.: Prentice-Hall, 1974.

Kmenta, Jan, *Elements of Econometrics.* New York: Macmillan, 1971.

Koutsoyiannis, A., *Theory of Econometrics.* New York: Harper & Row, Pub., 1973.

Leser, C. E. V., *Econometric Techniques and Problems* (2nd ed.). New York: Hafner, 1974.

Madansky, A., *Foundations of Econometrics.* Amsterdam: North-Holland, 1976.

Maddala, G. S., *Econometrics.* New York: McGraw-Hill, 1976.

Malinvaud, E., *Principles of Econometrics.* Paris: North-Holland, 1966.

———, *Statistical Methods of Econometrics* (2nd ed.). Amsterdam: North-Holland, 1976.

Mood, A. M., and F. A. Graybill, *Introduction to the Theory of Statistics* (2nd ed.). New York: McGraw-Hill, 1963.

Murphy, James L., *Introductory Econometrics.* Homewood, Ill.: Richard D. Irwin, 1973.

Naylor, T. H., *Computer Simulation Experiments with Economic Systems.* New York: John Wiley, 1971.

———, ed., *The Design of Computer Simulation Experiments.* Durham, N.C.: Duke University Press, 1969.

Netter, J., and W. Wasserman, *Applied Linear Statistical Models.* Homewood, Ill.: Richard D. Irwin, 1974.

Pindyck, R. S., and D. L. Rubinfeld, *Econometric Models and Econometric Forecasts.* New York: McGraw-Hill, 1976.

Rao, C. R., *Linear Statistical Inference and Its Applications* (2nd ed.). New York: John Wiley, 1975.

Rao, Potluri, and Roger LeRoy Miller, *Applied Econometrics.* Belmont, Calif.: Wadsworth, 1971.

Richmond, Samuel B., *Statistical Analysis* (2nd ed.). New York: Ronald Press, 1964.

Sprent, Peter, *Models in Regression and Related Topics.* London: Methuen, 1969.

Theil, Henry, *Principles of Econometrics.* New York: John Wiley, 1971.

Tintner, Gerhard, *Econometrics.* New York: John Wiley, 1965.

Valavanis, Stefan, *Econometrics: An Introduction to Maximum-Likelihood Methods.* New York: McGraw-Hill, 1959.

Wallis, K. F., *Introductory Econometrics.* Chicago: Aldine, 1972.

Walters, A. A., *An Introduction to Econometrics.* London: Macmillan, 1968.

Wonnacott, Thomas H., and Ronald J. Wonnacott, *Econometrics.* New York: John Wiley, 1970.

———, *Introductory Statistics* (2nd ed.). New York: John Wiley, 1972.

Yamane, Taro, *Statistics: An Introductory Analysis* (3rd ed.). New York: Harper & Row, Pub., 1973.

Zarembka, P., ed., *Frontiers in Econometrics.* New York: Academic Press, 1973.

Zellner, A., *An Introduction to Bayesian Inference in Econometrics.* New York: John Wiley, 1971.

index

a

b

c

d